South Park Scene, by Robert E. Jensen

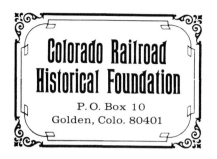

Colorado Railroad Historical Foundation
P. O. Box 10
Golden, Colo. 80401

Colorado Rail Annual No. 12
1974

MANAGING EDITOR
Cornelius W. Hauck
ASSOCIATE EDITOR
Gordon Chappell
CONSULTING EDITOR
Robert W. Richardson
PUBLISHED AND DISTRIBUTED BY

the Colorado Railroad Museum

BOX 10, GOLDEN COLO. 80401

Library of Congress Catalog Card Number 70-102682
Printed and Bound in the United States of America
Layout and Production: Cornelius W. Hauck
Typesetting: Quality Typesetting Co.
Printing: Feicke Offset Printing Co.
Binding: C. J. Krehbiel Co.

Second Printing — 1979

ISBN 0-918654-12-2

THE SOUTH PARK LINE

A Concise History

Chappell, Richardson & Hauck

published by the Colorado Railroad Museum
as the

Colorado Rail Annual No. 12

A Journal of
Railroad History in the Rocky Mountain West

Colorado Railroad Museum Box 10, Golden, Colo. 80401

Contents

Upper: Rocky Point, Boreas Pass; lower: Dome Rock, Platte Canyon; opposite: The Palisades, Alpine Pass. (Al Dunton Coll.)

Preface

"THE SOUTH PARK! . . . the most picturesque of pioneer narrow gauge railroads in a state once saturated with picturesque narrow gauge railroads . . . the South Park railroad has won an enduring and perhaps excessively prominent place in the history of Colorado."

So begins co-author Gordon Chappell in our treatment of Colorado's famed South Park narrow gauge line in this, our twelfth, COLORADO RAIL ANNUAL. Begun as the independent Denver, South Park & Pacific, control was soon sold to the Union Pacific, but hard times brought control back to Colorado through Court administration of the succeeding Denver, Leadville & Gunnison Railway. Subsequently the South Park became a key part of the new Colorado & Southern, in 1899, which in turn became a part of the Burlington System. Born as a weak and undernourished baby, the line blossomed into a robust if gangling teenager, only to succumb at retirement age to dismemberment and an early demise.

For reasons which we hope will become evident to you as you read this book, the South Park has always held an especial fascination and appeal for narrow gauge railway enthusiasts. Questions directed to the staff of the Colorado Railroad Museum have indicated that this interest has not waned in the least as the little railroad has receded further into the shadows of the past. Two large books on the subject have long been out of print and generally unavailable. Thus the Museum resolved to fill this void with a new, concise history of the line over its entire career.

Gordon Chappell, a frequent contributor to Colorado Railroad Museum publications, extensively researched the first dozen years of the railway's life to present a thorough history of the line's creation. Bob Richardson, Museum Director and co-founder, spent many long hours sifting through the voluminous Colorado & Southern records at the Colorado Railroad Museum as well as other sources in order to document

the operations of the line since the 1890's. Your Editor has filled in other areas in order to bring you a clear and complete picture of the little railroad, its nature and its history.

Cornelius W. Hauck
Cincinnati

The Museum

The Colorado Railroad Museum had its beginnings back in 1949, when co-founder Robert W. Richardson began accumulating railroad memorabilia at Alamosa, Colorado. Cornelius Hauck later lent his support to Bob's efforts, and in 1958 the two founded the present Museum at Golden. Through their efforts an historically invaluable collection of artifacts and records of early-day Colorado railroading was saved from destruction and preserved as a living record of a fascinating bygone era.

The Colorado Railroad His-torical Foundation was organized in 1966, with the encouragement of Bob and Cornelius, to carry on this work for the future. The Foundation is a non-profit (tax deductible) educational institution governed by a Board of Trustees. The specific purpose of the Foundation is to further the preservation of western railroad history through operation of the Colorado Railroad Museum. The Foundation's operation of the Museum is administered through an Executive Director, a position ably filled by Bob Richardson. Many interested

6

This page: Webster from Kenosha Hill, Wm. H. Jackson Photo (State Historical Society of Colorado Coll.). Following page: The Snow Trials, by Thomas A. Hauck.

railroad history buffs and others concerned with preservation of important aspects of America's heritage have already joined the Foundation's membership rolls. It is hoped that many others will become active supporters of the Museum's work through membership in the Foundation.

Our program has also gained the encouragement of the State Historical Society of Colorado, the American Association for State and Local History, and many other groups.

Membership in the Foundation can be your tangible expression of support for the museum, and as a member you will be able to take pride in a project you have helped to further. You will have an opportunity to meet the officers of the Foundation, to attend the Annual Meeting of the Foundation, and to take part in all of the Foundation's activities. Memberships begin at $10.00, and that part above $5.00 is tax deductible, as well as are all donations.

An active organization and an interested membership is the first prerequisite to the eventual success of our mission — won't you help by joining?

John Evans:

Building the South Park

Gordon S. Chappell

THE SOUTH PARK! To the average Coloradan this term signifies one — perhaps the most beautiful — of a number of great, high, mountain valleys, surrounded by ranges of even higher peaks, which are scattered throughout the central Rocky Mountains. But to the Coloradan sensitive to the history of his state, it calls to mind the most picturesque of pioneer narrow gauge railroads in a state once saturated with picturesque narrow gauge railroads. It was a railroad known variously as the Denver, South Park & Pacific, the Denver & South Park, the Denver, Leadville & Gunnison, the South Park Division of the Union Pacific, the South Park Division of the Colorado and Southern, and simply as *The South Park!*

An economist would undoubtedly view the South Park railroad as a mere footnote to Colorado railroad history. It was a streak of rust from end to end during much of its existence. It was poorly surveyed, poorly located, poorly engineered, poorly financed, and in financial trouble during most of its history. It lost every serious competition in which it engaged with its various rivals. As one among Colorado's many narrow gauge lines, it succumbed thirty years before the last of them passed from the scene, excepting those now strictly carriers of tourists. Its main line to Gunnison operated for less than thirty years before abandonment, and then only intermittently, being closed during many winter sea-

sons. Yet, perhaps because of its obsolescence during much of its history, because of the quaint and impractical Mason "bogie" locomotives employed during the line's first two decades, and because of the spectacular scenery visible from virtually every inch of the line's trackage, the South Park railroad possesses even beyond the grave a quality of intrigue, a fascination beyond compare, while other contemporary narrow gauge lines lie neglected in the scrap bin of history. Its significance small, its appeal great, the South Park railroad has won an enduring and perhaps excessively prominent place in the history of Colorado.

Railroad schemes had begun to proliferate in Colorado Territory even before the first railroad had penetrated its boundaries. Colorado promoters had failed to lure the main line of the first transcontinental railroad through the heart of Colorado due to the formidable ranges of mountains which any such railroad would have to pierce to the west of Denver. Instead, the Union Pacific was constructed through what is now Wyoming during the late 1860s along the much easier route of the Overland Trail, which crossed the Continental Divide at a comparatively low elevation over topography relatively easy for railroad construction. Thus it bypassed the worst of the Rocky Mountains — and Colorado Territory — by going to the north. Denver had to settle for — and itself build — what amounted to a branch feeder line, known as the Denver Pacific, which finally connected Denver with Cheyenne, Wyoming, in June 1870, a little over a year after the completion of the transcontinental railroad at Promontory Summit, Utah.

Shortly thereafter another railroad penetrated Colorado from the east, the Kansas Pacific. Its entry into the Territory brought with it one of Colorado's greatest railroad builders, a Pennsylvanian named William Jackson Palmer. Palmer, a veteran of the Pennsylvania Railroad and a subordinate official in the Kansas Pacific management, was already drawing up in his head plans for a great railroad system of his own, connecting Denver with Mexico City. This line, organized in 1870, was the first important railroad to use the narrow track gauge of three feet, most railroads having accepted a standard track width of four feet, eight and one half inches. Palmer's narrow gauge would prove economical in construction, especially in mountainous regions: cuts and fills would be narrower, thus smaller and less costly; locomotives and cars would be smaller and cheaper; curves could be sharper, thus allowing a narrow gauge railroad to negotiate twisting mountain cañons with greater ease than a standard gauge.

One of Palmer's associates, Governor A. C. Hunt, had already been active in Colorado railroad plans. In February 1868 Hunt and others had organized The Denver, South Park & Rio Grande Railroad Company, intended to penetrate the South Platte River Cañon, cross the South Park, descend Trout Creek Pass to the valley of the Arkansas River, follow the Arkansas south, cross Poncha Pass and run down San Luis Park to the Rio Grande, following that river to Santa Fe, the capital of New Mexico Territory.

This scheme, like Palmer's Denver & Rio Grande Railway organized two and a half years later, envisioned a north-south railroad connecting Denver with Santa Fe and, in the more ambitious Palmer's case, further south all the way to Mexico City. And this was the scheme, although by a route which bypassed the South Park, which the Denver & Rio Grande management followed faithfully during the first decade of their railroad's existence. To be sure, Palmer's planning included branch lines penetrating the mountains to reach the rich mining camps to the west of his railroad trunk line, but in his thinking they remained for many years secondary in importance. Here he was missing the main chance his railroad had to prosper: the immense traffic in both freight and passengers both to and from the wealthy mining camps growing like wildfire throughout the Rocky Mountains.

This was not true of a former physician and ex-governor of Colorado, Dr. John Evans. From the early 1860s he had been fully cognizant of the mineral wealth which lay in the mountains, and eager to rake off some of that wealth for himself in the form of tariffs paid for transportation. Evans was a man difficult to assess: like many men, a man of contradictory traits. He was probably no better and no worse than the average frontier capitalist. To his admirers he was a statesman, a builder, a founder of universities, a capitalist of great vision, a man of great energy, a constructive force in the development and growth of Colorado. To his critics he was a political and economic opportunist of the worst sort, amoral, a man without principle, ruthlessly ambitious, a follower of the path most expedient for John Evans. The blackest mark in the whole history of white settlement of Colorado, the indefensible massacre of Cheyenne Indians at Sand Creek on November 29, 1864, occurred while he was Territorial Governor and with his complicity, and he bore much of the responsibility for that sad episode. Whether he was as fine a man as his admirers described him as being, or as self-serving and evil as his detractors thought, he was clearly a man to seize opportunity and turn it to his own advantage. And the initial oversight of the Denver & Rio Grande Railway management in not pushing aggressively into the mountain mining regions from the beginning left John Evans a shining opportunity which he was quick to grasp.

Evans had played an important role in Colorado's first domestically sponsored railroad — the Denver Pacific, connecting Denver with the Union Pacific at Cheyenne in 1870. But he had also been active in efforts to build a railroad into the rich mining regions nearest to Denver, along Clear Creek and its tributaries, centering among the mountain towns of Black Hawk, Central City, Idaho Springs, Georgetown, and Silver Plume. In this arena, however, Evans was not destined to succeed. Instead of the various firms Evans backed, it was the rival Colorado Central which constructed narrow gauge trackage into the nearby mountain mining regions. Instead of Evans, it was W.A.H. Loveland, in an on-again, off-again relationship with the Union Pacific, who tapped the wealth of these mining districts, and preempted occupation of the most feasible railroad route into the region — the precipitous cañon of Clear Creek above the town of Golden.

But although Evans lost to Loveland in the competition to build a railroad into the Central City and Georgetown mining districts, he and the city of Denver defeated Loveland and the town of Golden in the more important competition for political and economic pre-eminence in Colorado Territory; the territorial capitol was wrested away from Golden and moved to Denver, and Loveland's various schemes for isolating Denver by building a network of railroads to and from Golden which by-passed Denver all failed. Thus Denver won its competition with Golden for pre-eminence among Colorado's cities, as it would soon win a similar competition with the more distant Colorado Springs. And Evans, with his friends, his power, and his economic backing centered in Denver, prospered accordingly.

Thus having lost the competition for construction of a rail line to the nearest mining camps up Clear Creek, by the summer of 1872 Evans began to focus his attention upon the next nearest mining center of prominence, the mining district around and above the town of Fairplay, a hundred miles to the southwest of Denver on the western edge of the great South Park. Evans' new scheme incubated in Denver financial circles in July, August and September, 1872 and finally hatched on September 30 when Evans and Denver banker David H. Moffat, Jr., Attorney Bela M. Hughes, Civil Engineer Leonard H. Eicholtz, financier Walter S. Cheesman, banker Charles B. Kountze, and other prominent Denver businessmen including Henry Crow, Joseph E. Bates, Frederick A. Clark, F. Z. Salomon, John Hughes and J. C. Reiff, met and organized *The Denver, South Park and Pacific Railway Company.* Their new firm was capitalized at $2,500,000 in 25,000 shares worth $100 each. The Articles of Association of the railway were filed with the Secretary of State of Colorado Territory during the noon hour on October 1, 1872, and the *Rocky Mountain News* reported the filing on the following day.

The Articles of Association indicated that the route of Evans' new railroad was to be from Denver

> by the most feasible route thence to a point in the South Park in Park County in said Territory, such point to be determined by the Board of Trustees of said company after careful surveys are made, with extensions and branches of said Rail Road and Telegraph Line to be constructed, however, under new companies or organizations.

Two days later the *Rocky Mountain News* interpreted this to mean that the DSP&P Railway would follow the route of one of the earlier Evans schemes which had foundered — the Denver, Georgetown & Utah — all or at least part of the way to Georgetown, deflecting somewhere from that line of railroad into the South Park. Evans had organized the DG&U after the Colorado Cen-

tral had gained control of the best route to Georgetown up Clear Creek Cañon, so his DG&U proposed to follow an alternate and much less satisfactory route heading from Denver southwest up Bear Creek to the vicinity of George M. Morrison's stone quarries, then northwest to the mouth of Mount Vernon Cañon, up Mount Vernon Cañon and over the ridge into the upper reaches of Clear Creek Cañon and on to Georgetown. Evans' railroad schemes often seemed to feature the most impractical routes, such as this one, but of course he had lost the competition for the best route through Clear Creek Cañon as early as 1870.

Clear Creek Cañon and, several miles to the south, Mount Vernon Cañon both lay about due west from Denver, and both of them provided avenues of access through the foothills of the Front Range of the Rockies, although one had to climb an impressive grade even to reach the mouth of the latter. But access through either of these cañons was to the Clear Creek mining districts and, if one went beyond to cross the main range, to the valley of the Blue River, from which one could pass south over Fremont Pass to the valley of the Arkansas River or westward to the tributaries of the Grand River (later to be known as the Colorado). But nowhere from the proposed route of the Denver, Georgetown and Utah was there an easy access to the South Park region.

South of Mount Vernon Cañon, however, lay three more breaches in the ramparts of the Front Range, namely the cañons of Bear Creek, Turkey Creek, and most southerly, of the South Platte River. As a route for the railroad to the South Park, Bear Creek Cañon seemed at first more attractive, if only because Morrison's stone quarries and coal deposits, only 16 miles from Denver, seemed to offer a source of freight traffic to feed money into a struggling company's coffers during expensive construction over a long route to the much more distant gold and coal mines of the South Park itself. Platte Cañon and Turkey Creek Cañon initially had much less to offer in the way of traffic, besides which their apparent steep and winding character intimidated the prospective railroad builder. Consequently, that fall some of the same Denver men who were promoting the South Park railroad organized the Morrison Stone, Lime and Townsite Company to establish a town near the Morrison stone quarry on Bear Creek.

It was typical for railroad promoters of that era to organize such townsites along their railroads or along prospective routes of their railroads not only to encourage the growth of industry which would feed the railroad profitable traffic, but also to make money directly from the sale of town lots. Land which was cheap prior to arrival of a railroad tended to escalate greatly in value once a railroad had reached it; thus the railroads, with the advance knowledge of where and when they intended to build track, could profit much from speculating in land and townsites and industries along their projected route. The Denver & Rio Grande management was expert at manipulating townsite schemes to their railroad's advantage, but John Evans and the South Park railroad's management were not far behind in adopting the practice.

Although the plans of the Denver, South Park & Pacific Railway now included construction of trackage to the new Morrison townsite, further investigation of the cañon of Bear Creek above Morrison did not encourage adoption of that route to the South Park. Turkey Creek Cañon, over the ridge to the south of Bear Creek, proved no more suitable. Once having entered either cañon, a railroad would have to cross a succession of major ridges and intervening ravines before reaching the South Park. By the spring of 1873, DSP&P Engineer Leonard Eicholtz had completed surveys to Morrison and beyond, and by April 2 had turned his attention to another survey which already had been completed for a distance of nine miles up the cañon of the South Platte. It was soon evident that despite its steep and winding character, Platte Cañon penetrated the mountains much further and was therefore much more satisfactory for railroad purposes on a route to the South Park than were Bear Creek or Turkey Creek Cañons. Following the South Platte and its tributaries, such a railroad would have to cross only one major ridge, at Kenosha Pass, to reach the broad, flat valley known as the South Park. It would nevertheless be an expensive project.

For reasons which were not spelled out, but which included an increase of capitalization by a million dollars and a more specific and much expanded statement of proposed routes, on June 14, 1873 the capitalists who had organized the Denver, South Park & Pacific Rail*way* reorganized the company, which had not yet built an inch of track, as the Denver, South Park & Pacific Rail*road*. The only change in the name of the new firm, therefore, was in the last half of the last word. In addition to increasing the capitalization of the firm to $3,500,000, the new Articles of Association described much more specifically a much more ambitious route than that described in the previous Articles:

> from the City of Denver to Morrison at the Bear Creek Canon and also to and through the Platte Canon and on the most feasible route to the South Park and thence to or near the town of South Park and to the Salt Springs — thence across the valley of the Arkansas River and through the Poncha Pass and across the San Luis Valley to or near the Town of Del-Norte and thence by the most feasible route to the San Juan mining districts in South Western Colorado — to be extended thence to the Pacific Ocean — with branches to Morrison — also to Summit County to be extended via the Middle Park to the Pacific Ocean — also to Dudley, and Horse Shoe, and to the head of the Arkansas Valley in Lake County in said Territory — to be located in divisions, after careful survey.

Thus the "Pacific" incorporated earlier into the railroad's name was, in these second Articles of Association, spelled out in reference to not one but TWO routes, and the San Juan mining districts centered around Silverton seemed then to be the most important objective beyond the South Park. It was an ambitious scheme for a railroad which had not yet been able to finance purchase of a rail.

At that time, Evans was trying to get an issue of $300,000 in county bonds approved by the voters of Arapahoe County (including Denver), but Alderman Barker offered an amendment, backed by the *Denver Daily Times*, to make the issue of bonds conditional on completion of 25-mile segments of railroad, the first to be finished in eighteen months with a year for construction of each additional segment, $50,000 in bonds to be issued to the company on completion of each segment on schedule until the road reached the specified 150-mile length. After this amendment was offered, Evans and the South Park management withdrew their petition for bonds during the third week of June, and on Friday, June 20, 1873, Evans petulantly told a *Denver Times* reporter that he was "done with the business and should have nothing more to do with it." Evans claimed that such conditions on issuance of the bonds would injure their sale to the extent of rendering them useless, and that he had proposed the only method of dealing with the problem of getting construction begun that was satisfactory to him, and if it did not satisfy the voters they could look to someone else to build a railroad to the South Park.

The *Denver Daily Times* chose at that point to editorialize, on June 21, 1873, about the concentration of Denver railroad schemes in the hands of a single clique, namely the Denver Pacific/ Denver, South Park & Pacific crowd:

> This brings us to another matter which will fit in here well — the subject of rail-road rings. They are a good thing to have in any growing community. They are a necessity,

for without them, railroads would not be built. But every community should have more than one. One alone is sure sooner or later to get such a control of transportation matters, as to hold the people in a vise and employ their power to the detriment of the people. Two, each against the other, and each striving for public support, will hold each other in check and do as near right as these combinations can be expected to do. We need another railroad ring in Denver, and if nothing is to be done on this South Park scheme so lately proposed, it is time to organize one.

It is well to remember that in the summer of 1873 the Denver & Rio Grande Railway was headquartered in Colorado Springs and its management was advancing the commercial interests of that city, while the Colorado Central was headquartered in Golden and attempting to advance the fortunes of Golden. That left Evans and the circle of businessmen who were behind both the Denver Pacific and the Denver, South Park & Pacific as Denver's only domestic circle of railroad promoters. As Evans was the most prominent member of that clique, the newspaper's comments were a slap at him. But far from following the course of withdrawal from such activity which his first petulant response to disappointment promised, by June 23 he and other members of the Denver Board of Trade were hard at work drawing up a proposal for another acceptable bond issue. It passed on July 28, and the Evans group began planning for construction.

As was the common practice in building a railroad, the management of the Denver, South Park & Pacific organized a construction company known as the Denver Railway Association, which began construction of grade on a line to Morrison in mid-August, 1873. It was already reasonably certain that a line to Morrison would in part be a dead-end branch intended to serve local industry, rather than part of a main line going through Morrison en route to the South Park. Engineer Leonard Eicholtz was already at work on preliminary engineering surveys up Platte Cañon for the main line, and in fact had to interrupt that work on July 30 to set the stakes on the already-surveyed Morrison line and organize the construction forces. By August 24, Eicholtz had one grading crew at work on the 9.7 miles of the Morrison Branch above where it split off from the route to the South Platte Cañon, a second force at work on the line between Denver and the mouth of the canyon, and a third at work in Platte Cañon itself. The junction of the two lines, 6.4 miles from Denver, was known at first as "Morrison Junction" although "Bear Creek Junction" would soon become the official name. Contracts

for ties were due to be let on September 1, 1873. The *Rocky Mountain News* predicted that trains would be running to Morrison in three months — the usual overly optimistic estimate of a frontier newspaper regarding railroad construction.

While winter weather soon slowed and then stopped construction of grade, surveying continued, and that winter Engineer H. R. Holbrook pushed a detailed construction survey up Platte Cañon. He and Thomas Winters, accompanied by a packer with two burros loaded with provisions and instruments, worked their way up the South Platte in mid-December, 1873, reaching 31 miles above the mouth of the cañon on December 21. The winter weather was a positive asset — the river was thoroughly frozen over in most places so that they could literally walk on the water, and where not completely frozen, there were nevertheless convenient ice bridges which afforded them comparatively easy passage.

Holbrook found the first eight and a half miles of construction from the mouth of the cañon to be the most expensive, averaging, he estimated, $11,600 per mile for the cost of grading and bridging. These were, of course, the most expensive items of construction, which would total $110,000 out of the $174,685 which he estimated was the total cost of that segment of track. Holbrook figured on using 3,000 cross ties per mile, allowing for perhaps 200 to be culled as rotten or substandard, at a cost of 34½ cents each. Spikes and Fisher rail joints would cost about $560 per mile; iron rail, weighing 30 pounds per yard, a mile requiring 47 tons, would cost $39,950 for 8.5 miles. The cost of labor for laying a mile of track would be $500 per mile, or $4,250 for 8.5 miles. Surveying and leveling would cost $5,000 for the 8.5 miles, and a water station for engines would cost an estimated $600.

The next 9.5 miles of construction to Buffalo Creek would cost only $6,000 per mile for grading and bridging, the other costs being the same as on the first section, except that additional water stations and buildings such as depots would cost $4,000. For the 13 miles from Buffalo Creek to Estabrook's Park, grading and bridging jumped up to an estimated $8,000 per mile, but were still considerably cheaper than on the first 8.5 miles. Holbrook submitted these estimates on December 26, 1873, and on January 14, 1874, handed in additional figures on sections from Estabrook's Park to Hall's Valley, 18 miles, thence to Kenosha Pass, about 6 miles, and from Kenosha Pass to the mining camp of Fairplay, 26 miles — a total of 101 miles of trackage from Denver to Fairplay costing $1,354,090 exclusive of motive power and rolling stock. One should note that excluding such expensive but necessary items as motive power, rolling stock, and operating capital, that estimate of cost comprised 39 per cent of the total capitalization of the railroad, without bringing it anywhere near its announced objective of the San Juan mining region in the southwestern corner of the Territory, much less to either of its projected termini on the Pacific Ocean.

As spring approached in 1874, the thoughts of railroad promoters such as Evans naturally turned to construction, and on March 1, his Denver Railway Association negotiated a construction contract with the Denver, South Park and Pacific Railroad for construction of 150 miles of railroad from Denver to Fairplay, across South Park and Trout Creek Pass, to the confluence of Trout Creek and the Arkansas River. According to this contract, the railroad was to be constructed in divisions from Denver to Morrison, from Morrison Junction to Buffalo Creek in Platte Cañon, from Buffalo Creek to Hall's Valley near Webster, from Hall's Valley to Fairplay, from Fairplay to the salt works in the South Park, and from the salt works to the mouth of Trout Creek on the banks of the Arkansas. Each division was to be turned over to the railroad company for operation upon its completion.

Thus by the spring of 1874 the Denver, South Park and Pacific still had not reached Morrison, but by then the firm *had* placed orders for locomotives and rolling stock. The *Denver Daily Times* reported on Tuesday, March 17, 1874, that Dawson and Baily of Connelsville, Pennsylvania, planned to ship the first DSP&P Engine, a locomotive named "Fairplay", during the following week. On the following day the newspaper reported that the railroad had contracted with Hallack Brothers Lumber Company for construction of thirty flat cars, five coal cars, five box cars, one first class passenger car, and one first class baggage car. These were all to be eight wheeled cars, 26 feet long and seven and a half feet wide. On Tuesday, March 24, 1874, the *Times* announced that the rails and the first locomotive for the DSP&P were expected during that week, and that the first bridge over the Platte and two over Bear Creek were ready for rails, as was much of the grade. Later that week the paper announced that "The last touches to the first division of the grade of the Denver & South Park road are just being put on, preparatory to the laying of the iron" and that 300 tons of rail were en route from Cincinnati.

That *Denver Daily Times* item employed an abbreviated form of the railroad company's name which would become common, to the extent that the initials "D&SP" would even be cast into the iron components of some of the railroad's locomotives. Yet the correct and proper name of the company was *Denver, South Park and Pacific Railroad,* and the correct initials were DSP&PRR — initials which local wags soon claimed to signify "Damned Slow Pulling And Pretty Rough Riding". Possibly the commonplace but inaccurate shortening of both name and initials (to "Denver & South Park" and "D&SP" respectively) by local citizens, business firms and newspapers stemmed from the fact that the stagecoach line operated by W. C. McClellan and R. J. Spotswood which connected Denver with Fairplay, Leadville and Oro City was called the "Denver & South Park Stage Company". Once the railroad was completed to Morrison, this stage line would operate from that point, connecting with trains at Morrison and thus serving as an extension of the railroad. Perhaps in addition to this confusion of names there was also an element of public pessimism regarding the "& Pacific" in the railroad's name, and local citizens may have regarded Denver and the South Park region as more reasonable termini for a locally sponsored railroad. Whatever the reasons, the Denver, South Park & Pacific Railroad became commonly and inaccurately known as the "Denver & South Park" even before it had laid a rail.

On the evening of March 29, 1874, a Kansas Pacific freight train hauled the Denver, South Park & Pacific Railroad's first locomotive into Denver. "The locomotive looks similar to those on the D.&R.G.R.R., and is of about the same weight," reported the *Denver Daily Times,* adding, that "It is besmeared with tallow to prevent rusting, and, of course, looks anything but handsome. A few hours' work will make her look as pretty as a picture." On the following day the *Times* added some technical details to its description of the locomotive, and reported that the wooden cab was built of black walnut and ash, and that the tender was painted to correspond with the cab. On April 4, the newspaper reported:

The iron for the Denver & South Park railroad has commenced arriving in Denver and the track-laying will be begun shortly. The new engine for this road has been "switching" for the Denver & Rio Grande road, and is found to work admirably.

Thus from the very beginning, although there was a deep-seated and basic rivalry between the South Park railroad and the Denver & Rio Grande, the two rivals could work together at some times and in some particulars: thus the D&RG could offer its shop facilities and its yard trackage as well as its expertise to ready the first South Park locomotive for operation at a time when the South Park itself had not yet laid a single rail.

The upper view was apparently taken not too long after the South Park was opened to traffic, and shows the road's little mixed train at the terminus of the Morrison branch. The engine appears to be No. 1, the Dawson & Baily mogul that was the line's first motive power. Below is DSP&P No. 2, the Platte Canon, obtained second hand (but hardly used) from the Kansas Central. Also a Dawson & Baily product, this handsome eightwheeler was larger than No. 1, and lasted long enough to be included in the Denver, Leadville & Gunnison roster of 1889. (Upper, R. B. Jackson Coll.; lower, Denver Public Library Western Hist. Coll.)

South Park railroad construction crews commenced laying ties on the South Park grade at the Denver Terminal Grounds on April 18, 1874, and by April 29 several miles of ties were bedded in place. S. A. Hutchins had subcontracted with the Denver Railway Association for the job of laying the track. Meanwhile, E. F. Hallack had gone East to order the car trucks and other metal parts for the freight and passenger cars his lumber firm was building, and the car trucks were expected to arrive during the first week of May. Enemies of the railroad charged that the rails now on hand were of inferior quality; if they were, and there seemed to be no evidence to support the charge, another eleven car loads of them arrived on the Kansas Pacific on April 30, with five more arriving May 5.

"Track Laying Commenced," announced the *Denver Daily Times* on Monday, May 18, 1874, marking the spiking down of the first rail on the Denver, South Park & Pacific. The article, on page 3 of the newspaper, continued:

Track-laying on the sixth railroad from Denver — the Denver, South Park & Pacific, commenced today, the sixth anniversary of the breaking of ground on our first road, the Denver Pacific. The road-bed is prepared for the iron all the way to Morrison, except for a short distance where the ties are not yet imbedded. It is expected that the iron will be laid and ready for the running of trains in ten days or two weeks. Hallack Bros. will have six or eight flat cars ready this week.

It was not until the morning of May 21 that Hallack Brothers received the trucks for 20 cars and could thereafter complete the cars and turn them over to the railroad for service. Until then, the DSP&P construction forces very likely employed leased Denver & Rio Grande cars. By the end of May 26, rails has been laid to just beyond the Platte Bridge. About three miles of grade near Morrison still awaited ties. "The engine is running satisfactorily," reported the Denver *Times,* and it added that eight flat cars, the type most useful in construction, had been completed by Hallack Brothers, while the work on the passenger cars was progressing.

On June 4, 1874, the *Times* reported further South Park progress:

Track-laying has been completed a quarter of a mile beyond S. S. Woodbury's ranch, between three and four miles from Denver. Work has progressed slowly on account of the men being obliged to bed some of the ties, as well as lay the rails. But the party have nearly reached that division of the road where the ties are already bedded, and as soon as it is reached a mile a day can be completed with ease. At the upper end of the road, near Morrison, ties have been delivered in suffi-

cient number to finish the road to that place. The frame work for one of the passenger cars is now being made at the shop of Hallack Brothers.

During the recent storm a big cottonwood lodged against the [Platte] bridge and shook the structure from end to end. With the assistance of the engine the tree was brought parallel with the current and sent down stream. Father Platte thus put in his first protest to the obstructions of his channel.

The first pleasure trip over the South Park road occurred yesterday. A couple of ladies came to the track, stopped the construction train and got aboard. They rode to the end of the track and back, and were highly delighted.

Governor Evans and a number of invited guests took a ride out to the end of the track this forenoon and made an inspection of the work.

By June 9, seven miles of track, to the mouth of Bear Creek, had been completed by South Park track-layers, and the entire line to Morrison now had ties in place. The construction crews therefore expected to complete a mile a day.

"The cars already constructed and those in progress are larger than those on the Rio Grande," reported the *Denver Daily Times,* "the company claiming that larger cars can be used with safety." By the evening of Saturday, June 13, the track over which these cars would roll had been completed to Arnett's Station on Bear Creek at the mouth of Turkey Creek, which the *Denver Daily Times* reported was 14 miles from Denver and only two from Morrison. "Two mixed trains will run each way per day, of which Mr. Ben Gilman, formerly of the Denver Pacific, and more lately of the Texas Pacific, will be conductor," commented the newspaper. It went on to claim that beyond Morrison Junction, seven miles of the main line from the mouth of Bear Creek to about half a mile beyond the mouth of Platte Cañon had been graded. By June 16, the DSP&P had 13 flat cars, and Hallack Brothers expected to finish the first two box cars during the ensuing week, and to complete four "Dolly Varden" or excursion cars, the latter probably converted flat cars, by the first of the following week. One such excursion car was being painted, a second was well under construction, and a third had just been commenced. On the evening of June 17, 1874, track was finished to the hogback or ridge about one third of a mile short of Taylor's old stage station. The bridge over Bear Creek was under construction, but not quite ready for rails. The railroad construction crew, operating from a tent camp on McBroom's ranch, planned to jump ahead and lay track beyond the incomplete bridge.

The track-layers apparently reached Morrison on or by Saturday, June 20, 1874, although it would take another four days to complete the yard tracks and switches and other necessary work. The *Denver Daily Times* described the initial excursion run by the Denver, South Park & Pacific Railroad, which was apparently a free trip for railroad officials and prominent Denver citizens who were invited guests:

> Saturday afternoon about 3 o'clock the engine "Fairplay" drew up a train of flats to the Larimer street crossing of the South Park railroad — seats being constructed of cross-ties. There a party boarded it consisting of ex-Governor Evans, Col. Eicholtz, Dr. Robinson, W.R. Thomas of the News, Henry Crow, Esq., C. B. Kountze, of the Colorado National, and other prominent citizens. The party stopped to inspect the coal banks, and visited the "Railroad camp" on John McBroom's ranch, near the mouth of Bear Creek canon, and then proceeded to Morrison. Arriving there they all adjourned to the sulphur springs, and one of the party declares that it was a rich sight to witness the descent of the city gents over the stones and through the bushes to the spring — no trail having yet been made — and then after a cooling drink to witness the labor expended in getting back. Returning to Morrison, they besieged the house of Mr. George Morrison, where fresh milk, buttermilk, wine and cake were very acceptable and heartily enjoyed. The party then returned to the train, and at 7:40 o'clock were back in Denver. About a hour and a half was consumed in going up, and an hour and a quarter in returning.
>
> The [rail]road is completed past the road crossing at Morrison, and beyond the Fairplay road and Taylor's Hotel.

In Morrison, a 40 by 100-foot white stone hotel was under construction, and a supplementary row of tourist cottages was planned on the edge of the bluff near the new hotel.

The *Rocky Mountain News* reported the laying of the last switches on June 23, 1874, and that same Tuesday Hallack Brothers placed four excursion cars and two box cars on the track. The *Denver Daily Times* reported:

> By Friday, when the first excursion takes place, six excursion cars will be ready, thus furnishing ample accommodations for 350 persons. A box car will be taken along, in which to place boxes, baskets and whatever a party may desire to carry to a pic-nic. Workmen are now engaged in putting the groves about Morrison in suitable condition for these excursion parties.

Also in Morrison, the stage company was preparing to put up stage barns, for upon completion and opening of the railroad to that town, the Fairplay stage line would commence running its stages from Morrison rather than from Denver, passengers riding the railroad for 16 miles. Denver newspapers meanwhile advertised the coming Friday excursion sponsored by ladies of the Lawrence Street Methodist Episcopal Church, with tickets priced at $1.50, half price for children.

The excursion on Friday, June 26, 1874, actually the second excursion on the railroad, introduced the Denver, South Park and Pacific Railroad to the public for the first time. The *Denver Daily Times* recorded details of the great event:

> At a little after 8 o'clock the train consisting of six excursion coaches and one baggage car, with about 150 passengers, left Larimer street. The first stopping place was the newly laid out town of Valverde, destined to be a delightful suburb of Denver. Here the engine was supplied with water by the use of a pulsometer, a novel method introduced for the purpose by this company. The train then proceeded, soon leaving the Platte River, and coming to the Morrison division of the road, which extends along Bear Creek to the new but thriving town of Morrison. Arriving at the town the eyes of all were attracted to the fine stone hotel in process of erection by J. P. Bailey & Co., the new brown-stone front just being completed for the residence of Mr. Morrison, from whom the town is named, the new stores and dwelling houses being built, besides numerous other improvements in progress. All, however, soon took refuge in the cool and delightful groves cleared and fitted up with benches and tables for the convenience of excursionists. The majority took basket dinners in the groves, others were courteously entertained by Mr. Pease, proprietor of the Morrison House. After lunch some made a trip to the grand scenery of Turkey Creek canon; some occupied themselves in fishing for speckled trout, here found in abundance. Nearly all improved the opportunity of visiting the sulphur spring, which, by the way, is more medicinal in its qualities than most of the other springs in the Territory, containing evidently little sodium and much sulphur and iron. The scenery in and about the town is varied — it is graded all the way from the beautiful to the sublime. A clear flowing stream, delightful shade trees, flowers, and the rocks that crown our "everlasting hills," all come into the picture.

Governor Evans was on the train, and, since it was a church benefit excursion, he had the odd experience of purchasing a ticket to ride on his own railroad. Two days later, on Sunday, another excursion went to Morrison, leaving at 9 a.m. from the Denver terminal, and leaving Morrison to return at 6 p.m. A third excursion was run on Tuesday, June 30, this one sponsored by the California Street Methodist Episcopal Church, and requiring five excursion cars. A fourth excursion, run by the First Congregational Sabbath School, was scheduled for July 2.

According to the *Denver Daily Times,* the Denver, South Park & Pacific line between Denver and Morrison began operating regular trains on Friday, July 3, 1874, although another source claimed that the trackage officially opened for business on July 1. The schedule published in the *Times* on July 3 called for two round trips daily from Denver; one leaving at 6 a.m. with arrival back in Denver at 9:30; and one at 5 p.m., with arrival in Denver at 9:30 p.m. This was, of course, a "mixed" train consisting of freight cars with one or more passenger cars on the rear end.

On July 9, Freight Agent A. S. Hughes announced in the Denver newspapers that the "Denver, S. P. & P. Ry." would receive freight at the temporary freight depot on the corner of 6th and Larimer streets between 9:30 a.m. and 4 p.m. Meanwhile, the South Park railroad continued to do a brisk business in church excursions on its Morrison line.

Less than a week after the official opening, on July 7, Hallack Brothers turned over to the railroad its first genuine passenger car, a first class passenger and baggage combination car named "Auraria". "It is finely painted, of a dark color, with appropriate stripes and trimmings," reported the *Denver Times.* The car was probably either a dark stained wood or a chocolate brown, and the trimmings probably consisted largely of gold leaf, with possibly a touch of red or yellow. Another passenger car followed a month later.

The real passenger cars especially were needed, for the Morrison line was engaged in a thriving passenger business, especially excursion trips, and the "excursion" cars had some limitations. Nor were all excursions to Morrison. On the evening of July 25, for example, the Denver Turnverein ran a trip only eight miles out to a point along the Platte called Petersburg, where a dancing platform had been built. Thus far no accidents had marred the operation of the railroad, but on one of the many excursions passengers feared one. On an excursion train returning from Morrison on the evening of August 2, with the cars being pushed by the engine, which was probably running backwards due to a lack of yard trackage in Morrison, a passenger lost his hat out of the window in the vicinity of the bridge over the Platte. He immediately began jerking the bell cord and shouting for the train to stop. Unaware of the lost hat, the other passengers envisioned various calamities: the bridge ahead of them having collapsed, the boiler about to burst, the train about to collide with a telegraph pole or some other obstacle. In a panic, they unloaded in all directions "with the agility of cats." Fortunately the train was running slowly. It stopped and

picked up those who had hastily jumped, none of them much the worse for wear other than a Mr. Potter who had lost a fine gold watch chain in the scramble. "The pilgrim didn't get his hat," added the *Denver Daily Times* in its report of the affair. But the following morning a railroad official went out to the site, and Mr. Potter did get his fine gold watch chain back.

"The sixth Denver railroad is rapidly becoming the pet of the people," claimed the *Times* on August 12, adding that: "Already we hear passengers say that the regular cars are crowded." The newspaper viewed the South Park railroad as "the best we have to give strangers a sight of Colorado farms . . ." By mid-August the railroad was advertising completion of a pavilion in Morrison which made that terminus an even more attractive magnet for weekend and evening excursions, and the number of summer Sunday school trips, not all of them on Sundays, would gain the Morrison line the sobriquet of "The Sunday School Route." On August 24, the railroad operated a Monday evening "Moonlight Excursion" to Morrison, one train leaving Denver at 5:15 p.m. and leaving Morrison to return at 8 p.m., a second train leaving Denver at 9 and leaving Morrison to return at midnight. The band which was to perform at Morrison Grand Pavilion would go out on the first train from Denver, serenading the passengers en route. Tickets were priced at a dollar per round trip, with 50 cents extra charged for dancing at Morrison. The Unity Church ladies followed up with another moonlight trip with dancing at Morrison on August 26. The latter turned out to be the largest and most successful excursion of the season. The new stone hotel had been completed and opened, and the recently erected Morrison Springs Pavilion or Grand Pavilion was only a few steps from the South Park depot, connected with it by a plank walk, and on the edge of the charming Bear Creek. It was indeed a pleasant place to have a party.

At this time the DSP&P owned only the one 2-6-0 Mogul-type locomotive. Even on occasions such as August 24 when the railroad operated two evening excursion trains, it was possible to handle both with a single engine, the announced schedule and the short 16-mile distance allowing such operation. It was also undoubtedly possible for the South Park railroad to lease a Denver & Rio Grande locomotive in an emergency.

Another locomotive did make its appearance briefly on the South Park railroad that month, but it belonged to neither the South Park nor the Denver & Rio Grande. A street railway called the Denver & Swansea had been organized in Denver, and on August 20, 1874, received the first of five "dummy" engines it had ordered; this was a small Baldwin-built steam locomotive entirely encased in a wooden body which looked like that of a small yellow horsecar, in order to disguise it so that it would not frighten horses and teams while it operated up and down the city streets. The odd little locomotive was rendered serviceable in the Denver & Rio Grande shop, and on August 25 Denver & Swansea engineer S. D. Paxton took her out for a run on the D&RG Railway, opening her up at one point to a speed of 37 miles per hour. On Thursday, August 27, the little dummy engine took a heavy Denver & Rio Grande passenger coach filled with excursionists up the DSP&P line to Morrison, making scheduled time easily, and on August 28 the little yellow locomotive made another trip to Morrison, this time with John Evans and a number of invited guests in the party. Named "Governor Gilpin" after Evans' predecessor in office and the Territory's first governor, the little yellow steam dummy was probably the oddest piece of motive power ever to operate on the South Park railroad. The Denver *Times* reported that she handled the Morrison run smoothly at 27 miles per hour.

While excursion and passenger traffic on the South Park's Morrison line was growing at a rapid rate, freight business was growing apace. One train from Morrison to Denver on September 15, 1874, carried one car of passengers, one loaded with limestone, one with lath, one with lumber from the mills along Bear Creek, five car loads of building stone from Morrison's quarry, and one of miscellaneous "less-than-car-lot" freight. Furthermore, two miles east of Morrison, or fourteen from Denver, near the western base of Mount Carbon, coal deposits promised to supply the railroad with even more traffic. The *Denver Daily Times* reported on September 16, 1874, that partners named Hodgson and Eaton had struck a fine vein of coal and expected to be shipping coal to Denver in a short time. This mine was on land belonging to one Francis Gallup, and it lay immediately adjacent to the South Park track. A mile south of the track, a Dr. Wenrich was busily opening another coal mine, and one mile north of the track a Mr. Wilson proposed to tap the same coal deposit, a long north-south vein. The Denver newspaper welcomed the introduction of this new competition into an "already active" Denver coal market, hoping that the new nearby source of coal would result in lower prices. But the coal discovery was of even greater significance for the Denver, South Park & Pacific Railroad: hitherto during its first two months of operation the South Park's locomotive had burned

coal mined at Cañon City far to the south, and hauled to Denver by the Denver & Rio Grande Railway. Once these mines near Morrison started to produce it, it would be able to burn Mount Carbon coal mined adjacent to its own trackage and shipped over its own rails, hence cheaper and from a more accessible source. Morrison coal could therefore fuel South Park railroad operations in the Denver vicinity and during construction through Platte Cañon and over Kenosha Pass, until the railroad reached a second source of the black fuel in the South Park itself.

On September 25, 1874, the South Park line capped its opening season of operation with an excursion to Morrison featuring both domestic and imported dignitaries. Secretary of the Interior Schuyler Colfax and his wife, Governor Stephen Elbert, ex-Governor John Evans and his wife, and numerous prominent citizens were in the party. Entertainment was provided by one Earl Reid, and the *Denver Daily Times* Reported:

> After a half hour's singing in the Pavilion, where the rippling of the waters commingling with the music, and the moonlight pouring through the grove and bathing the surrounding heights, made the whole scene seem like a fairy dream, and charmed all, the company went to the Evergreen Hotel, where a parlor concert was given. The splendid Steinway piano was presided over by Mrs. A. R. Dyer, while Mrs. Cole, Misses Ross, Butler and a number of other of our best amateur performers participated. An oyster supper was served, and after the repast, Gov. Evans introduced to the audience the distinguished guest, Mr. Colfax, who made a few brief and pertinent remarks . . . .

At 10:30 p.m. the excursionists returned to the railroad cars, and the DSP&PRR returned them to Denver. And on October 1, the brand new Evergreen Hotel, which had hosted the party of excursionists on September 25, held its official "Grand Opening", which of course occasioned another South Park excursion on that date, including two extra trains.

During that first three months of operation, the Denver, South Park & Pacific Railroad's line to Morrison earned $5,982.73, compared with operating expenses of $4,470.91, for a net earning of $1,511.82. Of course this was after a construction expenditure of $163,391 for the 16-mile First Division between Denver and Morrison, an average cost of $10,212 per mile. If that rate of earning remained steady, it would take 26 years to pay the cost of construction of the Morrison line, not counting interest.

Now that the railroad had reached Morrison, it was destined to remain there for longer than anyone connected with the DSP&P envisioned.

John Evans had scored a major accomplishment in building those 16 miles of track during the summer of 1874, because the Panic of '73 had dried up capital throughout the United States, and the mid-1870's were depression years in Colorado, as elsewhere in the nation. From the very beginning, the Denver, South Park & Pacific management had experienced difficulty in raising capital, and had Evans not had a banker brother who was a partner in a Cincinnati iron foundry, he might not even have been able to purchase the rail necessary to reach Morrison. Completion of the miniscule 16-mile branch to Morrison did not significantly change that picture; it was still nearly a hundred miles to Fairplay, the first important gold-mining camp which the railroad could hope to reach, and those miles encompassed much tougher construction problems than were encountered between Denver and Morrison. There were difficult years ahead.

The initial South Park construction firm, the Denver Railway Association, had exhausted its resources in building the Morrison Branch, and in an effort to revitalize the project, Evans and his associates organized, on October 12, 1874, the Denver Railway and Enterprise Company, capitalized at $500,000, divided into 500 shares worth $1,000 each. "The object of this company," reported the *Denver Daily Times* on October 15, "is to undertake the grading, construction and equipment of the South Park railway, the opening up of quarries, etc." The Articles of Association of the new firm stated the purposes in greater detail:

> To open and work quarries, prepare stone, make lime from the rock and plaster of Paris from the gypsum, market coal, make plank, lath, shingles, and lumber. Undertake the grading, construction and equipment of The Denver South Park & Pacific R.R. or any part thereof as well as furnishing or procuring the Right-of-Way and Depot grounds therefore and the furnishing and erection of all buildings, bridges, tanks, and other things necessary and applicable to such Railroad in the creation of business for the same, including the laying out of Towns at Stations on the Line thereof and promoting the settlement and improvement and the Sale of Lots or other disposition of same.

One week after incorporating this firm, on October 20, John Evans left for New York to seek additional capital, but would experience little success there in selling South Park railroad securities.

Operation of the Morrison Branch meanwhile underwent several changes in the time table. Effective October 6th, the evening "Morrison accommodation train" was scheduled to leave at 4:30 instead of 5:15, and would arrive in Morrison at 6 p.m. The morning "Passenger" schedule remained unchanged. Then on Sunday, November 1, the "Winter Time Table" went into effect. The "Passenger" left Denver at 8 a.m., and returned at 6:15 p.m., being scheduled as trains 1 and 2. The "Accommodation" left Denver at 3 p.m. and returned at 11:15 a.m., constituting trains 3 and 4. Operating with the one locomotive, this odd schedule apparently meant that the morning passenger train to Morrison returned as an "Accommodation" train, and the afternoon "Accommodation" train to Morrison returned as the "Passenger".

Up to this time the Denver, South Park & Pacific Railroad had operated quite satisfactorily with the single Dawson & Baily 2-6-0 18-ton Mogul locomotive *Fairplay*, with the only known exceptions being the two trips of the Denver & Swansea engine *Governor Gilpin* out to Morrison and back. But construction of the Denver & Swansea was tied up in litigation, and the little yellow "dummy" engine stood dead on a side track near the Denver & Rio Grande shops. "The action of the courts has made her a practical as well as a theoretical dummy," commented the *Denver Daily Times* on October 19.

At the beginning of November, however, the Denver, South Park & Pacific received its second engine, a Dawson & Baily 21-ton 4-4-0 "American" type locomotive purchased second-hand from the Kansas Central. The *Denver Daily Times* noted on November 3, 1874: "The 'Platte Canon' is the name of a narrow-gauge engine which has arrived for the Denver & South Park railway," and the *Rocky Mountain News* reported that same day, "A NEW narrow gauge engine called 'Platte Canon,' for the Denver & South Park railroad, arrived a day or two ago." The precise date of its arrival via the Kansas Pacific, which according to the *News* would have been either November 1 or November 2, seems to have escaped both newspapers. But the *News* went on to add, "It will be ready for service soon."

With two engines on its roster, the DSP&P would not be crippled or forced to lease motive power if one locomotive broke down; it was thus a successful, independent, 16-mile railroad. Although he was experiencing great difficulty in selling South Park securities, John Evans had great hopes for his little railroad, to the extent that he counted on the now humming business of the Morrison Branch to serve as a springboard for further construction.

Even before the Morrison Branch was completed, the DSP&P management came under fire for not building its railroad fast enough, and Evans seized upon a letter from a concerned citizen of Fairplay as an excuse to set forth the South Park management's plans for expansion and the reasoning behind them. He then took steps to have his lengthy and detailed letter published in the usually friendly *Denver Daily Times* on Friday, June 5, 1874.

First, Evans dealt with the suspicion on the part of skeptics who feared that the plan to build the South Park railroad in divisions concealed some nefarious plot to finance many such divisions when in fact the company might not succeed in building more than the first one. Such could be the result of inflation and escalating costs, but there was also the implication that the whole project could be an elaborate swindle to line the pockets of Evans and his associates, as South Park rivals lost no opportunity to insinuate. Evans bridled at such insinuations, and attempted to sooth Fairplay's George Pease on that question:

> I assure you that there has never been any other purpose on the part of the Denver, South Park & Pacific railroad company and its promoters, than to build its entire line of road as set forth in its published plans, and that, too, as rapidly as they can secure the means for the purpose.
>
> Those plans wisely contemplated completing the road and putting it into operation in divisions. In this way the country and the city of Denver derive a benefit from each division, as soon as opened for business. In no other way can the means invested in the road be made to pay as it progresses. And in this way alone can we certainly prove the value of the enterprise which is necessary to secure the money to build the road.
>
> The first division of sixteen miles to Morrison will be completed in the most substantial manner, and put in operation in a few days with a fair prospect of immediately doing a good business. A large amount of the grading has already been done on the second division of thirty-two miles to Buffalo creek, and it is expected that the grading on this division will be nearly or quite all completed with the means already provided for. When this is done it is believed that the forty-eight miles of road in these divisions thus near completion will furnish ample security for the amount of money that will be required to complete and put in operation the second division; and also to do the grading on another division of the road, say to Bailey's or Hall's valley; and in case the first forty-eight miles of the road, thus put in operation, shall do a good business, it will give security for the means to complete it to Hall's valley; and doing a good business, it will enable us to raise the money to complete it to Fairplay. And so it will be extended beyond to the salt works, and to the Arkansas valley, and its extension to Del Norte, division after division, as rapidly as

by the various means at command the money can be provided for the purpose.

> The railroad company will issue its bonds secured by a first mortgage on the whole line of its road, which will be placed in the hands of reliable trustees, whose duty it will be to receive the proceeds of their sale and see to the faithful application of the money to the construction of the road. The traffic contracts already agreed for, giving a drawback on eastward bound business, will provide a large sinking fund for these bonds, which will be placed in the hands of the trustees, which will largely increase their value. They will not be issued until after the first division of the road is completed and in operation, and a large part of the second division is graded, so that there will be a substantial basis of security for an amount of the bonds sufficient to complete the second and grade a third division of the road as above suggested.
>
> Without the amount that is being expended on the road by the association, from their private means and free from the aid given by Arapahoe county, as a basis of security for additional funds, there would be no reasonable hope of disposing of any part of said first mortgage bonds. This certainly is the case since the financial crisis. Therefore, we are pursuing the only practicable plan for building the road. And I assure you, that the entire amount of the proceeds of the Arapahoe county bonds will be honestly and faithfully applied to the construction of the road, together with large amounts of money advanced by the association from its other resources, to make such basis of security. Any surmise or statement to the contrary is not only libeleus [sic] but calculated to retard the construction of the road.

Evans went on to say that the Denver Railway Association relied for its profits on making the stock of the railroad company, which it would receive in payment for construction, more valuable. Hence this construction firm would find it advantageous to build the road economically but well, so that it could be operated cheaply but nevertheless do a good business. Evans insisted that it was necessary to demonstrate the railroad's profitability by placing each division of it in operation as soon as it was completed if the management was to obtain more capital for further construction.

He answered in detail the criticism that by investing in the townsite company and industries at Morrison, the railroad management had taken steps which would retard rather than promote further construction, and tend to end the railroad at Morrison:

> You refer to the property interests of the Association at Morrison, and elsewhere on the line of the railroad, as liable to retard the progress of or defeat the construction beyond

certain points. But . . . the influence of these interests will have precisely the opposite effect. If the acquisition of a valuable interest at one point on the line will enable the Association to raise the means to extend the road that far, the same will be true of points beyond. The prospect of realizing considerable aid from the enhancement of the value of lands at the stations on the line of the road, in which the Association would acquire an interest, has been openly discussed as a part of the plan for raising the means to build it from the commencement of the interprise. Without this prospect it could neither have been successfully inaugurated nor carried forward, as it has been up to this time. And it is difficult to see why, if through the aid of this influence we are enabled to raise the money to build the road to any point, it will not be equally as efficient in aiding us to extend it to another and another end of the route.

To illustrate I may say that in contracting for rolling stock the Association has already put in as cash in payment a large amount of real estate at double the amount paid for it. And as in the establishment of stations on the line they have already received liberal donations of interests in the property benefitted, it has greatly enhanced their means and strengthened their ability to build the road. The only difficulty in building the road is to raise the means, and as this is a perfectly fair and legitimate source from which to derive them, why should any one desiring the road built, object?

But of course as Evans well knew, many of those who objected were in fact involved in rival railroad schemes and did not want to see the South Park succeed. Evans went on:

But you can readily see how a failure to secure such interests may retard the building of the road by leaving the association without the aid they would give. Some persons have taken a false view of this matter, doubtless supposing the road could be built without aid, and instead of assisting us have retarded the work by refusing to give us the right of way. Others have refused to divide the profits on the location of stations, or to sell at reasonable prices lands on which stations might be advantageously located. The former of these make us pay court charges or exhorbitant prices for the right of way, out of means that would otherwise be applied to building the road. The latter refuse us the aid which would materially help us to go forward without costing them anything and deny themselves the benefit of the location of stations on their lands. In these cases fortunately, the company have the right to locate their stations, and as it is but proper and is necessary that a part of the benefits the road confer shall go towards its construction, they will exercise it.

In other words, if landowners, settlements or towns along the line did not provide right-of-way

or depot grounds on terms that suited the railroad, the South Park management would bypass such locations in favor of others who met their terms. By following this policy, the South Park and other Colorado railroads held the power of life or death over the commerce of many an infant community, and although there were some situations and locations in which such power did not work, in many others it was absolute.

Evans acknowledged that many landowners, far from opposing the South Park railroad, had given free right-of-way over their land, and in other ways encouraged the expansion of the railroad. Citizens of Morrison were apparently among those who had helped:

And at the town of Morrison the association has acquired a large interest in the quarries and land on which the town is laid out. At the mouth of Turkey creek it has secured a valuable interest in coal lands and arranged for an interest in lands on which a town will be laid out. By these interests alone the association expect largely to develop business for the road; provide it with cheap coal; cheapen the cost and improve the quality of building material in Denver; build up important towns and an attractive watering place [resort]; and realize enough from these operations to build the nine miles of branch road to Morrison, and so enhance the property of the liberal and enlightened parties aiding the enterprise as that they will also be largely benefitted.

Thus if Evans and the railroad management were willing to use the railroad's great economic power as a club with which to beat those who opposed them, they were also willing to offer the carrot of mutual profits to encourage those who aided them — or so his theory stated.

Elsewhere in his lengthy letter, Evans outlined some of the collateral investments the South Park management had made in 1874:

The association has already made contracts or agreements for lands or large interests therein, at the first station from Denver (Valverde); at a station to be located near Littleton; at one to be located at the Platte cañon, and at one to be located near the mouth of Buffalo creek. They are also in negotiation for like interests at other eligible points both in the valley and in the mountains on the line of the road. And they have commenced such negotiations at the mouth of Geneva Gulch, at Hall's Valley; at Hamilton; including an interest in the coal mines there; at Fairplay and at the Salt Works. And they propose to do so at other points at an early age. And as in the way I have suggested, the progress of the work will largely depend upon the success of these negotiations, we hope to be met by parties interested in a spir[i]t of liberality in our endeavors thus to raise a part of the means to build a railroad that cannot fail to be a great public benefit.

Evans' letter touched on some other interesting points. He said that he and his associates "undertook to build the South Park railroad because of its great importance to the city of Denver, in which its [the Denver Railway Association's] members are largely [financially] interested; as well as to secure the trade and develop the country to which it is to extend." He went on to add that the investors had justification for wanting a reasonable profit on their investment.

This letter, of course, was written before completion of the Morrison Branch. Unfortunately, in the years following completion of that line, Evans and his associates were to discover that their very real accomplishment counted for little in securing the additional financing they needed to extend the line up Platte Cañon. The depression years of the mid-1870s were not conducive to great railroad projects, and completion of the Morrison Branch exhausted Denver's resources at that time.

But they would not cease trying. The initial construction firm, the Denver Railway Association, had commenced work not only on the Morrison line, but on the main line through the South Platte Cañon, in mid-August 1873. The *Rocky Mountain News* of August 24 reported that in addition to the grading crew then at work on the Morrison line, another was on the main line between Denver and the mouth of Platte Cañon, while a third was at work in the cañon itself. On July 4, 1874, when the Morrison Branch was nearing completion, the *Denver Daily Times* reported that the grading from Morrison Junction to the Platte Cañon was about two thirds completed. The remaining third was under contract, and would presumably be built as soon as the railroad had secured legal right-of-way. At that time, the Denver Railway Association hoped to grade the line up the cañon to Buffalo Creek during the fall and winter of 1874-75, while water was low and before the spring rise.

In October 1874 the firm's resources had been exhausted, and it was replaced by the Denver Railway & Enterprise Company, which on March 8, 1875, negotiated a new contract with the DSP&P Railroad, whereafter it resumed grade construction between Morrison Junction and Platte Cañon, and accomplished very little more than its predecessor. Denver, still in a nip-and-tuck race with Colorado Springs for economic primacy in Colorado Territory, and seeing the South Park railroad as one more asset in its aspirations, pushed and prodded the railroad's management. The *Rocky Mountain Herald* of March 4, 1876, boasted of Denver's prospects:

The railroad relations, and the geographical situation of Denver, . . . destine its permanent prosperity as the "commercial centre" for Colorado at large. And not only for Colorado at large, but also for northern New Mexico and southern Wyoming, will Denver eventually become the great depot for distribution, and the great entrepot for exchange. Like Chicago to the old Northwest, or St. Louis to the Mississippi Valley, or San Francisco to the Pacific coast, this growing giant of the Great Interior is destined to do the business which her grand central situation, and her great railway radiation, shall eventually supply and control.

But then the newspaper revealed that these great prospects for the future were followed by a very large "if":

But more especially will this be so, by the construction of the D.&S.P. railway to the southwest, which will give us the outlet and inlet to and from the rich mining counties of the South Park and the San Juan country. With this sixth and best artery of trade opened to the southwest, Denver can safely claim to be both the commercial centre and the railroad centre of Colorado and surrounding Territories.

All of this had come into focus at a meeting of the Denver Board of Trade (an early Chamber of Commerce) the previous Thursday evening, at which Evans had insisted that the DSP&P lacked only $150,000 to insure completion of the track into the South Park region. A leading Denver merchant introduced a resolution which was passed with enthusiasm:

Resolved, That the extension of the South Park railroad to Buffalo Creek, or Bailey's ranch, is of the greatest importance to the prosperity of Denver.

Resolved, That we will earnestly cooperate with the Denver Railway & Enterprise Company, in their effort to secure subscriptions to the remainder of the stock of the company, and especially enough to enable it to pay for grading and tieing the road to Buffalo Creek.

Resolved, That a committe[e] of six be appointed by the chair to urge upon our citizens the propriety and importance of making such subscriptions.

Unfortunately, the project remained moribund.

On July 6, 1876, a third construction company, the Denver & San Juan Construction Company, was incorporated with capital set at $350,000, capital which was finally obtained with great difficulty. The *Railroad Gazette* notified its readers on July 28, 1876, that:

The Denver & San Juan Railroad Construction Company gives notice that bids will be received at its office in Denver, Col., until

Aug. 10, for the grading of this road from the mouth of Platte Canon to the South Fork of the Platte . . . The work will be let in mile sections, and approximate estimates of the quantities given. Bidders will state a price per cubic yard for solid, loose rock and earth excavation; also a price per cubic yard (of 25 feet) for culvert masonry, slope and retaining walls and rip raps. Plans, profiles and specifications will be ready for examination by Aug. 1. The work will be paid for monthly in cash.

The *Gazette* item implied that the grade from Morrison Junction to the mouth of Platte Cañon was virtually complete, and added that work in the cañon would "be heavy and difficult."

The Denver & San Juan Construction Company resumed construction in mid-August, 1876, and apparently received a financial boost early the following year. The *Railroad Gazette* of February 9, 1877, reported that the DSP&P management had executed a mortgage for $2,500,000 to the Farmer's Loan and Trust Company of New York, and planned to issue bonds under this mortgage to complete the road to Fairplay.

Evans had written in mid-1874 that the grade between the mouth of Platte Cañon and Buffalo Creek was "the most difficult and expensive part of the whole line . . ." The *Rocky Mountain News* of October 12, 1877, described construction of just that section. The *News* reporter and several companions drove a buggy out along the South Park grade, passing the towns of Petersburgh and Littleton and the ranches of Brown, Skelton, Hussey, Lilley, Shallabarger, Archer, Strong, Lehow and Gallager, the latter at the entrance to Platte Cañon. Up to that point they had found the grade completed and ties distributed alongside, "in readiness for the finishing gang and the iron." After an hour's rest, they drove their buggy on the completed grade six miles up the cañon to Cecil A. Deane's tie camp at the end of the finished construction. The reporter described the difficult character of the work:

In many places they have been obliged to let their men down with ropes secured to overhanging masses of rock. A drill hole would be made with great difficulty, and the drill left within; then another a few feet away; then a tie would be lowered upon the projecting drills, and a footing was thus secured for the men to put in the first blast. Thus they worked down through many feet of the hardest granite, the powder and [nitro]glycerine and dynamite rending away the rocks, and thus half tearing from the solid mountain wall, half stealing from the river's bed, a pathway for the iron horse. Thus for weeks and months have these fearless and energetic men labored within a few miles of our city. The ringing of the steel upon their anvils, the .nking of the drills, the steady stroke of the

hammer, the sharp bang and sullen roar of the blast have not indeed been heard; but their results are to be seen all along the great mountain gorge, and the work has so far progressed that its chief difficulties may be said to have been overcome, and that which remains to be accomplished is but a small part of what has already been completed. "The back-bone of the canon is broken", complacently remarked Mr. Bartlett, as he stood looking at one of Chatfield's sixty-foot rock cuttings, and pointed up the canon to where some of Wood's gang were hanging by their eyelids to a precipitous cliff.

The *News* reporter found that in addition to the six miles of completed grade, which still needed several bridges or culverts, one mile was nearly completed, and work had just begun on the remaining one and a half miles of the contract. Isaac W. Chatfield had sixty men at work, and the other contractor, Robert Woods, had sixty-five. The cost of that grading, according to then-current estimates, was $4,000 for the first mile up from the mouth of the cañon, $8,000 for each of the next three miles, $15,000 for the following mile, $17,000 for the mile after that, and $18,000 per mile for the remaining two and a half miles. From the mouth of Platte Cañon the grade ran along the north bank of the South Platte for three and a half miles, crossing on an iron bridge to the south bank for the next three and a half miles, then recrossing on a second iron bridge to follow the north bank to the forks of the stream. Above the forks, Kennedy and Madge had a force of 35 men at work, and between there and Bailey, five grading crews were at work.

The *Rocky Mountain News* described the construction camps in the cañon that fall:

Deane's tie camp is situated on the south side of the river, just where a little stream comes down from the mountains, and opens a roadway to his large timber tract not far distant. Here he proposes to build a store and hotel, for which he is now moulding brick, as well as a saw mill. A post office has been applied for. Chatfield's camp is directly opposite, on the north bank. A little farther up the gulch — known as Wolfert's — is the engineer's camp, over which Mrs. Bartlett presides with much grace and hospitality. Up the canon three-fourths of a mile, on a shelf of the rocks, are the white tents of Wood's graders, and to which supplies have to be transported by a circuitous, if not a dangerous, trail. The men are quiet and well behaved. Few accidents, and still fewer deaths, have occurred. On few public works have the lives and comfort of the men been more carefully protected or provided for. The food furnished is excellent, and is well served. 'Boston', the cook at the tie camp, is a famous caterer, and dishes up on tin[plates] a most palatable meal, of boiled beef and potatoes, pork and beans, rice, pickles, bread and butter, pie, tea and coffee — which we must admit would be all the more inviting, even to a hungry, tramping editor, if served with the civilizing china, and silverware, napkins, table cloths, etc.

The tie cutters had a job no less difficult than that of the graders. Deane's men had to construct roads to deliver ties to either the grade or the river bank, and they floated some of the ties down to collecting booms downstream. So far, Deane had delivered 60,000 ties on a 100,000-tie contract. The ties were six and a half to seven feet long and seven inches on the face on which rails were laid, and a mile of track required 2,800 of them.

This expensive construction up Platte Cañon had the customary effect on the Denver, South Park & Pacific's construction firm; it collapsed that fall. Consequently on November 24, 1877, the management organized the *fourth* construction firm designed to build the railroad to the South Park, this one named the Denver & South Park Railroad Construction and Land Company, thus adding to the confusion in the railroad's proper name by giving a bit of legitimacy to the popular title, "Denver & South Park". On November 26, the new firm took over the old construction contract, and *Railroad Gazette* reported on December 14 that "the new company intends to begin work at once." According to the *Denver Daily Times,* Evans had meanwhile obtained a $300,000 loan, probably with the help of his brother in Cincinnati.

Tracklaying resumed during the spring of 1878, and on the afternoon of Saturday, May 4, the DSP&P operated the first passenger and excursion train over the new line, departing from the 6th & Larimer Street depot at 2 p.m. "It was composed of the engine number two, named *Platte Cañon,* the passenger coach *Auraria,* a box car and a flat car, all well filled," reported the *Rocky Mountain News* on the following day. The trip to the end of track, which then was at the mouth of the South Platte Cañon, required fifty-five minutes. The newspaper continued:

The rails were just entering the canon but the track layers had fallen back a quarter of a mile this side where they were engaged putting in a Y which was completed in time for the engine to turn around for the trip home.

The *Denver Daily Times* reported that on May 23 the last of the iron needed to complete the road all the way to Fairville had been shipped. Tracklaying had meanwhile resumed from Morrison Junction and by May 24 had reached the second bridge in Platte Cañon, which was not quite finished. The 94 foot span was soon completed, and on May 27 South Park director W. S. Cheesman took a small party of guests by train to the end of track, then a mile beyond the second bridge.

While construction progressed, a bank excursion had been scheduled to go up the cañon, but its sponsors cancelled when they learned that the railroad would allow them only a short time in the cañon. Evans apologized in a letter dated Wednesday, May 29, 1878, and explained the railroad's problem:

Our two locomotives are taxed to their utmost capacity by forwarding iron and doing the regular business of the road. Until the arrival of our new engine, "Oro City," which left Taunton, Mass. in care of a messenger Monday last week, and is expected on Saturday next [June 1, 1878], we shall be unable to offer any other facilities for excursion parties than a ride to the canon and immediate return.

On Friday, May 31, the DSP&P received a number of box and flat cars from the car-building firm of Barney & Smith of Dayton, Ohio, apparently the second lot of cars received from that firm that year. The next day another construction train consisting of seven South Park cars loaded with iron and other material steamed out to Platte Cañon. The Kansas Pacific, meanwhile, was carrying into Denver a steady stream of construction material consigned to the narrow gauge line.

By Saturday night, June 1, 1878, the South Park end of track was 32 miles from Denver, or 12 miles above the mouth of Platte Cañon and two miles above the forks of the South Platte. The Lawrence Street Methodist Episcopal Church scheduled an excursion for the following Saturday, and the *Denver Daily Times* complained that "The South Park road is over-burdened with applications for excursions, and more trains and days are demanded than the road and calendar can supply."

On the night of Sunday, June 2, 1878, a Kansas Pacific freight train brought the Denver, South Park & Pacific its third engine, the *Oro City,* a 2-6-6T 22-ton "bogie" locomotive. The *Denver Daily Times* of Monday, June 3, 1878, described the diminutive machine:

It was made by the Mason Machine Company, of Taunton, Mass., and when polished and brightened will make a fine appearance. The tender, instead of being separable from the engine, as is the usual custom, is joined directly to the cab. The cab is finished off in nice style and can be closed so as to entirely shut out cold, storms, winds, etc. For this the engineer and fireman will doubtless be appropriately thankful. The engine will be set up immediately and go into actual service.

When construction of the South Park resumed and additional locomotives were required, the road turned to the Mason Machine Works of Taunton, Massachusetts, and between 1878 and 1880 acquired 19 of William Mason's unique 2-6-6T "bogie" engines. The first of the group was No. 3 the Oro City, shown in service at left (Denver Public Library Western Hist. Coll.); the official builder's photograph of No. 15 the Breckenridge is reproduced below (Art Wallace Coll.).

The engine was fired up for a trial trip on Wednesday, June 5, and proved satisfactory.

A storm on June 4 knocked one bent out of the Dutch Creek trestle on the South Park railroad above Littleton, but did little other damage, and the following day the newspaper advertised the "First Grand EXCURSION to the Forks of the Platte Canon." The excursion train, scheduled for June 8, was supposed to leave the South Park depot at 6th and Larimer at 8:30 a.m., and tickets were for sale for three dollars. The Episcopal Church ladies were planning to serve hot tea and coffee at a large tent pitched at the terminus of the trip, and a brass band was scheduled for entertainment. On June 6, the DSP&P's new engine, *Oro City,* made its first real trip up the line, taking 14 cars up into Platte Cañon and carrying a committee of men and women to test the route for the next day's excursion and put up the pavilion and other fixtures. After this initial excursion, the railroad management planned to defer other excursions until the line was more adequately equipped.

On June 7, a "great tent" was taken up into the cañon to be erected at Dome Rock where the excursion was to terminate, and by the day of the excursion, June 8, the tracklayers had reportedly reached a point six miles above the forks of the stream. About 140 people went on the church excursion that day.

On June 10, two more box cars and eight pairs of passenger car trucks consigned to the DSP&P arrived on the Kansas Pacific's evening freight train from the east. According to the *Denver Daily Times* construction of bridges was causing a delay in tracklaying; nevertheless, on the evening of June 17, 1878, the South Park end of track reached Buffalo Creek, 38.6 miles from Denver.

As a further spur to South Park construction, the *Denver Daily Times* reported on June 19, 1878 that at least one hundred wagon freighters were constantly employed in hauling merchandise between Colorado Springs and Leadville. "It is manifest destiny," reported the *Times,* "that the Denver & South Park road will soon reach a point where it will control this traffic if vigorously pushed forward." In the *Times'* view, the Denver South Park & Pacific Railroad was a decisive factor in Denver gaining preeminence over Colorado Springs as the commercial capital of Colorado.

Track was due to be completed to Pine Grove on June 26, 2.7 miles beyond Buffalo Creek and still 12.4 miles short of Bailey's. Stagecoaches and wagon freighters which had connected with the South Park line at Morrison until this time now began shipping to and from the end of track at Pine Grove.

Meanwhile three "elegant new passenger coaches" had been shipped from Dayton, Ohio, for use on the DSP&P, and the railroad scheduled a July 4 excursion.

The new cars arrived in Denver on the Kansas Pacific on Saturday, June 29. The *Denver Daily Times* described them:

> They are finely finished and will perfectly answer all requirements, both of beauty and utility. They came from Dayton, Ohio, over broad-gauge roads, broad-gauge trucks having been substituted for the narrow-gauge wheels, which were sent upon a flat car. The combination passenger and express car is named "Hall's Valley." The passenger cars are named "Geneva" and "Leadville."

The new cars undoubtedly got their first workout on the July 4 excursion. At 8 a.m. a train of five cars pulled out of the Colorado Central depot at 16th Street and ran down to the Denver, South Park & Pacific depot, where another car was added to the train. A second train of four cars left the South Park depot at 6th and Larimer Streets at 8:30, the two trains together carrying about 600 people. The coupling bar between the engine and the first car of the second train broke when the train reached the first bridge in the cañon, and the train had to return for hasty repairs, not departing again until 10 a.m. But the first train had been making frequent stops along the line to let groups off for fishing, sketching, picnicking, etc., so that the second train reached Pine Grove only fifteen minutes after the first one. The *Denver Daily Times* commented:

> Such crowds are very trying for conductors, inevitably, but Conductor Greenslit, of the larger train, and Conductor Hanna, of the smaller, managed to get through without getting cross, and to go through the squeezing, inattentive, noisy, inquisitive crowd, answering countless useless questions over and over again, forcing curious spectators from risky perches on the roofs of cars, and giving more information to the hour than the best versed lecturer possibly could in twice the time — always courteous and always smiling. Mr. Hawkins, the company's photographist, was along, and took plates of several points of interest while the train or an excursion party was a part of the view.

The newspaper commented that the "carrying capacity of this road was crowded to its utmost, hundreds not especially interested in the celebration in the city by the temperance orders taking advantage of the low rates offered to escape the heat, dust and confusion of the town for the cool, shady resorts of the mountains."

The Denver, South Park & Pacific railroad was

At Platte Canyon (or Waterton), MP 20.43, the line entered the canyon, and 3½ miles further crossed from the north to the south bank of the stream on an iron truss bridge. This "first bridge" is shown above, looking upstream, shortly after completion; a construction tent is still in evidence at left (Museum Collection).

After passing through Dean's, or Deansbury (later Strontia Springs), the line crossed back to the north side on another ("second") iron bridge, about 3½ miles above the "first" bridge. The view of Second Bridge at right shows it upon completion, with the surrounding right-of-way littered with construction refuse. Below, Mason bogie No. 10 the Granite was posed on the bridge by William H. Jackson for this dramatic view (both photos, Museum Collection). Over the years this location would prove to be a favorite for photographers of the South Park.

As soon as the South Park's tracks penetrated the scenic upper reaches of the Platte Canyon it became a prime attraction not only for excursionists but also for commercial photographers. Jackson, Weitfle, Chamberlain and others quickly transported their cumbersome gear up the canyon to record views of the South Park's little Mason-powered trains posed in carefully chosen scenic surroundings. Of particular interest is the view on the page opposite, showing a construction train backed into a siding at Buffalo Creek to permit the westbound mixed to steam by. (All photos, State Hist. Society of Colorado.)

now progressing steadily up the cañon of the North Fork of the South Platte River, and with the nation and Colorado recovering from the depression years of the mid-1870s, the outlook was brighter, especially as Leadville was a booming mining camp and a great source of rail traffic. The October 11 issue of *The Railroad Gazette* reported the road open for business to Bailey's, 53.7 miles from the South Park depot in Denver, and on Wednesday, November 20, 1878, Engine No. 4, the *San Juan,* arrived on a Kansas Pacific flat car on the evening freight. "The style of its construction is much the same as that of the 'Oro City,' now running on the same line," reported the *Denver Daily Times* on November 21; "It is christened the 'San Juan,' and was made by the Mason Machine Works, of Taunton, Mass." It was another 2-6-6T "bogie" locomotive, a type which was to become closely identified with the South Park railroad.

While one type of engineer, the locomotive engineer, was steaming up the *San Juan* for its trial trip, another type of engineer, the civil engineer, was scouting the passes in the Park Range for a feasible route to Leadville. The stated objective of the Denver, South Park & Pacific was still the San Juan Mining Region in the southwestern corner of the state, but the booming silver mining camp of Leadville was much closer and exerted a much stronger attraction for a struggling railroad. Surveyors drew up plans for crossing the mountains either from the north end of Hall's Valley to approach Leadville via Tenmile Creek and Fremont Pass, or further south from the South Park to the Arkansas Valley, then heading north into Leadville. To protect both routes, Evans and his associates followed the Denver & Rio Grande practice of incorporating, on December 13, 1878, separate railroad companies to occupy each route. The Denver, South Park & Ten Mile Railroad Company was organized to

> locate, construct, own, operate and maintain a single or double track narrow gauge railroad and a telegraph line from the most feasible point of connection with the Denver South Park & Pacific Railroad in Park County, Colorado, by way of the confluence of Ten Mile Creek with Blue River in Summit County aforesaid and along the valley of the Arkansas River, by way of Leadville to Twin Lakes.

Its alter ego, the Denver, South Park & Leadville Railroad had been incorporated to

> locate, construct, own, operate, and maintain a single or double track narrow gauge railroad and a telegraph line from the most feasible point of connection with the Denver, South Park & Pacific Railroad on Trout Creek in Lake County, Colorado, through and along the

Valley and Canons of the Arkansas River, by way of, or near Leadville to the mines of its vicinity in the same county.

Which of these lines would the Denver, South Park & Pacific build? In time it would adopt the absolutely unpredictable alternative of building variations of BOTH, reaching Leadville at different times from two different directions. But at the time these firms were organized in December 1878, that denoument to railroad rivalries in the Rockies still lay several years in the future.

The railroad situation in Colorado was complex indeed as the new year of 1879 dawned. In an inauspicious move one of the South Park's financial backers began to rock the boat. *Railroad Gazette* of December 20, 1878, told its readers that the President of the Kansas Pacific Railway, which held a large block of Denver & South Park Construction & Land Company stock, had filed suit seeking receivership of the construction firm, claiming that it was mismanaged. The suit was unsuccessful, but undoubtedly caused Evans some nervous moments. He certainly had enough other problems to contemplate without being diverted by a stockholders' revolt.

Leadville was the focus of his problems. None of the four major railroads which operated lines into the mountains west of Denver had envisioned Leadville as their major objective. The Denver & Rio Grande was headed to Mexico City and perhaps to the San Juan region; Leadville was an afterthought. The Denver, South Park & Pacific was headed to the South Park and the San Juan region; Leadville was an afterthought. The Atchison, Topeka & Santa Fe was headed to New Mexico; Leadville was an afterthought. The Union Pacific's subsidiary in the mountains, the Colorado Central, was heading for the mining region west of Denver; Leadville was an afterthought. Unfortunately all four railroads had the same afterthought, and all at about the same time. This situation fostered intense rivalry and swiftly shifting alliances. The Denver & Rio Grande and the Atchison, Topeka & Santa Fe fought bitterly over the Royal Gorge route to Leadville, in America's most famous railroad war, yet during part of that period the Denver & Rio Grande was controlled by the Santa Fe company. The Denver, South Park & Pacific and the Santa Fe company would form an alliance which spelled out cooperation and shared trackage in an effort to reach Leadville, yet interlocking contracts gave the Denver & Rio Grande a legal veto over the pact. The Denver, South Park & Pacific and the Denver & Rio Grande would agree to share trackage between Buena Vista and Leadville and between Nathrop and

Gunnison, but later would become the most bitter enemies. The Union Pacific would abandon its proposed line to Leadville from Georgetown, and instead absorb the Denver, South Park & Pacific as a U.P. route to Leadville. All of these complex maneuverings, and more, would occur in a space of about five years.

The rivalry between the D&RG and the AT&SF is pertinent to the South Park railroad's history only in that it drove the AT&SF and the South Park together — and in that it delayed construction of a line through the Royal Gorge long enough for the South Park to enter the Leadville race. Due to the Royal Gorge rivalry and the efforts of the Union Pacific crowd to freeze the Santa Fe line out of northern Colorado traffic, AT&SF Vice President and General Manager William B. Strong initiated discussions with John Evans about the first of December, 1878. At 11 p.m. on December 28, after a final eight-hour session of negotiation, AT&SF President Thomas Nickerson and Vice-President F. H. Peabody signed an agreement with Evans and the South Park management which signified the injection of AT&SF capital into the DSP&P which would guarantee completion of its construction to Leadville. *Railroad Gazette* subsequently quoted a New York newspaper's description of the terms of the agreement:

The contract provides for the purchase by the Atchison, Topeka & Santa Fe Railroad Company from the Denver & South Park Construction & Land Company, which has charge of the building of the Denver, South Park & Pacific Railroad, at par and accrued interest, of $700,000 of the 7 per cent. gold first-mortgage bonds of the last-named road. The purchase money is to be deposited with the Farmers' Loan & Trust Company, of New York, and is to be applied, first, toward the payment of the outstanding indebtedness of the construction company, and second, to complete the construction and equipment of the Denver, South Park & Pacific Railroad. The Atchison, Topeka & Santa Fe Company receives $700,000 of the capital stock of the Denver, South Park & Pacific Company, in order to maintain its control of that company. The issue of the first-mortgage bonds of the South Park Company is limited to $1,000,000, the $700,000 bonds received by the Atchison, Topeka & Santa Fe being deemed canceled and destroyed.

To guarantee the construction of the South Park Railroad $350,000 first-mortgage bonds of the company are to be pledged to the Atchison Company, and deposited with the Farmers' Loan & Trust Company. The contract also provides that whenever the Pueblo & Arkansas Valley Railroad (which practically is part of the Atchison, Topeka & Santa Fe road) shall be extended from its point of intersection with the Denver, South Park & Pacific road, near Trout Creek, on the Arkansas River, to Leadville, or any points beyond that place, the South Park Company shall have the right of joint trackage over the extension upon the payment of a monthly rental of 8 per cent. per annum on one-half of the actual cash cost of the construction of the track so far as used. The right of joint use of track upon the same terms over any extensions constructed by the Denver, South Park & Pacific Company connecting with the Pueblo & Arkansas Valley road is also confirmed to the Atchison, Topeka & Santa Fe Company. All extensions to the San Juan mining region by either the South Park or the Pueblo & Arkansas Valley Company are also to be subject to the same provisions of the agreement, which are to be perpetual. The tracks thus used in common are to be kept in repair at the joint expense of the two contracting railroad companies according to the traffic of each company upon the tracks so jointly used.

The agreement went on to specify a 25-year freight pool and a uniform rate structure, ending with a stipulation that both the South Park and the Pueblo and Arkansas Valley would complete and equip their roads to the point of their junction near Trout Creek on or before July 10, 1879.

The whole agreement was rendered void, however, because the lease by which the Atchison, Topeka & Santa Fe controlled the Denver & Rio Grande contained a clause which gave the Rio Grande stockholders veto power over any traffic agreement which the AT&SF might negotiate with Rio Grande rivals. L. H. Meyer, Trustee for the Denver & Rio Grande bondholders, vetoed the Santa Fe-South Park agreement in January. The South Park would have to build on to Leadville without any help from the Santa Fe.

While all this negotiating had been going on in Denver and New York, the South Park was continuing to do that very thing — build towards Leadville. By December 31, 1878, the end of track had reached Slaght's, 58.1 miles from the DSP&P depot at 6th & Larimer Streets in Denver, and during the year the company had extended its track a mile north from the depot in Denver to the new Denver Union Terminal. It had also constructed a .3-mile spur from one-half mile east of Morrison on the Morrison Branch south to Soda Lakes. *Railroad Gazette* reported that the Denver, South Park & Pacific had built 51 miles of track in 1878 (not counting the two small extensions), an impressive total when compared with the amount built during the previous three years — none.

On January 17, 1879, the South Park end of track reached Hall's Valley, soon to be renamed Webster. Here the railroad established another

33

temporary interchange point for the stage lines and wagon freighters which operated their business from the end of track to Leadville over Mosquito Pass, and other mining camps in the mountains.

On February 4, 1879, the Denver, South Park & Pacific Railroad bought its fifth locomotive, another 2-6-6T "bogie" engine built by the Mason Machine Works of Taunton, Massachusetts. But this engine was slightly smaller than the *Oro City* and the *San Juan*, with cylinders 12″ x 16″ instead of 13″ x 16″ as on the other two Mason machines, and with 34-inch drivers, three inches smaller in diameter than the other two. Its weight, too, was lighter, an even 21 tons. Furthermore, the engine was second hand. It had been built in January 1878 for the Kansas Central narrow gauge, arriving in Leavenworth, Kansas, on January 31, 1878, on a Chicago, Rock Island and Pacific flat car. The engine was named *L. T. Smith* and the *Leavenworth Daily Times* of February 1, 1878, described it as "one of the neatest little engines ever used in the West" and a "handsome piece of workmanship." The *Times* thought that being named for Mr. L. T. Smith was a "sure indication that it will always be on time," while the rival *Public Press* predicted that the engine "like its namesake, will be puffing and blowing all the time." The agent for the railroad declared that he had not seen a "neater piece of machinery in a long time."

Unfortunately the *L. T. Smith* jumped the track near Soldier Creek Bridge about two miles from Onaga, Kansas, on the evening of Wednesday, February 6, 1878, on one of her trial runs. She rolled over an embankment, the result being that the cab was "considerably mashed", although the engineer-fireman, a Mr. Parks, escaped without injury. The errant locomotive was rerailed on Tuesday, February 12, and on the following day the *Holton Signal* published a rumor that the *L. T. Smith* would be returned to the manufacturer. The engine was undergoing repairs on February 27, although by March 6 it was still without a cab, and on May 1 the *Signal* repeated the rumor that it would be returned to the Mason company, being too heavy for the railroad. Although the *Leavenworth Daily Times* noted that the rumor lacked confirmation, on June 11 it had to swallow those words and report that the engine was being returned to the manufacturer that very day. "It is so constructed that it does not work well on their track, and will have to be refitted," claimed the *Times*. The Mason works thus had a little over seven months in which to rebuild its wayward engine. Sold to the South Park on February 4, 1879 as No. 5, and named *Leadville*, the locomotive

arrived in Denver on a Kansas Pacific freight on the night of February 18, 1879.

The railroad on which the new locomotive would operate was making steady although slow progress. Construction from Webster to the summit of Kenosha was the most difficult the locating engineers had encountered since the first six miles up the South Platte Cañon. After making a horseshoe curve in Hall's Valley the railroad line consisted of continual sidehill cuts and involved a large quantity of heavy rock work for the grading crews, with steep 3.9 per cent grades and seemingly endless curves. By March 29 there were 350 men at work on the grading. George Crofutt, writing the text for a new guidebook that April, described the South Park railroad's progress:

WEBSTER — is the end of the track, 70 miles from Denver. It is a few miles east of the "Kenosha Hills," over which the company are grading their track, by a zig zag route to gain elevation, and enable them to reach the South Park, ten miles distant. Once in the Park, the labor of grading is very light, and we understand it is the design of the company to push the building of their road vigorously, toward the great silver regions to the westward, of which, Leadville is the recognized center. At this time, the greater portion of travel from Denver for the South Park, Fairplay, and Leadville take this route. The distance to Leadville is about 65 miles, but a new wagon road is soon to be opened, reducing the distance to about 45 miles. Four and six horse coaches leave Webster on arrival of the cars.

One Albert Sanford would later recall departure of a South Park train from Denver for the end-of-track at Webster during that spring of 1879, when he was a young boy:

"The Morning Passenger" train had been backed in, headed by two engines that took turns "popping" the safety valve. Already there were many passengers boarding to find the best seats and a place for bundles that varied in size from an ordinary bed roll to a fairly complete prospecting outfit, which, before leaving time, were frequently gathered up by a pair of brawny brakemen and thrown promiscuously into a box car ahead . . . To original equipment that was used on the Morrison Branch, a few new coaches had been added, and, on this occasion, a "special" was attached to the rear.

Now, among my railroad friends, was "Long Bill" Draper, a brakeman who was stationed at the entrance to the special with a list of those having reservations. Something happened "up ahead," Draper was called from his post, and, hurriedly passing the list to me with orders to admit no others, disappeared, and a thrill came to me that has never been duplicated . . .

I had completed an examination of this roll of honor, discovered that with few exceptions,

This exceptional Weitfle photograph captures the spirit of Webster when it was "end of track" and trans-shipment point from rail to stage or wagon for the arduous journey to Leadville and other camps. The long South Park narrow gauge train on the rough, unballasted pole-tie track, the mounds of baggage and freight scattered on the station platform, the timbers and tents in the background are all integral parts of the scene. (Denver Public Library Western Hist. Coll.)

Kenosha Pass provided the DSP&P with an exit from the Platte Canyon into the road's namesake Park. From Webster the track climbed nearly a thousand feet in less than seven miles; altitude at the top of the pass was 9,991 feet. Top, DSP&P 42 (ex-No. 6 Tenmile) is standing at Webster with a waycar in this late-1880s view, while a long freight can be seen descending the east slope of Kenosha on the hillside above. Center, a construction train with a load of pole ties is at the top of Kenosha, headed west; some of photographer Collier's equipment is at right. (Both, Museum Collection.) Bottom, another Mason (probably No. 5) poses for its picture on the west slope of the pass. (State Hist. Society of Colorado Coll.)

I knew every man by sight, when my first test came with the arrival of a carriage and I checked in David Moffat, Walter Cheesman and Eben Smith.

In the meantime Draper returned and another carriage rolled up in a cloud of dust and its occupant jumped to the ground before the vehicle stopped. A large, broad-shouldered man with a heavy, drooping moustache, who seemed to know everybody and everybody knew him, came up. He was a man whose millions had just begun to be poured out of the [silver] carbonate beds of Leadville, with a good part, even then, being so invested in Denver that makers of new maps began to give the city more prominence — Horace A. W. Tabor — and he had time to grasp the hand of this passenger brakeman and say, "Howdy, Bill."

The next arrival came in an express wagon, seated with the driver, with an overcoat and a man-size carpet sack, the only baggage . . . He did not jump from his perch but rather made the descent backwards with a firm hold on the seat, as an old farmer would do. The smile of that expressman, as a fee and a tip, too, no doubt, was handed him, broadened as his passenger said, "Tom, you made it in good time, but I don't think you missed that darn sprinkling cart six inches. Goodbye, good luck." This man, short and rather stout of build, was dressed in "digging clothes" that showed stains from mine drippings and candle grease, with trousers tucked in the tops of heavy boots. He also wore a heavy dark moustache, "burnsides," reaching half way down his cheeks and kindly eyes, shaded by heavy brows. Some one asked as he was being cordially greeted by all, "How is the 'Morning Star'?" This was John L. Routt, owner of one of the latest bonanza strikes and governor of Colorado.

Both engine bells are ringing and two men, apart from the crowd, are so engrossed in conversation over freight and passenger problems to Leadville that, apparently, the time card is forgotten. "Stuttering Billy" Jackson, the conductor, hurries to them, and, partly overcoming his impediment to speech, says, "Don't want to rush you and the Colonel, Governor, but we're ready to pull out," and as "Billy" waves a signal to Engineers Frank Kaub and "Little Joe" Horgan, the president of the South Park Road, John Evans, and "Bob" Spotswood, the veteran stage man, get aboard as the long slack of the train starts the rear car with a jerk.

The passengers would find Webster to be a booming end-of-track town where diminutive balloon-stacked Mason locomotives shunted freight cars back and forth while wagon freighters loaded merchandise outbound for Fairplay and Leadville and other arriving wagons disgorged piles of silver ingots for shipment east. Here the iron horses mingled with the four-footed variety, as Spotswood & McClellan stage coaches loaded passengers for the spectacular ride over Mosquito Pass. Here was the supply base for the graders building the 6.8 miles of grade to the summit of the ridge which separated the South Park railroad from the South Park region. "We have not got over the Kenosha Hill as quick as we expected last fall for the reason that we filled up those deep ravines with embankments entire instead of putting in trassel work as originally contemplated," Evans wrote on May 6, 1879, adding that "We begin tracklaying tomorrow." Thus it was a conscious management decision to build the railroad solidly at the beginning, rather than to resort to time-saving but costly expedients such as tall timber trestles which would eventually have to be replaced, which helped to slow the progress of construction. It seemed a wise and economy-minded move—except for the factor that the South Park was racing other narrow gauge lines for entry into the mountain mining towns, so that ultimately lost time might prove more costly than installation and later replacement of temporary trestles.

It was not until 1 p.m. on May 19 that the tracklayers completed spiking their rails down on hand-hewn "pole" ties at the summit of Kenosha Pass, 9,991 feet above sea level. They thus reached a mountain crossing which for the next year would be the highest point attained by any railroad in North America, exceeding the Denver & Rio Grande's 1877 record set at Veta Pass by 749 feet. At 3:30 p.m., two and a half hours after track had reached Kenosha, the first DSP&P train pulled up to the summit.

Grading crews, of course, were at work far ahead in the vast valley known as the South Park. The Board of Directors had adopted the final surveys for construction from the town of Jefferson on the South Park side of Kenosha Pass to the vicinity of the mouth of Trout Creek on April 15, 1879, while the end of track was still at Webster, and on May 24 they adopted a further survey from the mouth of Trout Creek up the Arkansas Valley through Buena Vista to Malta, three miles below Leadville. The company had advertised for bids for construction along the first of these two surveys immediately. Not only was construction across the South Park relatively problem-free, even the grade down the west side of the pass to the valley floor was comparatively easy to build. That does not mean that the South Park was entirely flat, however; there were hills to be climbed and hills to be outflanked, creeks to be crossed, and crossed again, but none of these posed difficulties on the order of those experienced in the first few miles of Platte Cañon or between Webster and Kenosha. *Railway Age* reported that the grading crews had reached Jefferson in mid-May and the tracklayers were expected to arrive there by May 20, 1879. Three hundred men were at work on DSP&P construction, pushing the railroad forward at a rate of one half to three quarters of a mile per day.

That same month John Evans was still seeking some agreement with the Santa Fe to eliminate the duplication of plant which construction of two parallel narrow gauge rail lines from the foot of Trout Creek Pass to Leadville would create. On May 6, 1879, he wrote the prominent banker, Mahlon D. Thatcher, a lengthy letter in which he outlined his plans to attempt a last-ditch effort to avoid cut-throat competition over this route. He also mentioned the status of its construction:

> It seems too bad too that we should build two roads from Trout Creek to Leadville when one track ought to answer — By the way we have our location for an independent line all the way [to Leadville] completed and our engineers say will have a cheaper line than the A.T.&S.F. though our grades and curves will not be quite so good. We expect to be at the Arkansas river on or soon after the time proposed. And shall be able to raise all the money necessary without the sale of a bond if we so elect.

Meanwhile, just as Leadville had diverted Colorado railroads from earlier goals, the booming Gunnison region west of the main range of the Rockies beyond the Arkansas Valley similarly beckoned the South Park and its competitors. As early as May 20, 1879, John Evans wrote Eicholtz,

> The finding [of] a pass over to Elk Mountain via Chalk Creek, Cottonwood or Marshall Pass as soon as possible for our road is of the utmost importance to my negotiations as you know. Don't think your observations without barometer or cords will do me any good. If anything prevents you from making thorough reports, such as made on the Poncha Pass, don't fail to send me word in time to get Maj. Evans to send some one else to do it.

Eicholtz, of course, had scouted these passes earlier without making any measured survey, and John Evans did not regard such preliminary work as adequate. He opened his letter by saying that "Chatfield goes up in the morning and takes the 'Rod', 'Tape Lines', & 'Barometer' with him — I had no better express line to send [them] by."

But although Evans wanted hard data on a possible route to Gunnison, that did not mean he was yet willing to give up plans to build via Poncha Pass to Del Norte and the San Juan region. He continued:

> If we can get a good route to Elk Mountain as we have over Poncha pass by your report we will get all the money we want. But I am

impatient of not getting reports. I wrote you yesterday [May 5, 1879] what to do about the work in Poncha. If necessary to occupy the difficult points put more men on. Don't fail to send maps & profiles as quick as possible so I can finish up & file.

Thus in May 1879, as the end-of-track of the Denver, South Park & Pacific Railroad progressed slowly down the west slope of Kenosha Pass into the South Park, through that great valley and beyond over Trout Creek Pass, DSP&P surveyors prepared to tackle the various approaches to the Collegiate and Saguache Ranges to find a route to Gunnison.

The easiest of the passes mentioned by Evans was Marshall Pass, an offshoot of Poncha Pass, but its liability lay in the fact that it crossed the range far south of any direct route to Gunnison. Had Eicholtz adopted that route, the South Park would have found it necessary to loop far south to cross the Saguache range, then head northwest to reach the Gunnison mining region. Thus Eicholtz chose to enter the main range of the Rockies via Chalk Creek Cañon, using one of several possible passes to cross the range, a route he had scouted during the last week of April.

Thus South Park surveyors were already at work laying out a rail route to Gunnison before the DSP&P end-of-track had crossed the South Park. Meanwhile, *Railway World* described the experience of riding to the end-of-track while it was still at Kenosha Pass:

> At present this ride over the South Park is by no means a comfortable one. Travellers who have been accustomed to Palace Sleeping Cars for night travel find an all night ride in a narrow gauge car with low backed cushionless seats not a little fatigueing and hardly a good preparation for 15 hours of stage coaching over the roughest of mountain roads.
>
> The scenes at the end of track, even at 5 or 6 o'clock in the morning, were extremely interesting and suggestive of our destination. The end of track of an unfinished railroad is always a busy place; but at the summit, besides the shanties of the workmen, the heaps of construction material, and the temporary station, there were piles of base bullion, looking like pig lead and car loads of high class silver ore in small sacks, waiting for transportation to Denver, besides groceries and merchandise of every description, machinery, household goods, hay, grain, and almost every other necessity of modern civilization all ready to start through the park and over the range to Leadville on wagon trains. A short distance from the station were the camps and corrals of the wagon trains. A few were loaded ready to start, and the teamsters were hitching up their mules, each team consisting of 6 or 8 mules which pull two wagons, one chained behind the other.

Westward from Kenosha track-laying progressed steadily, and the first South Park train reached the vicinity of the South Park coal mines, a point which the railroad would name Como, on June 21, 1879. *Railroad Gazette* of June 27 reported the end of track at Hamilton, 90 miles from Denver, or two miles beyond the measured location of Como; in fact, Hamilton may have been an earlier name for Como. Although on August 8 the same journal reported the grade work complete all the way to the Arkansas River at the foot of Trout Creek Pass near Buena Vista, the end-of-track was still far behind, and Governor Evans reported on September 1 that 92 miles of main line were in operation, or only two more than were in service over a month earlier — hardly the "mile-a-day" of track-laying claimed by Denver newspapers.

Fairplay, not far beyond Como, had been eclipsed by Leadville as the important objective of the Denver, South Park & Pacific, and because of this and because of the terrain involved, the railroad would not build its main line through that town. A direct route between Como and Fairplay encountered the Red Hills which the railroad could outflank more easily than it could cross. The railroad would reach Fairplay by a branch line backtracking ten miles from Garos on the floor of the South Park, and there was not as much urgency about completion of trackage to Fairplay as there was to reaching the Arkansas River.

Another problem faced the South Park management during the fall of 1879, as was indicated by the *Denver Tribune* in September:

> It was rumored on the street that the Denver & Rio Grande managers intend to sue out a writ of injunction to prevent the Denver & South Park from going into the Arkansas Valley . . . That such a proposition has been broached by the Denver & Rio Grande managers is positive. Whether they will dare to carry it into effect is a question which a very few days will decide. The aim of the plan is clear. The Denver & Rio Grande claims the right of way along the Arkansas River, and they desire to prevent the South Park from continuing its construction just as they stopped the Santa Fe. The completion of the line is of such great importance, both to the South Park and the people of Leadville, that any sum these people will claim may be raised to prevent the stoppage of construction. The South Park managers have the Santa Fe experience as a guide, and they know how effective the canon litigation was in stopping the Leadville extension [of the AT&SF] from Canon City. Whether the fear of similar obstacles may move them to pay the Rio Grande managers into letting them alone, time will settle. If the writ is served and the matter put in litigation, it is safe to say that Leadville will have no

railroad this year, and perhaps not next.

Thus by September, 1879, the Santa Fe company (and its Pueblo & Arkansas Valley narrow gauge subsidiary) had lost its chance to build up the valley of the Arkansas to Leadville, and the South Park management faced as a rival in that arena the Denver & Rio Grande.

Progress continued, however, on the line to Gunnison, which faced no threat such as litigation. By that fall, Eicholtz and his surveyors had selected Altman Pass as the most desirable of several possible crossings of the range reached by the valley of Chalk Creek, and the engineers made plans for a long tunnel under the pass which they would call Alpine Tunnel. This would necessitate about four miles of wagon road, departing from the Williams Pass toll road in the floor of the valley and following "Tunnel Gulch" to its end, then curving south in a horseshoe to climb up to the site of a tunnel construction camp. Work on the tunnel would thus begin long before work on the grade beyond the Arkansas Valley had even been started, and on October 30, 1879 the South Park management asked for bids for building Alpine Tunnel:

Notice to Railroad Contractors
Denver, South Park and Pacific Railroad Company.
President's Office
Denver, Colo., Oct. 30, 1879.

Sealed Proposals will be received at this office until the 18th proximo for the construction of the tunnel about 1,600 feet long on the extension of the road of said company, from the Arkansas Valley to the Valley of the Gunnison, at Alpine Pass, head of Chalk Creek. The time at which the contractor will agree to complete the work will be an element of importance in the bids. Plans and specifications may be seen at this office for one week preceding the letting. The company reserves the right to reject any and all bids.

By authority of the board of trustees.
John Evans, President.

The DSP&P let the contract for construction of Alpine Tunnel to M. Cummings & Company on November 25, 1879, with the stipulation that the tunnel be completed by July 1, 1880. This meant the immediate beginning of construction of a tunnel at an elevation of 11,600 feet at the onset of winter on the spine of the continent. The terms were impossible!

Meanwhile, Evans' negotiations with the Santa Fe had collapsed and he had commenced negotiations with Jay Gould and the Denver & Rio Grande management. With the Santa Fe out of the picture and the Rio Grande in, it still seemed illogical to him for two railroads to build parallel lines into Leadville. The terrain between Buena Vista and

Leadville was not as restrictive as the Royal Gorge, so that the Denver & Rio Grande, whatever its threats and despite its prior claim to the best right of way, could not convincingly claim that the topography allowed room for only one rail line — its own. In addition to these factors, the prominent financier Jay Gould found it advantageous at this moment to lend his weight to maneuver the Rio Grande and the South Park interests into a peaceful accord rather than cut-throat rivalry. The result was a Joint Operating Agreement signed by officers of both railroads on October 1, 1879. By its terms, the Denver & Rio Grande would build and own trackage from the vicinity of Buena Vista to Leadville, granting the South Park the right to use the same trackage for its own trains for a fee. The South Park, on the other hand, would build trackage to the Gunnison Country, granting the Denver & Rio Grande the right to operate its own trains over those rails for a fee. Since the D&RG was still blocked at the Royal Gorge, it was envisioned that the South Park would reach Buena Vista first. Therefore Denver & Rio Grande crews would commence construction of an isolated segment of their railroad between Buena Vista and Leadville, and the South Park would supply them with track material shipped in over the South Park railroad to Buena Vista at a special low rate to be determined by negotiations. The *Colorado Springs Gazette* claimed further that by this agreement the South Park left the San Juan region, its initial stated objective, to the Denver & Rio Grande.

The Denver, South Park & Pacific was an increasingly busy railroad that fall, while Jay Gould, John Evans and William Jackson Palmer maneuvered for position. Its original locomotives were still in service: in fact No. 2, the *Platte Cañon*, chose Saturday, September 13, to back towards a mis-aligned turntable at Morrison, thus dumping its tender into the turn-table pit. The railroad now had many more engines on order from Mason, so taxing that builder that the DSP&P had to purchase additional motive power from Baldwin, as well as three more used Dawson & Baily engines. The railroad's rolling stock was also multiplying, and the *Denver Times* described in October an item of especial interest:

> The new Pullman palace car recently built at Detroit for the Denver & South Park railroad . . . is the first narrow gauge Pullman ever constructed for any road. It is named the *South Park* and is a very handsome car, built very similar to the standard popular sleepers of the broader gauges. The body of the coach is eighteen inches narrower than those built for the standard, and the aisles in proportion.

> The berths are also smaller than in the larger cars, and are each intended to hold but one person. The exterior of the car is painted the regulation color and ornamented in the Eastlake style. The interior is elaborately finished in mahogany, upholstered in crimson plush, hung with silk curtains and fitted with silver-plated rods and lamps. The ceiling is handsomely frescoed, and the interior arrangements are elaborate and are strictly first-class. The *South Park* is the forerunner, as it were, of a numerous band to come. Three more sleepers of precisely the same construction have been ordered, and are expected to arrive in a few days. With these valuable acquisitions the South Park road will be second to no narrow gauge railroad in the world in the efficiency of its stock. With Horton reclining chair cars and Pullman sleepers, the public ought to be well satisfied with its accommodations.

Construction of the line across the South Park continued at a snail's pace. By October 30, the end of track had reached Weston, 107 miles from Denver. In fact, the Denver, South Park & Pacific did not do as well as it had in 1878, for by December 31 it had completed only 46.6 miles of track that year to a point 166 miles from Denver, 3.8 miles short of the summit of Trout Creek Pass. The company had built 51 miles of track in 1878.

One matter which diverted effort from main line construction was the necessity of building two short mine branches near Como. Both east and west of the main line at this point were coal mines which had been opened up in the 1870s. The Lechner or Upper Como Mine to the west lay in the foothills of the Park Range, and coal from this mine had been hauled by wagon to Fairplay and other markets. To the southeast, down Park Gulch, lay a more productive mine named for W. H. King, the county clerk and postmaster. The South Park railroad had invested in this mine, just as it had obtained interests in the coal mines and other industries near Morrison.

A 3.32-mile long branch line to the King Coal Mines, leaving the main line about ¾ of a mile short of Como at milepost 87.4, was completed and put into service in 1880. These mines were located on the west side of a low ridge composed of a soft, granulated, sandy shale which made tunneling exceedingly difficult. Even with the use of cross-bars and lagging, sand would readily flow into the mines and fill them up. Furthermore, they contained explosive gas and were dangerous mines to work. Nevertheless, the King Coal Mines were busy producers, for they turned out a fine locomotive fuel. King soon became a sizeable community with 60 wooden company houses.

The Lechner Mine was not quite so attractive, nevertheless the DSP&P also built a 1.4-mile long spur northwest from Como to this mine in 1880.

On January 10, 1880, President John Evans wrote Jay Gould, who had been purchasing South Park stock, regarding the current status of the company, and commented on the progress of construction:

> We are pushing tracklaying toward Buena Vista but the construction force meets many delays on account of want of punctuality in parties upon whom we relied to furnish timbers, &c. Hope to get better organized for our extension.

As the DSP&P crossed Trout Creek 27 times negotiating the valley from the summit of the pass to the Arkansas River, the need for bridge timbers was apparent. On January 16, Evans wrote Gould: "The road will be opened to Buena Vista in about two weeks if the weather permits work . . ." Evans was, as usual, unduly optimistic. On February 6, Evans wired Gould in New York: "South Park reached the Arkansas today. If Rio Grande will go ahead track may reach Leadville as soon as iron can be laid." *Railroad Gazette* subsequently reported that DSP&P trains commenced regular operation to Arkansas Station on the east bank of the river on February 11, 1880. This location was several miles south of Buena Vista, and that distance included a bridge over the Arkansas. The 150-foot steel span was slung across the river on February 14, and South Park trains first reached Buena Vista on March 3, 1880.

Evans' February 6 telegram to Gould, of course, anticipated immediate beginning of Denver & Rio Grande tracklaying from the vicinity of Buena Vista north to Leadville on the grade previously constructed by the Santa Fe subsidiary, the Pueblo & Arkansas Valley Railroad, in accordance with the Joint Operating Agreement of October 1, 1879. This would have been a disconnected segment of Denver & Rio Grande track, however, as the Denver & Rio Grande was still stalled in the Royal Gorge by litigation with the Atchison, Topeka & Santa Fe, and although the Royal Gorge War was supposedly ended by the "Treaty of Boston" or the "Tripartite Agreement" of March 27, 1880, the Santa Fe managed to drag matters out until April 5, and it was not until then that the D&RG could resume track-laying. Thus the D&RG would not reach Buena Vista for some time; nor would it undertake premature construction from Buena Vista north, since such construction would benefit the South Park railroad more than itself, both in giving the DSP&P early access to Leadville and in giving the South Park freight revenue for hauling track material to Buena Vista from Denver. No, the D&RG would wait until its own end-of-track reached Buena Vista before building northward to Leadville.

The Joint Operating Agreement also envisioned the South Park using D&RG track southward from the point where it reached the Arkansas River at the foot of Trout Creek Pass to whatever point it chose to diverge west towards Gunnison. The point of divergence had been selected as Chalk Creek, about five miles south of Arkansas Station. With the Rio Grande railroad still stalled in the Royal Gorge, the DSP&P impatiently commenced construction southward on the Rio Grande grade, building the track itself as far as Nathrop, where it turned west again towards the Collegiate Range. By mid-March it had laid three of the five miles of track. The Denver & Rio Grande did not reach South Arkansas (Salida) until May 20, and was not at Nathrop until June 1, by which time the DSP&P was building track westward across the broad valley of the Arkansas towards the Chalk Cliffs. The D&RG construction forces proceeded onward, absorbing about five miles of DSP&P track from Nathrop to the vicinity of Arkansas Station, then building several more miles of their own track to reach Buena Vista on June 9. Construction continued throughout the summer, and the D&RG railhead pushed into Malta on June 29 and reached Leadville on July 20, 1880.

In accordance with the Joint Trackage Agreement, by July 2, 1880, the South Park was operating daily passenger trains between Denver and Malta, three miles short of Leadville, and on July 16 the DSP&P added two daily freight trains to that terminus. And thirteen days after the D&RG completed construction of track to Leadville, the DSP&P scheduled its own daily passenger and freight trains into that booming city.

And booming it was, so much so that the immense traffic the South Park was profitably handling gave rise to the claim that the DSP&P was the most profitable railroad enterprise ever undertaken in the United States! But what may have been true for a brief period of several years would have to be tested over the long haul of a half century to determine whether any such claim could stand the wear of time. Certainly as of 1880, the DSP&P had suffered more lean years than fat ones!

Having reached Leadville, the focus on South Park construction shifted back to Alpine Tunnel, where the construction forces were facing great difficulty. The weather at an altitude of nearly 12,000 feet during the middle of winter was indeed "alpine". The contractors had faced great difficulty in building their road up Tunnel Gulch and erecting their construction camps in December snows, and the men commenced excavating the curved entrance to the eastern portal early in

For a brief period the South Park and D&RG jointly operated the line up the Arkansas from Buena Vista to Leadville. Above, switching the Buena Vista yards is a South Park Dawson & Baily mogul — second hand from the Cairo & St. Louis, its wooden pilot lost in some mishap. (Museum Collection.) Below, Main Street in Buena Vista; the two story building houses a "railroad hospital." (Denver Public Library Western History Coll.)

Leadville, objective of the feverish railroad race between the DSP&P and D&RG, looked like this at the time, the view being east along Harrison Avenue. The Clarendon Hotel is at left, but the rationale behind the log structure in the middle of the street is not at hand. (Neal Miller Coll.) The old map reproduced in part below reflects the grandiose expansion schemes of the South Park's management in 1880.

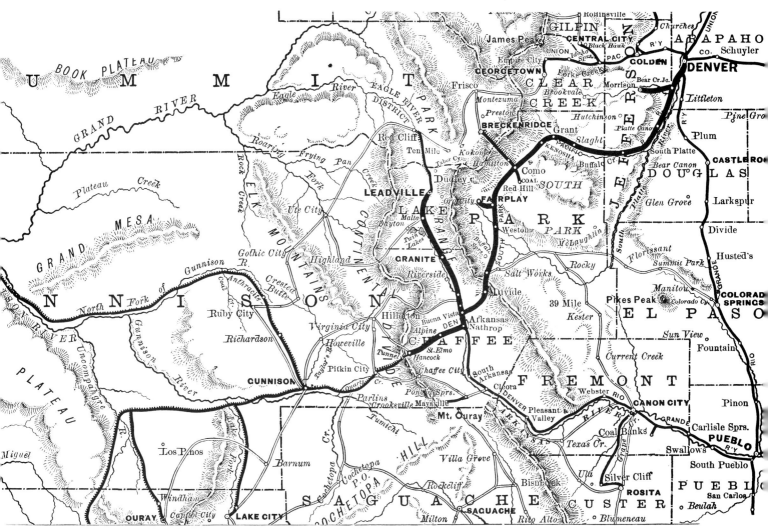

January, 1880. Instead of solid granite, the ridge through which the tunnel was being dug and blasted turned out to be composed of slide rock and decomposed granite, rubble debris which over the eons had fallen from the slopes of the mountains on each side, all of it veined with troublesome streams of water. Itinerant laborers, experienced miners from Leadville, a gang of blacks, all picked and dug away at the ridge, but the progress could be measured in inches, and nearly every inch gained had to be timbered using 12 x 12-inch beams of California redwood with heavy lagging between them. Few laborers lasted long in temperatures which reached — 40° F. On January 8, 1880, the DSP&P let contracts for grading and tie delivery not only between the foot of Trout Creek Pass and Alpine Tunnel but on the other side of the tunnel towards Gunnison. By March, progress on the tunnel itself was so slow, the management discussed at length the possibility of constructing a switchback over the pass pending completion of the tunnel, as the Atchison, Topeka & Santa Fe had just done in crossing Raton Pass. But although construction of such a switchback was not impossible from engineering considerations alone, except in summer its construction and operation would have been rendered nearly impossible by the brutal weather which enveloped Alpine Pass during most of the year. The idea of building a switchback over the summit of the pass was rejected.

By April, M. Cummings & Company had completed only 150 of 1,771.1 feet of tunneling. Consequently in May, Eicholtz began negotiations with the firm of Fitzgerald, Cushing and Osborn of Lincoln, Nebraska. Early in June he notified the Cummings firm that they had lost the contract and on July 12, 1880, the Fitzgerald firm signed on to do the job.

Construction of grade and tracklaying up Chalk Creek progressed much faster than the digging of Alpine Tunnel. *Railroad Gazette* of July 16 reported that DSP&P track had reached Hortense, at the entrance to Chalk Creek Cañon six miles west of Buena Vista, and on August 28 the *Gunnison Review* announced that the DSP&P had commenced running passenger trains as far as Heywood Springs, which was a half mile short of the end of track at Hortense. On the far side of the range, the *Gunnison Review* reported that the DSP&P had purchased all the rails needed to reach Gunnison, and on the west side of Alpine Pass ties were being delivered and piled at Quartz Creek ready for use. In Gunnison itself, stonemasons were at work on a new stone depot for the DSP&P at the corner of 9th Street and York Avenue.

The Joint Operating Agreement gave the Denver & Rio Grande trackage rights over the DSP&P west of Nathrop, and the *Rocky Mountain News* of October 10, 1880, announced the operation of D&RG trains over the 5.8 miles of DSP&P track between Nathrop and Hortense, where passengers changed to stages for the ride over Williams Pass to the Gunnison region. The *Rocky Mountain News* of December 23 announced that the line was open to Alpine (later called Fisher), 12.2 miles short of the tunnel, and by the end of the year the end-of-track had stretched another 4.4 miles to St. Elmo, 16.9 miles west of Nathrop. Alpine nevertheless remained the terminus of operations for some months, and a Denver & Rio Grande Railway employees' time table of January 9, 1881, showed two D&RG passenger trains between Nathrop and Alpine each day. Train No. 77 left Alpine at 5:35 a.m. passing Hortense at 6:35, arriving at Nathrop at 7 a.m., departing Nathrop as No. 76 at 7:50 a.m. and arriving at Alpine at 9:15 a.m. The evening train, No. 75, left Alpine at 4:50 p.m. arriving in Nathrop at 6:15 p.m., departing at 8:50 p.m. and arriving back at Alpine at 10:15 p.m.

Momentous changes, meanwhile, had taken place in railroad strategy in the Rockies which would doom this cooperation between the South Park and the Rio Grande and result in the most bitter enmity. Jay Gould, having failed to gain complete control of the Denver & Rio Grande, had been investing in the Denver, South Park & Pacific. Evans had in fact been playing Gould and Palmer off against one another in negotiations for purchase of stock, and in the end it was Gould who won. The practical effect of this shift in stock ownership was that the Denver, South Park & Pacific would become a subsidiary of the Union Pacific Railroad.

The agreement between the Denver & Rio Grande and the Atchison, Topeka & Santa Fe of February 1880 had involved a third party — hence the name "Tripartite Agreement". That third party was the Union Pacific, and like the Santa Fe road, it agreed not to build into the mountains of central Colorado, territory which was to be left to the Denver & Rio Grande. Gould's purchase of controlling interest in the South Park broke the spirit if not the letter of that agreement. William Jackson Palmer, president of the Denver & Rio Grande, had been caught napping by the Santa Fe when the Royal Gorge War began; he would not be caught napping again. If Gould's interest in the South Park gave the Union Pacific control of the line over Alpine Pass to Gunnison, then the Denver & Rio Grande would build its *own* line to Gunnison, over Marshall Pass, thus breaking the Joint Operating Agreement it had made with the Den-

The junction of the Rio Grande and South Park at Nathrop is shown above, about 1880-1881, looking south. The D&RG track from Pueblo passes the substantial stone station at left; the DSP&P track from Denver turns off at the stub switch in the foreground and passes to the right of the station and the Nachtrieb Hotel. At left, the scene as viewed from the hills to the east. The South Park track can be seen swinging around past the Hotel (center) and behind the low hill beyond; a D&RG engine is switching the brief yards (left). (Upper, Mal Ferrell Coll.; left, State Hist. Society of Colo. Coll.)

As soon as the South Park's track had penetrated the Chalk Creek Canyon and train service begun, William H. Jackson made a photographic tour over the line, posing his little "mixed" train (engine No. 3, the first of the Mason bogies, with box car and coach) at various scenic locations. Page opposite top, the train is near Hortense, and bottom, near Cascades. The view on this page left is near St. Elmo. (Top. opp., Museum Collection; others, Denver Public Library Western Hist. Coll.)

Although the photo at right is clearly stamped "Rainbow Falls, Chalk Creek, DSP&P RR", the train is identifiable as a D&RG train. The D&RG did have joint traffic rights over the South Park between Nathrop and Alpine (Fisher) for a brief period; however, further investigation indicates that the locale is actually on the D&RG's Blue River Branch above Leadville, despite the photographer's identification. (Denver Public Library Western History Collection.)

ver, South Park & Pacific. During the second week of September, 1880, the D&RG let contracts for grading a line towards Gunnison, a week later men were driving pilings for the railroad bridge over the Arkansas at Salida, by October 2 grading crews were at work, and on October 21 the track-layers spiked down the first rail on the D&RG's Gunnison Extension.

Denver & Rio Grande employees' time tables continued to list the two daily passenger trains each way on the "Alpine Branch" from Nathrop to Alpine until December 4, 1881; whether they actually operated that long is unknown. Evans was furious with Palmer for commencing a D&RG line to Gunnison, just as Palmer had been furious with Evans for selling DSP&P control to Jay Gould of the Union Pacific. But although that part of the Joint Operating Agreement which left construction to Gunnison entirely to the South Park lay dead, the D&RG still sought what profits it could reap from sharing trackage as far up Chalk Creek as Alpine, and from the mileage revenues it received from letting South Park trains operate from Buena Vista to Leadville, and the South Park was wholly dependent upon 35.5 miles of Denver & Rio Grande trackage for its entry into Leadville. But the consequences of Evans' sale of South Park control to the Union Pacific were not finished with Denver & Rio Grande construction of an independent line of its own to Gunnison; now the South Park would have to build a line of *its* own to Leadville. The ramifications of this stock transfer would thus reverberate throughout the Rocky Mountains for another four years, with much unnecessary duplication of railroad track and plant.

Evans remained associated with the DSP&P even though it was under Union Pacific control, and he and his Denver cronies soon discovered to their dismay what U.P. control could mean. At the beginning of the new year, 1881, the Union Pacific announced that the Denver, South Park & Pacific, although technically still a separately incorporated company, would be operated as the South Park Division of the Union Pacific Railroad. And before a week was out, Union Pacific headquarters in Omaha had issued a new tariff sheet which drove DSP&P freight rates sky high. Evans immediately wired Sidney Dillon in protest and on January 6 wrote Assistant General Manager T. L. Kimball:

> The rules about coal load rates are turning all through business over the Rio Grande, and the new local rates have literally suspended business along the line. Many of our best customers will be bankrupted by it and the road left without traffic unless changed at once. Orders to agents not to ship without prepayment of freights, issued from Omaha today, don't touch the case. Unless a change is made soon, the business will be ruined and the road will not pay operating expenses.

The following day he protested to Jay Gould himself:

> The legislature is now in session, and many members propose to regulate our tariffs and prohibit all pooling between Railroads in the state &c &c.
>
> Just at such an unfortunate time, Mr. Vining (without any consultation either with me, Col. Fisher, or Col. Hughes, our late Gen'l Freight Agent, who had arranged our tariffs, and made our rules, revised them again and again to get business and make the most out of it) issues a new tariff raising prices on our local business to a prohibitory point, and adopting rules which will throw most of the through freight on to the Rio Grande, and increase operating expenses greatly.
>
> For instance, we had at great pains got up cars to carry 12 tons, and thus save dead weights. He charges double rates for all over 8 tons in our car load rates.
>
> The quarries at Morrison produce a great amount of freights, and mainly belong to the South Park Company. His rates for stone and lime are double the highest we had ever been able to get. This suspends work at your own quarries, and throws the business onto the D&RG.
>
> We had with great care worked up a lumber, wood and tie business from the forests on our road, and by liberal rates for timber from our own lands had built up a very large and profitable traffic at high rates from this source. Vining's tariff on the products of the forest are so great, that the business is suspended. His charge for wood from Buffalo, is double that we had, and is nearly as much as wood is worth.
>
> It has not only stopped shipments, but will bankrupt the men we have induced to go on our road to do business. Coal too is put at prohibitory rates. Some ordered before knowing the rise is refused at the depot because the freights are more than the price of the coal in the market.
>
> This unfortunate blunder is followed up today with orders not to ship any more to parties refusing to take these goods and pay more freights than the goods are worth, unless freights are prepaid.
>
> Of course this makes the matter (serious as it is) ridiculous in the extreme.
>
> The road will not pay operating expenses long under such management.
>
> The master of transportation, Mr. McCormick, says his empty cars are filling the side tracks for want of business already. If continued much longer, this management will ruin the property. It will now require a long time to reestablish the business interrupted.
>
> Perhaps the most unfortunate aspect of the case is that it comes just as our Legislature is

Gunnison, 1880: heralded as the future "Pittsburgh of the west" and objective of a costly railroad-building race between the South Park and the D&RG. Unprepossessing as it may appear here with its raw mud street, it did feature an "Oyster Depot" with "New York and Baltimore Oysters received daily" (left) and an "Art Gallery" (right). (Gunnison Camera Center photo).

convened. The men whose business is interrupted both builders, shippers, quarrymen, lumber men, wood choppers, &c raise a great hue and cry against the oppressions of the U.P. monopoly as they call it and demand legislative protection.

The papers have been pointing out shortcomings of the U.P. and praising the D&RG to our detriment for a week or two, and now urge legislation. Our board of trade last night took up the question and appointed a committee to prepare a bill. We had a pretty solid sentiment against any legislation at this time lest it interfere with building roads when this blunder was made. Now, I fear it will be difficult to prevent hostile legislation.

I doubt the practicability of operating the South Park road from so great a distance as Omaha, where local questions can't be well understood.

And to add insult to injury, it now appeared that the U.P. was going to dispense with Evans' services. At a conference in New York he had been led to believe that he would run U.P. affairs in the Colorado mountains, with the position of President of the Colorado Central and the South Park. In January 1880, Sidney Dillon suspended that arrangement, and Evans wrote Gould:

As I now hold a place of nominal responsibility without any definition of my authority I ask to know your wishes, and that of the U.P. Co. before the matter gets any more unpleas-

ant. Of course I cannot stand in a place to be censured for acts I sought to correct without any control over them.

Evans, of course, had made a pile of money from the sale of his South Park stock, so he really had little reason to feel personally hurt. Anyway, his protests did no good, and in fact Gould got out while he could, selling his South Park and U.P. interests before U.P. President S. H. H. Clark could ruin both roads.

Construction of the tunnel at Alpine Pass continued throughout the winter and spring and into the summer of 1881, and at 8:30 a.m. on July 26, 1881, the crew working from the west end broke through to the east. The crews from east and west then got into an argument over who should be first to pass through the opening, an argument resolved by giving that honor to one of Superintendent Osborn's children, who was followed by Mrs. Osborn and another woman, then the chief engineer, P. F. Barr, who gave the crews ten dollars for beer.

There was still much work before the railroad could reach Gunnison. The tunnel had to be enlarged, snowsheds built at appropriate locations on both sides, and track built through it. As a matter of fact, track had just been built into Hancock, 4.8 miles west of St. Elmo and still 3.2 miles short of the tunnel on that same day the tunnel heading was broken through, July 26. On the following day, July 27, the Denver & Rio Grande end-of-track on its Gunnison Extension had successfully crossed Marshall Pass and was only 23.1 miles of easy valley construction from Gunnison, while the South Park railroad had 43.5 miles of track-laying to do, in part through difficult mountain terrain, even presuming the grade was finished all the way to Gunnison, which it was not. The South Park had lost the race, although the management gamely claimed it would run South Park trains into Gunnison within six weeks. They would not even succeed in six *months!*

The Denver & Rio Grande operated its first train into Gunnison on August 6, 1881. It was another two weeks before the South Park end-of-track even reached the east portal of Alpine Tunnel. Defeat in the race to Gunnison took much of the starch out of the South Park effort. It progressed listlessly throughout the end of the year. On November 19 the *Gunnison Review* reported that construction between the tunnel and Gunnison had been shut down until spring except for some work in the tunnel, while the *Pitkin Mining News* claimed that work did not actually stop until December 2. Some work continued in the tunnel, and the first engine passed through that month, then all lay

dormant until April, 1882. Construction of track and grade resumed then west of the tunnel. Grading crews had spent much of 1881 chipping away at the great granite cliff faces west of the tunnel, where they built a great rock wall to retain the fill on which the grade would rest as it passed these rock "Palisades" descending towards the floor of Missouri Gulch. It was slow, hard work, and although much had been done in 1881, much more remained to be done in 1882. The grade had been largely completed between the tunnel and Gunnison in 1881, but winter snows and spring thaws had brought down rocks and placed them on the grade, and caused minor washouts elsewhere. Many ties had been bedded in 1881, but many more remained to be placed in 1882.

On May 1st, 1882, three locomotives pushed a snowplow from Hancock up to the tunnel, opening the track to the summit for the first time that year. Using rail on hand, track-layers may have begun work west of the tunnel, where the sun would be more likely to melt snow off the grade, as early as April 15. On May 12 the DSP&P advertised for 300 men to lay track not only between the tunnel and Gunnison but as far as Elk Mountain to the north of Gunnison. The end of track reached Woodstock, 3.3 miles west of Alpine Tunnel and in the great curve in Missouri Gulch at the base

This snowy scene shows the tunnel crews at work on the east portal of Alpine during the winter of 1880-1881. The pace of work does not appear here to be very active. (State Hist. Society of Colorado Coll.)

As soon as track was completed through the tunnel and down the west side, William H. Jackson appeared to record the breathtaking vistas on film. The view at right, looking south along the Palisades, shows the track going downgrade towards the valley below. This dramatic view was often reprinted and imitated over the years. The view below, taken about the same location but looking upgrade towards the tunnel, is perhaps less splendid but more terrifying; the valley below seems miles beneath the narrow shelf holding the track. No derailments here, please. (Denver Public Library Western Hist. Coll.)

of the Palisades, about June 3, 1882. By June 12 they were only a mile further. The South Park scheduled regular train service as far as Woodstock to begin on Tuesday, June 20, but a landslide at the east portal of the tunnel intervened and delayed the opening of that segment of track one day.

By the evening of July 11, 1882, the rails had reached within a half a mile of the city limits of Pitkin and one mile of the Pitkin depot grounds. At 3 p.m., July 12, 150 workmen and the construction train reached the depot where they were met by an enthusiastic crowd of citizens, who gave them "three rousing cheers" and the customary welcoming speech. The track-layers had thus covered 9 miles in one month.

After the construction train, the first train to arrive in Pitkin was a special train consisting of an engine and one Pullman sleeping car carrying Sidney Dillon, Leonard Eicholtz and other dignitaries. It had left Alpine Tunnel behind Engine 11, a 2-6-6T Mason locomotive named *Ouray*, and halfway between the Tunnel and Pitkin, near Midway Tank, a casting on one side of the locomotive broke. The engineer stopped and made some jury-rigged repairs, then started down grade again, hoping to get into Pitkin with power on only one side of the engine. But the engine got out of control and ran away downgrade. The porter on the sleeping car became excited and yelled for people to jump and several did, a Mr. James Canfield breaking his ankle in the process. Meanwhile the conductor was busy uncoupling the sleeper from the locomotive, after which he stopped the car by clubbing down the handbrake. The engineer got his engine back under control, and set it out at the siding at Quartz. Her sister Engine 10, a 2-6-6T called *Granite,* was called off the construction train to take the sleeping car on into Pitkin.

The Denver, South Park & Pacific Railroad commenced regular train service into Pitkin on July 13. Engine 57 meanwhile headed construction trains south towards Parlins, 11.9 miles short of Gunnison. By Wednesday, August 30, the South Park end of track was at Biebel's ranch, three miles from Gunnison.

The South Park installed crossing frogs at their junction with the D&RG Crested Butte Branch in Gunnison on September 4, after which they could run trains through to the west end of town. On September 5, the railroad finished its Gunnison water tank, and the turntable was nearing completion. That evening Gunnison celebrated the arrival of the South Park railroad with a wild party featuring free beer.

Gunnison, of course, was not to be the terminus of the Denver, South Park & Pacific Railroad — at least it was not to have been under the Evans management, but what the Union Pacific management in Omaha would do might be another matter entirely. What Evans' intentions were in terms of objectives were spelled out not only in the articles of incorporation, resolutions of the board of directors and various amendments to the articles, but also in the names given to South Park locomotives while he was still in charge of the railroad: *San Juan*, No. 4; *Tenmile*, No. 6; *Lake City*, No. 8; *Ouray*, No. 11; *Ruby*, No. 13; *Breckenridge*, No. 15; *Eureka*, No. 16; *Silverton*, No. 20, *Crested Butte*, No. 22; *Rico*, No. 26; and *Roaring Fork*, No. 27. All of these locomotives had been built before the end of 1880 and before Evans left the road. Each of those names represented a serious South Park objective at one time or another — and the names of intermediate engines not listed above represented, with few exceptions, points already reached by the railroad.

Some of these South Park objectives dated from the second incorporation of the company in June 1873. The San Juan region was an objective spelled out in this document, and as the DSP&P expected to reach it via Poncha Pass and Del Norte, the town they were obviously heading for was Silverton. However, the South Park railroad was attracted to Gunnison instead, and in the meantime the Denver & Rio Grande occupied the Santa Fe locations over Poncha and Marshall Passes, and building westward from Veta Pass reached the San Juan region at Durango in the summer of 1881, building north that fall and winter to reach Silverton during the following summer. Another Denver & Rio Grande branch reached Del Norte. The early enthusiasm which the Denver, South Park & Pacific managers had evinced towards construction of a line via Del Norte to Silverton vanished once the competition had already reached those towns.

That left three other rich mining towns on the northern edge of the San Juan region which the Denver & Rio Grande had not tapped, and all of them more readily accessible from Gunnison than was Silverton. These were Lake City, Ouray and Rico, in order of their location east to west. On February 10, 1880, the South Park management had amended the Articles of Association adding authority for the railroad to build via the Uncompahgre Valley, Ouray, the San Miguel Valley and the Dolores Valley to Arizona, and via Ohio Creek Pass to the Elk Mountain coal fields, over Kebler Pass to the north fork of the Gunnison, down that stream to its confluence with the Grand (Colorado) River, and on westward to Utah, with a branch down the Roaring Fork Valley. Both of these lines could be projected to the Pacific Coast as stipulated in the Articles of Association, but presumably that would require incorporation of the DSP&P in Arizona, Utah, Nevada and California before the railroad could actually build track in those states. The *Denver Daily Times* of March 18, 1880, described these South Park plans, adding an item or two not actually stated in the amendments:

> At Gunnison City the line branches. The Utah extension will follow up Ohio Creek, thence to Anthracite Creek, thence down Anthracite Creek to the North Fork of the Gunnison, down the North Fork to the Main Gunnison River, and thence by way of the Grand River to the State line.
>
> The other branch from Gunnison will run down the Gunnison to the Grand Canon of the Gunnison, where it crosses the river and passes in a southwesterly direction via the Uncompahgre River to the State line. The Lake City branch leaves this line just before reaching the Lake Fork of the Gunnison and runs up this Fork to Lake City. The Ouray branch runs up the Uncompahgre to Ouray.

Thus the Arizona Extension of the Denver, South Park & Pacific Railroad included branches to Lake City and Ouray; and Rico, although not mentioned above, would be on the main line of the extension. *Railroad Gazette* noted on October 1, 1880: "The South Park Company will push their extension from Gunnison City through to Rico as soon as possible." At that time, of course, the Denver & Rio Grande had not yet built over Marshall Pass, and no railroad approached any of these towns closer than the South Park line then under construction to Gunnison. But in the two year delay occasioned by construction of Alpine Tunnel, the Denver & Rio Grande reached Gunnison, followed the proposed South Park route through the "Grand Cañon of the Gunnison", more properly termed the Black Cañon, actually commenced grading of a branch line to Lake City, and surveyed a line to Ouray. As with Del Norte and Silverton, DSP&P enthusiasm for reaching Lake City, Ouray and Rico evaporated once the Denver & Rio Grande won the race to Gunnison and beyond.

That left the Utah Extension. In the fall of 1881, the Denver & Rio Grande had built a branch from Gunnison to Crested Butte; but it followed a different route than the Ohio Creek line proposed by the DSP&P, and it showed no signs of being anything more than a dead end branch. Consequently, the Denver, South Park & Pacific put construction forces in the field to build over Ohio Creek Pass, over Kebler Pass, down the North Fork of the Gunnison and the Gunnison proper to

the new town of Grand Junction at the confluence of the Gunnison and the Grand (Colorado) Rivers.

This line the South Park undertook to build. South Park surveyors had run a complete final location as far as the Utah Border via Grand Junction by the fall of 1882, and construction west of Gunnison had commenced in 1880. The *Gunnison Review* of November 19, 1881, reported grading completed all the way from Alpine Tunnel to Ruby above Ohio Creek Pass near the summit of the descent into the valley of the North Fork of the Gunnison. This was something of an exaggeration, but work was in progress all along the line, and much indeed was finished. As late as January 26, 1882, a hundred South Park graders were at work on this line, and the *Pitkin Mining News* of January 27 claimed that most of the grading between Gunnison and Irwin above Ohio and Kebler Passes was finished except for three miles just south of Ohio Creek Pass. Those three miles included the only heavy rock work on the line, and involved a huge stone fill and grade chiseled out of the cliff face, both of which were about half completed, as well as several short sections of grade on which no work had yet been done. Below the loop at the foot of the grade which incorporated the stone work, grade was completed all the way back to Gunnison. But the *Gunnison Daily Review* of March 28, 1882 reported a rumor that the South Park had stopped all work between Gunnison and Ruby Camp on their Utah Extension. The Union Pacific management was apparently having its doubts about the wisdom of completing the line to Utah. Early in September, 1882, the South Park commenced tracklaying on this extension north from Gunnison, but with the limited objective of reaching the coal mines at Baldwin, 14 miles north of Gunnison and in the valley at the foot of Ohio Creek Pass. Construction of grade over the pass would not resume until 1892, leading then to a brief little railroad war with the Denver & Rio Grande near Kebler Pass, after which construction would halt for all time. Again, the Denver, South Park & Pacific had been outflanked by the Denver & Rio Grande, whose own Utah Extension had reached Grand Junction on November 21, 1882, before South Park track layers had even reached Ohio Creek Pass. Again the South Park had lost a railroad race — in fact was so far behind that it could hardly be called a race. The South Park railroad would never reach Utah, much less the Pacific.

In fact, the South Park was having enough trouble holding on to the Leadville traffic, and for several years had been building branch lines in the South Park region to exploit more effectively the center of its domain. The DSP&P management had under consideration a number of different lines reaching west from its main line through the South Park. On February 20, 1879, the *Fairplay Flume* discussed one possible short cut to Leadville by way of a tunnel through the Park Range west of Fairplay. That scheme was popular in Fairplay as it would place the town on the main line to Leadville rather than at the end of a ten mile branch. In August, 1880, the DSP&P had a survey crew running a line from Como to Breckenridge by way of Hoosier Pass.

That fall the railroad did begin construction of a branch line from Garos (17 miles beyond Como) 10.1 miles up the valley to Fairplay. Considerable grading was done before work was suspended in late November for the winter. Construction was resumed in April, 1881, but apparently at an agonizingly slow pace. The crew walked off the job in April for lack of pay; a 17½-foot deep cut stalled them in June; a small flood disrupted the grade in July; and a hail storm created havoc in August. Finally the *Fairplay Flume* was able to announce on September 15, 1881, that the track had reached town, although several weeks of additional work was required before the branch could be placed in service. U.P. officials apparently had difficulty negotiating for depot grounds on favorable terms, as the *Flume* of January 12, 1882, reported that the Fairplay depot was "still conducted on the box car plan". However, a permanent structure was soon begun, being opened to the public on March 16.

Fairplay was not to be the terminus of the branch, however; it was projected on to Alma, 5.3 miles beyond, a newer mining camp. A further extension ran from London Junction, just below Alma, 7.4 miles northwest to the London Mine on the eastern side of Mosquito Pass. This latter line was not constructed by the South Park, but by an independent corporation organized on February 16, 1882, by the management of the London Mine — and given the imposing name London, South Park & Leadville Railroad. Construction was begun that summer and the line was completed to the tramway of the mine in October. A rented D&RG locomotive — derisively called "The Teapot" by the South Park crews — was used until the line's new 2-8-0 arrived from Baldwin in late June, 1883.

The LSP&P never proved profitable to operate; among other factors, a switchback near the upper end of the line complicated operations, and although the firm talked of a tunnel under Mosquito Pass providing a short cut to Leadville, the project never materialized. By 1885, the LSP&P was in trouble, and reorganization as the South Park & Leadville Short Line Railroad failed to solve its problems. Before the end of the year the Union Pacific, which had advanced most of the track material, foreclosed and took over all of the capital stock.

A major branch from the Denver, South Park & Pacific Railroad extending west of the main line in the South Park was the Breckenridge Branch, construction of which began with the laying of the Lechner Mine Branch near Como in 1880. On April 6, 1880, the South Park directors decided to build to Breckenridge on the far side of the Park Range. The *Fairplay Flume* noted on November 11, 1880 that the DSP&P had completed two miles of grade on the Breckenridge Branch, but planned to lay no iron until the following spring. Later that month the newspaper reported the sale of the DSP&P to Jay Gould, which meant that it had passed into control of the Union Pacific.

Thus a branch to Breckenridge was a legacy of the Evans management of the DSP&P; the Union Pacific management did not originate the idea of crossing the Park Range. Under U.P. management, work resumed in 1881, and by June 16, graders were nearing the summit of the Park Range, 10.6 miles from Como, at Boreas Pass. About September 1, the grading crew which had completed its work on the Fairplay Branch moved to the Breckenridge Branch to speed construction. The *Fairplay Flume* claimed in October that the station at the summit would be called "Spottswood Station" after the co-proprietor of the stagecoach line which connected with South Park trains, but the proposed name failed to stick and the pass was called Boreas instead.

The Union Pacific halted work for the winter due to the severity of the weather on the pass, but in April, 1882, the grading crews resumed work on the 11.3 miles of grading from the summit to Breckenridge, while tracklayers commenced laying the 10.6 miles of track between Como and the summit. The company expected to complete the road into Breckenridge by July 4 and run an excursion between there and Como, but the end-of-track actually reached Breckenridge on August 2, 1882.

From Breckenridge, Evans had intended to extend the narrow gauge line north 8.9 miles to Dillon and another 4.2 miles to Keystone, in order to tap the business of the Montezuma mining district, and the Union Pacific management carried out this project by the end of the year. It immediately found winter operations over Boreas Pass to be exceedingly difficult.

A concomitant of construction of this branch

Wm. H. Jackson made these views of a mixed train (powered by Mason bogie No. 48) on the Fairplay branch in the eighties; Fairplay is at right, London Junction below. (State Hist. Society of Colorado Coll.)

The Rio Grande was first to penetrate the Tenmile and Blue River area, and benefited in location of grade. A D&RG mixed is shown in this Jackson view at Wheeler Flat (Solitude) (Denver Public Library Western Hist. Coll.) Below, a Buckwalter view of a South Park train at Robinson, further up the Tenmile valley, about the 1890 period (Museum Coll. from C. S. Ryland).

line over the Park Range, necessitating the use of helper locomotives from both sides, was the growth of the junction town of Como at the head of the branch into a major railroad center. The *Fairplay Flume* of April 28, 1881, noted the laying of foundations for a roundhouse and a locomotive shop at Como. Providing helper service not only for Boreas but for Kenosha and Trout Creek Passes as well, Como soon housed the most important facilities on the entire Denver, South Park & Pacific Railroad except for Denver.

Although the management had earlier adopted surveys which included a line from Dillon to Leadville, the management had expressed no intention actually to build such a line, until increasing friction between the Union Pacific and the Denver & Rio Grande led to litigation involving the Joint Operating Agreement under which the South Park operated its trains over D&RG trackage between Buena Vista and Leadville. When the U.P. management had raised freight rates to prohibitive levels, they drove much business to the Denver & Rio Grande, and such business once lost tended not to return. Thus the D&RG was hauling about 85 or 90 per cent of the traffic out of Leadville, while the South Park still had to pay about $10,000 per year for use of the trackage from there to Buena Vista. The South Park demanded either a lower trackage use fee or a greater share of the profits, and refused for awhile to pay their trackage fee, causing the D&RG to sue. Relations between the two railroads became increasingly acrimonious. Consequently during the summer of 1883, the Union Pacific management decided to construct its own line to Leadville!

The railroad had a choice of two routes. It could build 35.5 miles of track up the Arkansas Valley from Buena Vista to Leadville, or 32 miles of track from Dillon to Leadville. The fact that the line via Dillon required three miles' less construction certainly was not decisive in the selection of route, but the fact that it was 20 miles shorter to Leadville from Denver probably was decisive. Both Evans and the later Union Pacific management of the South Park consistently chose the shorter line between two points as the most desirable, without regard for difficulty of construction or operation. Similarly they chose the most permanent, hence the most expensive, forms of construction: under Evans, using fills on Kenosha instead of cheaper and faster-to-erect trestles, and building a great stone wall at the Palisades on Alpine Pass instead of using cheaper grading techniques, a practice the Union Pacific management of the South Park continued in the vast stone fill on Ohio Creek Pass. One liability of such construction was that if the project failed to reach completion, as did the Ohio Creek Pass extension, the company lost much more money for such expensive grading than if cheaper and even temporary techniques had been followed. The Denver & Rio Grande management understood these factors thoroughly and consistently built the easiest and cheapest line, which admittedly they might later have to spend money to upgrade. Nevertheless, by so doing they managed consistently to defeat the South Park in the race for territory, for instance building to Gunnison in less than a year while it took the South Park more than two and a half.

In yet another error in judgment, the Union Pacific management apparently did not make up its mind to build from Dillon to Leadville until July, 1883 — at least that was when it signed the initial contract for construction of the line to Leadville. Again, the Denver & Rio Grande had beaten the South Park company to the finish line, having extended a line of its own from Leadville north to Dillon by November, 1882, thus occupying the best location for trackage through Ten Mile Cañon and over Fremont Pass.

Construction of the South Park line to Leadville commenced on August 3, by which time three survey crews totaling 50 men were at work staking out the final location.

For very practical reasons competing railroads are forced to cooperate from an operational standpoint. One can never tell when one's own track or equipment may be incapacitated by natural disaster, whereupon to maintain service to and the loyalty of one's steady customers, it may prove necessary to lease motive power or rolling stock, or to make use of shop facilities or operate over the trackage of one's most bitter rival. Furthermore, when railroad rivalries in the operational sphere became too bitter, they raised the spectre of unsolicited court intervention and the possibility of legislative action to remedy such situations — and no railroad wanted those solutions. Consequently the D&RG continued to allow the DSP&P to use trackage between Buena Vista and Leadville and Macune and Nathrop, although on unfavorable terms, and even afforded the use of the Leadville yard for trains of construction material destined to aid the rival South Park. But when it came to blocking the new construction at the site and in the courts, it was another matter, and where it was possible to throw up either a physical or legal obstacle to South Park construction between Dillon (actually from Dickey, just short of Dillon) to Leadville, the Denver & Rio Grande would pull no punches.

Railway Age noted the construction of the new

1844. SUMMIT OF BOREAS PASS HIGH LINE COMO VIA BRECKENRIDGE TO LEADVILLE.

1843. TEN MILE RANGE SOUTH OF BOREAS PASS

The interesting views at left were taken by Alex Martin shortly after completion of the Boreas Pass line. Upper, a little mixed train headed by new Cooke mogul No. 70 (later C&S 7) stopped at the summit, next to the impressive stone engine house, while the lower photo shows the same train a mile further at Farnham. (Both, Don Duke-Golden West Books Coll.) On this page, a short mixed stops for a group photo at Rocky Point, on the west side of Boreas (R. B. Jackson Coll.), while below a light engine pauses on Nigger Hill (now Barney Ford Hill) overlooking Breckenridge in the valley below (Denver Public Library Western Hist. Coll.).

line in its issue of August 16, reporting that the contracts required completion of the 32 miles in 60 days and quoting the *Leadville Herald* to the effect that the work would require 12,000 men to meet that deadline. Carlisle & Corrigan of Pueblo had the construction contract. Among those hired were 200 Italian immigrants who boarded a South Park train at Denver Union Depot on August 13 for the ride to the scene of construction. *The Railroad Gazette* of August 17 erroneously reported that the project would require a long tunnel; the line would employ no such tunnel, but it would have to cross Fremont Pass to reach Leadville. By August 31 the Union Pacific had pulled a large force of laborers off of work on the Oregon Short Line Railroad and transferred them to Colorado to speed construction of the Leadville Extension before winter set in.

But winter weather was not to be the Union Pacific's major problem in constructing trackage to Leadville. On August 27, 1883, the Denver & Rio Grande filed suit and obtained a temporary injunction which prevented the South Park from entering upon D&RG right-of-way in Summit County. The injunction applied equally to D&RG snowsheds, snow fences and telegraph lines, and prohibited the Union Pacific forces from changing the course of Ten Mile Creek or any of its tributaries. As the Denver & Rio Grande in places wandered back and forth from one side of the creek and cañon to the other, it rendered South Park construction difficult. The Denver, South Park & Pacific filed a cross bill containing the rather weak argument that the nature of the country was such that it could not avoid coming within the Denver & Rio Grande's right-of-way at certain points. The DSP&P ignored the injunction until the Sheriff commenced jailing its civil engineers and laborers.

Nor was such legal action the only measure taken by the Denver & Rio Grande. A dispatch dated September 3 to *The Railroad Gazette* (published in the issue of September 7) reported a different sort of interference with South Park railroad construction:

> The Union Pacific people are having all sorts of trouble getting into Leadville, as their enemy, the Denver & Rio Grande, seems to be exhaustless in their filibustering resources. Injunctions and every device known to railroad men are adopted to retard the construction of the line on the Cummings & Finn switch [spur] to East Leadville. At a point where the Union Pacific expects to cross the Rio Grande a locomotive has been stationed for a week past, rendering it impossible for the construction force to complete the connection. At regular intervals the stationary locomotive is supplied with coal and water, and there it stands day and night.

The principle trouble the South Park faced was not in Leadville, however, but in Kokomo, north of Fremont Pass, where a combination of the topography and the Denver & Rio Grande's location rendered construction of the DSP&P trackage difficult without infringing on D&RG right-of-way. In November Judge Moses Hallett appointed a railway commission to report on the dispute, and its report, issued on December 5, 1883, recommended two alternatives to the proposed South Park location at Kokomo, one including two overhead crossings of the D&RG. Meanwhile, unwilling to await a final decision in the matter, the South Park constructed its own alternative — a switchback on the hillside above Kokomo which remained entirely free of the D&RG right-of-way, although it was a nuisance to operate. But in building the switchback, the Union Pacific encountered an irate land-owner who demanded an exorbitant fee for right-of-way, which would require the DSP&P either to settle for an outrageous amount or suffer the delays of condemnation proceedings through the courts. As the whole point of the switchback was to speed completion of a through line to Leadville, the DSP&P chose to settle rather than to condemn.

At 7 a.m. on February 1, 1884, while the DSP&P was still struggling to complete its track into Leadville from the north, the joint D&RG/DSP&P roundhouse in Leadville caught fire, and in an "incredibly short time", according to the *Leadville Daily Herald*, the "whole building was wrapped in flames." Efforts both of railroad forces, utilizing two steam pumps to throw water on the blaze, and of the Leadville fire department, which arrived a little later, were unavailing — there were no hydrants nearby to which they could connect their hoses.

Daybreak revealed the remains of six locomotives among the ruins, five of them Denver & Rio Grande, one belonging to the South Park railroad. It was fortunate for the DSP&P that it had only the one engine in the structure.

Elsewhere in Leadville, the DSP&P had several days earlier put twenty men at work breaking ground for a new freight depot, located on the west side of Hazel Street between Ninth and Tenth.

But all of this was preliminary to the main show. Several property owners in Leadville had tried to hold the DSP&P up for a fat price for their land. The right-of-way in contention consisted of a four block stretch which lay between Eighth and Twelfth Streets. The railroad had offered what it considered a reasonable sum for the land but had met only with refusal on the part of the owners. It is not clear whether the railroad then obtained condemnation of the land through legal process; what is clear is that they went ahead and built across these four city blocks anyway, and the manner in which the railroad proceeded suggested a *fait accompli*. On Friday, February 1, 1884, the DSP&P put between 300 and 400 men at work on the grade, and proceeded in the process to tear down two residences, whose occupants the South Park construction superintendent claimed to have placed in better dwellings than the ones destroyed. The construction forces commenced laying track at 8 p.m. that night, and finished at 4 a.m. on Saturday morning, February 2, 1884. The superintendent claimed that trains would be running over the new track by the following Tuesday, and indeed, on Tuesday, February 5, 1884, the first locomotive operated over the new line into Leadville, according to the *Daily Herald*, although the Union Pacific annual report claimed that this occurred on February 6. But the newspaper of the latter date reported:

> The completion of the South Park railroad to this city, which was shown by the running of the first locomotive over the new line into Leadville yesterday, is an event of no small importance. It means competition in freight and passenger rates to Denver, and through Denver to all the east. It opens up a new territory to the trade and enterprise of this city, and sets the business of Leadville free from the chains which virtually bound it to one road in the past. The South Park line is by far the shortest route to Denver, and it will tend to make the intercourse between the two cities much more intimate than it has heretofore been. Leadville and Denver will both reap great advantages from this connection, and they both have reason to rejoice over the completion of the great work which was ended yesterday.

Whether the DSP&P commenced regular service over the new line is not clear. The *Leadville Daily Herald* did not report in detail on this question, because when South Park trains could not make it across Boreas and Fremont Passes to Leadville, they could still operate over the D&RG north from Buena Vista through Malta. Unfortunately, the winter of 1884 proved to be one of the worst in the decade, and no sooner had the DSP&P completed its new and still uncertain trackage than winter struck with a vengeance. The DSP&P was soon forced to rely on a renewal of its contract for trackage rights with its bitter rival, the D&RG, in order to reach town. That the rival D&RG was willing to renew a trackage agreement with the South Park despite the rivalry was not especially surprising. The DSP&P had reached Leadville, so that further attempts to harass the Union Pacific

subsidiary would be pointless; besides, should the D&RG be blocked by flood, landslide or other natural disaster in the Royal Gorge, Brown's Cañon or elsewhere on its route to Leadville, it might one day wish to run its own trains over the DSP&P during such emergency. Consequently, when February snows blocked the South Park line over Boreas and Fremont Passes, the DSP&P continued running regular trains in over the D&RG. Even that line posed problems. The *Daily Herald* of February 23 reported:

> The South Park train got belated about a mile from town last night, owing to ice, and consequently delayed the Denver and Rio Grande, which was behind it. Some of the passengers walked across, and others took carriages, but at the time of going to press both trains were "stalled" within sight of the city.

On February 28, the newspaper reported that snow between the town and Little Frying Pan gulch was so deep that mines had to suspend ore shipments. One miner had managed to get through with a load of ore, but it required three days for him to make seven miles with his wagon.

That the South Park railroad should have trouble operating that winter over freshly built and therefore especially vulnerable trackage was not surprising. The problems experienced by the Denver & Rio Grande operating its well-established and parallel line over Fremont Pass illustrated the severity of the winter. On Sunday evening, March 9, 1884, a D&RG train consisting of seven locomotives and two coaches left Kokomo southbound to plow their way over Fremont Pass. They departed Kokomo at 10:30 p.m. and by 5 a.m. the following morning had only reached Alicante, 6.4 miles south of Kokomo. An engaged couple on the train elected to walk the twelve miles to Leadville, but after three miles of tramping through deep snow, they and other passengers who accompanied them gave up the attempt. At 9 a.m. on the following day, Tuesday, March 11, three men and three women decided to try to walk the distance again, and after a long, difficult walk, arrived in Leadville at 4 p.m. En route they found two dead locomotives, stalled and without fuel, just south of Bird's Eye, and four miles south of Alicante they found eight snowslides, several of them two thousand feet long and twenty feet high. With the D&RG's established operations over Fremont Pass this badly blocked, it was not surprising that the DSP&P's new and yet untried line was even less capable of operation.

Elsewhere, that terrible winter caused the South Park railroad equally serious problems. At 6 p.m. on Monday, March 10, a disastrous avalanche came down the precipitous slopes just west of the Palisades on the west side of Alpine Pass, utterly destroying the little railroad section house and town at Woodstock, killing a number of people living there. Rescue forces set out from both Alpine Tunnel and Pitkin, but could do little other than to dig the bodies out of the snowslide. The *Leadville Herald* noted on March 15, "The storms of this season have been of unusual severity. Snow-slides have been numerous, and in them many men have lost their lives."

Such snowslides frequently damaged the track as well as blocking train operation. Such densely packed snow would require the labor of hundreds of men to shovel the track free by hand, and in some instances it would prove necessary to dynamite the ice and the snow to break it free. New track was also especially vulnerable to washouts, and the spring melt from the deep snows of the winter of 1884 further damaged the South Park line. Consequently crews were at work all summer and well into the fall. Over parts of the route the snow was not sufficiently melted or cleared to enable men to work on the track until *July*. The first regular passenger train was not destined to operate over the route until September 30, 1884, the first eastbound South Park train departed on the morning of October 1. On the following day, the *Leadville Daily Herald* editorialized:

> The people of Leadville are to be congratulated upon the opening of the South Park "High Line" from this city to Como, which auspicious event occurred yesterday. The establishment of the new route changes the aspect of railroad affairs so far as Leadville is concerned in a manner that cannot fail to accrue to the benefit of the public. Heretofore the rivalry existing between the Union Pacific and the Denver and Rio Grande companies could not be conveyed to this city, for the reason that the latter company held the only track by which we could be reached and in consequence held its big rival at its mercy. The South Park company is now running its own trains over its own track between this city and Denver, and occupies a position where it can act as independently as its rival....

Thus the DSP&P had reached Leadville, where it now had its own freight depot and employed a residence at 327 8th Street as a passenger depot, pending completion of a new Union Pacific passenger depot to be built between 8th and 9th Streets. The company had already completed a water tank and a turntable for servicing engines, and the new eight-stall roundhouse was nearing completion.

The South Park now possessed its own line all the way from Denver to Leadville — a line 126 miles shorter than the rival D&RG route via Pueblo and Salida. However, even though it was nearly twice as long as the South Park's new route, the Denver & Rio Grande line had the bene-

fit of much easier grades — one low summit over Monument Hill on the Denver-Pueblo line, and a continuous moderate grade all the way from Pueblo up the Arkansas Valley to Leadville. In contrast the South Park had to climb from 5,186 feet at Denver Union Station to 9,991 feet at Kenosha Pass; down to 9,508 feet at Jefferson and then up to 11,493 feet in just a few miles at Boreas; 9,004 feet again at Dickey, only to climb back to 11,320 feet at Fremont Pass before dropping down to 10,208 feet at the Leadville depot. This roller-coaster route required much greater use of motive power, with many helper engines and the attendant higher costs; it was also much more vulnerable to severe winter weather problems, both as to disruptions of service and operating costs.

Other problems that faced the South Park in 1884 were not removed by completion of the new line. Because the Rio Grande had beaten the South Park to the Ten Mile region, that road had already established firm relationships with shippers along the line which were not easily broken. The myopic policies of the Omaha management in the early 1880s drove many shippers to the Rio Grande, and once gone they tended not to return. The Leadville boom itself had peaked; thus there was no new flood of traffic to tap. The parent Union Pacific, mismanaged, overextended, facing ultimate bankruptcy, had not been much help and would be even less in the future. Finally, a new threat was to appear on the horizon shortly — the construction of a new *standard gauge* railroad, the Colorado Midland, from Colorado Springs through South Park to Leadville and beyond. This in turn forced standard gauging of the Denver & Rio Grande line, and the South Park would become less competitive than ever.

One may easily conclude that the South Park railroad was ill-conceived and poorly managed during much of its history, that its routes were ill-chosen, that it was fated to lose in each competition with its peers. Yet its excessively arduous routes made it the single most scenic narrow gauge railroad that ever ran in the Colorado Rockies. There was hardly an inch of its track from Denver Union Station to the termini of either its Leadville or Gunnison Divisions, or any of its branches, that was not dominated by some of the most spectacular mountain scenery on the North American continent. Thus many decades after its demise, the term "South Park" calls to mind not only that great mountain parkland southwest of Denver ringed by the Colorado Rockies, but also the diminutive and intriguing narrow gauge trains that once ran there.

Leadville, final destination achieved by the South Park, offered the hospitality of the Hotel Vendome. The South Park approaches Leadville from Fremont Pass over a spectacular right-of-way carved out of the hillsides high above the valley floor; below, DSP&P No. 217 leads a short freight across a trestle being buried under a permanent fill, a few miles above Leadville (State Hist. Society of Colorado Coll.).

Outwardly, the South Park seemed to begin its period of Union Pacific stewardship auspiciously enough: its own lines completed to Gunnison and Leadville, the promise of a growing tide of freight to deliver to its Union Pacific connection at Denver, and 28 powerful new Cooke locomotives to speed its trains on their way — as here, with mogul No. 112 (later C&S 7) leading a consist of livestock, lumber and ore through the famed Second Bridge in Platte Canyon. (Wm. H. Jackson photo, Museum Coll.)

Transition:

The U.P. and Receivership

Cornelius W. Hauck

Absorption of the South Park into the Union Pacific system in 1881 proved to be something of a mixed blessing. It did result in the completion of the various extensions projected at the time, which might well not have been accomplished under the slow-motion Evans management. However, it was directly responsible for the collapse of the joint D&RG trackage rights agreement that in turn made further construction (of the Dillon-Leadville line) a necessity; it subjected the South Park to heavy-handed absentee management from Omaha that killed off traffic along its lines and drove off other traffic to the rival Rio Grande; and it drew the South Park into the Union Pacific's own web of troubles.

And troubles they were; troubles that had their basis in the origins of the railroad.

The idea of constructing a transcontinental rail line out across the unpopulated wilderness of the west in the 1860s was risky and speculative in the extreme. It was understood from the outset that, if the project was to be potentially profitable enough to attract the necessary venture capital, much of the profit would have to be realized through development of the lands through which the railroad would be built. And as these wastelands were largely government-owned, the government would then be a major beneficiary of the railroad's construction, and a logical participant in that construction through the providing of financial aid.

This was, in fact, what happened. But in their enthusiasm to build the line (and due to their weak bargaining position subsequently in dealing with the government), Union Pacific management obtained government aid on what later turned out to be onerous terms. Instead of being a co-speculator in the venture, the government became a preferred creditor with a lien on the property.

Further, a major error in the original economic projections for the transcontinental soon became evident: the main line from Omaha to Ogden could not be maintained as a profitable property without a network of supporting branch lines and feeder lines to produce traffic. This was, of course, the rationale behind the acquisition of the South Park; it was the impetus for the acquisition of feeder lines and construction of branches throughout the west. But terms of the government debt precluded the financing of such extensions on a long-term, consolidated basis, and as a result the Union Pacific entered the eighties with a large (and still growing) "floating debt" that made the road's financial structure shaky and unstable.

To service this debt and construct more branch lines, to pay dividends to its stockholders, *and* to pay interest and principal on the government debt was more than the railroad could manage. The road's officials decided early that the only course they could follow with any hope of success was to build the needed branches; to pay dividends so as to attract additional private investment for this expansion; and to relegate payments to the government to last, until the government debt could be refinanced on more equitable terms, and stretched out in payment on some realistic basis. However, the politicians — displaying the usual objectivity and perception of politicians — insisted loudly upon the government's being first in line for any returns from the railroad, to the exclusion of all others. The politicians were further inflamed by the gradual realization that foreclosure to force management compliance was not a viable alternative, since the government lien only covered the Omaha-Ogden main line, and the naked main line bereft of its branches was only of nominal value to anyone other than the Union Pacific. Hence foreclosure and sale of the main line could only result in its being reacquired by the Union Pacific, but at what would amount to a bargain price — thus accomplishing the refinancing that the railroad's management had been seeking in vain for many years.

Instead of cooperating with the railroad's management, the government turned to harassing them at every turn. This not only weakened the road, but scared off potential investors who might have helped solve the dilemma. In an effort to make a fresh start on the problem, in June, 1884, the Union Pacific brought in a new "reform" President — Charles Francis Adams, Jr. Adams had gained a national reputation as a railroad expert through his work on the Massachusetts Railroad Commission and his extensive writing on railroad affairs (and the shortcomings of railroad managements), and he had served a term as a government director on the Union Pacific board. It was hoped that Adams would revitalize the management of the road, improve its public image, and bring about some sort of rapprochement with Congress.

Adams tackled the task with vigor, and one of his first moves was to bring in S. R. Callaway as General Manager in place of S. H. H. Clark, whom he branded "utterly incompetent". Clark was, of course, the Manager responsible for the Union Pacific policies that had proven so ruinous to the South Park. Adams had no illusions about the South Park's attractiveness, however, and his opinions came out clearly a few years later during the Pacific Railway Commission hearings. His summation of the South Park's history must rank as a classic:

> The chief source of revenue of the road was in carrying men and material into Colorado to dig holes in the ground called mines, and until

it was discovered that there was nothing in those mines the business was immense. That was the famous mining boom of Colorado — for it was famous at the time — when every one was crazy. While the craze lasted, the railroad did a magnificent business. When it broke down, and these mines and villages were deserted — and they stand there deserted today — of course the business left the road. It was the same with all the Denver and Rio Grande as well as the South Park.

Adams did not think much of narrow gauges in general, and testified that he considered "the narrow gauge a first class nuisance". He went on to say that

> the whole theory of the narrow gauge is broken down; the theory under which it started was that it could have very much lighter rails, because it had very much lighter equipment, and it would require very much lighter structure; but since that, under the pressure of business, they have found it necessary to increase the weight of rails, and of locomotives, until they have got it up as high as the standard gauge was at the time the narrow-gauge roads were built; and the only ground it can possibly stand on now is that it can climb to points which the standard gauge cannot reach . . .

Adams' recounting of the history of the Union Pacific's acquisition of the DSP&P in subsequent testimony tempered his criticism a little, at least in regard to his appraisal of the judgement shown by earlier UP management.

> We bought the stock from Governor Evans. There was a sharp competition going on for the possession of that road between rival lines, as I have been informed. It was before I was a director. Governor Evans wanted to sell it; and General Palmer, of the Denver and Rio Grande, and Mr. Gould, on the part of the Union Pacific, were bidders for it; and Governor Evans played between the two, and he succeeded. At that time everything in Colorado was in that very inflated condition which usually precedes a great collapse. There was a state of artificial prosperity very marked. Finally, Mr. Gould, I think it was, on the part of the Union Pacific, closed the transaction with Governor Evans, and he (Gould) gave it to the Union Pacific, or the Union Pacific took the bargain of him . . .

> As things turned out afterward, it was a most extravagant price, but at the time it was not so considered. There never was such a collapse as that which took place in Colorado shortly afterwards that I ever heard of . . ..
> The road has not paid operating expenses for two or three years, but at the time we bought it and after it paid dividends on its stock (in the) year that preceded the collapse. I ought to state, in justice to the gentlemen who purchased this property, that after the contract was made for its purchase from Governor Evans they were offered a bonus of $500,000

The Union Pacific heavily advertised and promoted the South Park as a scenic attraction for tourists. Pictured here is a small train (Mason bogie No. 42 and DSP&P coach No. 9) provided for photographers' use in making scenic photos of the line. The upper picture (attributed to Mellen) shows the train posed in Box Canyon, east of Nathrop, while the lower photo (Wm. H. Jackson) shows the train west of Nathrop in the Chalk Creek Canyon, below Mt. Princeton. (Upper, T. G. Wurm Coll.; lower, State Hist. Society of Colorado Coll.)

for the bargain . . . I have no doubt General Palmer did make that offer; from what I know of him and from the statements I have received, I have never had the slightest reason to believe that there was anything that would not sustain a perfect examination in that transaction. It was an error of judgment, as things afterwards turned out; to that we are all liable. . . .

The Leadville business and the business to these mining camps up on the mountains . . . is increasing rapidly now. A million and a half (gross earnings), I think it was, last year . . . failed to pay its operating expenses and taxes by about $60,000 . . . in the ups and downs of railroad property, and especially in a region like Colorado, I should not consider the future of that road in any way hopeless.

Thus Adams seemed to hold out some hope that ultimately — perhaps with a new or renewed mining boom — the South Park might yet prove to be a valuable and profitable feeder for the parent road.

Unfortunately, Adams was more than preoccupied with the overwhelming problems facing the Union Pacific, and had little time for the South Park. The latter road continued to be operated as a minor branch of the transcontinental, with decisions made by and in the interests of Omaha. The expense of the Boreas Pass construction and costly winter operations over Alpine and Boreas continued to weigh heavily on the South Park, while the bulk of Leadville and Gunnison business continued to go (by design or by default) to the Rio Grande. Only the captive coal business from the Baldwin mines north of Gunnison seemed to hold promise.

After 1883 the South Park failed to earn its bond interest in any year, and the result was not surprising: in May, 1888, a representative of the bondholders had a receiver appointed. The following July the property was sold at foreclosure to a bondholders' committee, who in turn transferred it in August, 1889, to a new corporation — the Denver, Leadville & Gunnison Railway Company. Outside bondholders of the DSP&P were paid off in new Union Pacific bonds, while the UP now held all DL&G stock and bonds — the South Park had thus become a wholly-owned subsidiary of the big road. As might have been expected, tightening of absentee Omaha control did little for the South Park's fortunes, and the new DL&G continued in its predecessor's footsteps as a loser.

After 1882 John Evans no longer had any direct involvement in the operation of the South Park, but that did not end his involvement in railroad affairs, or his jousting with the Union Pacific. Even before his final departure from the South Park scene Evans launched a new venture — a standard gauge line projected to run from Denver to tidewater on the Gulf of Mexico. The new road was incorporated on January 25, 1881, and was christened the Denver & New Orleans. During 1881 and 1882 Evans managed to raise sufficient funds to construct the line from Denver to Pueblo, with a branch to Colorado Springs (the main line as originally constructed ran generally to the east of the Rio Grande line). But there it was to stop for a half dozen years. Not only did it become increasingly difficult to raise funds for western railroad ventures, but hostility and refusal to cooperate on the part of connecting lines — notably the Union Pacific — made profitable operation of the line anything but easy.

Evans was destined to be rescued by a partner from an unexpected source, a man who was responsible for building much of the Union Pacific and a close friend of Charles Francis Adams: General Grenville M. Dodge.

Dodge was already a national figure when he stepped into Union Pacific management as chief engineer in 1866, to give some badly needed direction to the floundering road and complete its construction across Wyoming to Ogden. After Union Pacific construction was completed, Dodge became interested in another transcontinental railroad project — the long-proposed southern transcontinental through Texas, New Mexico and Arizona. At least two railroads — the Southern Pacific Railroad Co. (no relation to the modern Southern Pacific) and the Memphis, El Paso & Pacific — had made early attempts to follow this route, and had built a few miles of track. In 1872 a new company, The Texas and Pacific Railway Co. (which had its origin in a congressional charter in 1871 for The Texas Pacific Railroad Co.) took over the Southern Pacific (now named Southern Transcontinental) and, in 1873, the Memphis El Paso & Pacific. Dodge was a board member of the new T&P and was appointed its chief engineer. The first section of the line, from Texarkana to Dallas, was completed in 1873, but the financial panic of that year stalled the road indefinitely; only after Jay Gould purchased the road from the original Texas backers was Dodge able to complete it to Sierra Blanca and El Paso in 1880.

In 1873, a Fort Worth group had chartered yet another little Texas road — the Fort Worth & Denver City. The panic of 1873 precluded any early construction, and the country northwest of Fort Worth was so slow to develop that there was little impetus for pushing the line forward. In 1881, after the T&P construction was completed, Dodge submitted a contract to the FW&DC, offering to construct their road to the Texas-New Mexico state line — where it would meet the Denver

At Denver, South Park patrons began their journey at the imposing stone Union Station, shown above in its original state (State Hist. Society of Colorado Coll.). At the Leadville end, the most imposing attraction was not the little brick depot but the huge, sprawling Arkansas Valley Smelting Works (from Mines & Mining Men of Colorado).

& New Orleans. The terms were accepted and Dodge quickly built the FW&DC as far as Wichita Falls. Construction was halted there, however, because of adverse political developments in Texas and because it was apparent that Evans' Denver & New Orleans was stalled at Pueblo.

The D&NO's problems were not easily resolved — money for Colorado railroad schemes simply dried up in the mid-eighties — and to keep from losing control Evans had to reorganize his road in 1886 as the Denver, Texas & Gulf. The FW&DC resumed construction, reaching Vernon in 1886, Washburn (near Amarillo) in 1887, and Texline in January, 1888. Because Evans was still stuck at Pueblo, Dodge organized a third company in 1887, the Denver, Texas & Ft. Worth, to lease and build trackage between Pueblo and Texline and operate the whole as a through route. This was accomplished by April, 1888, and the new system immediately proved a resounding success, quickly building up a profitable through traffic.

Dodge, however, felt that the DT&FW's ultimate chance for success lay in its becoming a part of the fast-growing Union Pacific system. Despite Evans' objections, Dodge and Ames combined the DT&FW and DT&G (plus a controlling interest in the FW&DC) with the Colorado Central and other minor UP Colorado properties into a new Union Pacific subsidiary — the Union Pacific, Denver & Gulf. The UPD&G was organized on April 1, 1890, with great expectations — expectations that were to be promptly thwarted by developments within the Union Pacific.

In his efforts to save the Union Pacific, Charles Francis Adams had charted a three-part course: 1. to improve operating efficiency and straighten out the road's tangled internal affairs; 2. to push extensions and acquire lines that would tap new territories and build up traffic; 3. to establish better relations with government and resolve the government debt problem. Unfortunately, the task proved insurmountable. Business in the eighties was spotty at best, and new competing roads (such as the Burlington, Rock Island, Santa Fe and Northern Pacific) cut into the UP's ability to generate the funds needed. Despite unremitting efforts, and the support of many in and out of government, no progress was made on the critical government debt problem — the politicians were having a field-day; inveighing against big business and railroad tycoons was a sure and cheap way to buy votes — never mind the facts or merit of a case. Finally, Adams threw in the towel, Gould took over and, in November, 1890, installed Sidney Dillon in the presidency once again.

Dillon, though aging and dispirited, did what he could. To attempt to meet the approaching maturity of the Federal debt he instituted a crash austerity program, with instructions to all officers to hoard cash, while Gould tried to shore up the road's finances in Wall Street. Their efforts merely postponed the inevitable. Dillon, exhausted, died in 1892, and Jay Gould also suddenly died; then Frederick L. Ames, the last of the original directors who had the strength to hold the road together, died in September, 1893. The road had become all but paralyzed by the overhanging government debt and continuous government interference, and the financial panic of 1893 brought the charade to a conclusion: receivers were appointed for the road on October 13, 1893.

Evans, Dodge and others concerned with the Colorado roads had been watching this unfold with increasing concern. Evans had been retained on the UPD&G board as a "maverick" director, and complained bitterly during the 1891-3 period that the UP was violating the agreement, "using" the DT&FW for its own ends and in the process ruining the railroad. Dodge, in less spectacular fashion, tried to combat the adverse UP policies, to no avail. In addition to Omaha's mismanagement, several years of crop failures hastened the downhill plunge. Thus, when the end was drawing near for the parent UP, the champions of the subsidiary lines were ready to move to protect their properties.

Evans, in fact, jumped the gun by applying for a receiver for the UPD&G alone on August 13, 1893, two months before the UP's bankruptcy, on the basis that his road had been "misused" to benefit the UP and that a local receiver should be appointed to correct the abuses. Dodge formed a UPD&G bondholders' committee to the same end, and became involved in endless pleadings before and negotiations with Judge Moses Hallett, in an effort to get a receiver appointed who was both capable and friendly to UPD&G interests.

Finally, on December 12, 1893, Hallett named Frank Trumbull as sole receiver. Trumbull was the 35-year old president of the Citizens' Coal Company, a Dodge nominee for the post, and as it was to turn out a happy choice.

Trumbull was not a stranger to railroad management. The son of a schoolteacher, he had started working in a bookstore in his home town of Arcadia, Missouri, at the age of 12, and at age 14 became deputy postmaster of Pleasant Hill. At 16 he went to work as a clerk for the Katy, later moving over to the Missouri Pacific where he became a freight auditor; in 1886 he became auditor of the Texas & Pacific, leaving that road in 1888 to enter the coal business in Colorado. He still kept in touch with railroad affairs during the 1888-1893 period, writing analyses of western railroads for New York and London investors. He thus had some useful background in railroad operation and finance — particularly with respect to railroads in financial difficulty — as well as being energetic, alert, and level-headed. And he apparently had the wisdom to accept help and advice from some of the knowledgeable and experienced men connected with the Gulf Route — in particular, Grenville Dodge.

While Trumbull and Dodge were struggling to reestablish the viability of the Gulf Route, the Union Pacific's receivers were coming to the conclusion that one of the burdens they no longer wished to shoulder was the South Park (DL&G) and its now constant deficits. Accordingly, they applied to the court in Nebraska to be relieved of responsibility for the road and to permit the bondholders (through the American Loan and Trust Company as trustee) to foreclose. This was done, the trustee filing the foreclosure suit in Federal District Court in Denver, that court having jurisdiction.

Dodge was immediately concerned lest the Denver & Rio Grande gain control of the South Park as a result of this receivership, thereby threatening the loss of mountain traffic from the South Park to the Gulf Road. He transmitted his concern to Judge Hallett, suggesting further that it would be most logical to include the South Park under the control of the same receiver as the Gulf Road. Judge Hallett apparently accepted this viewpoint and, on August 4, 1894, appointed Frank Trumbull as receiver of the Denver, Leadville & Gunnison Railway as well.

The addition of the South Park to Trumbull's railroad empire hardly lightened his burden. The line had been in trouble since 1883, when Union Pacific mismanagement and the peaking of the Leadville traffic had begun to take their toll. During the 1879-1883 period the South Park had been a very profitable enterprise, accumulating handsome surpluses after all expenses, interest and depreciation. Profits under the Evans management during 1879-1880 were nothing short of phenomenal, and even under Union Pacific management in 1881-1882 — when Omaha was doing its best to kill off local traffic on the line — the road managed to bring down a total of $342,447 additional to surplus. The handwriting appeared on the wall in 1883, however, when the road failed to earn interest charges, even though gross earnings held steady.

The year 1884 proved to be a disaster. The cumulative effect of UP mismanagement, the staggering costs of operation over Boreas and Alpine, deflation of the Leadville boom, and continued diversion of through traffic to the D&RG resulted in an operating ratio of 125%. Gross earnings, which had been running around a million and a half dollars for the previous three years, dropped to $1,194,069, while operating expenses, which had been averaging less than a million, two hundred thousand, leaped to $1,491,061.

Management reacted by cutting costs wherever possible, but the South Park was an expensive road just to keep open for operations. Its only hope of profitability lay in generating a high volume of traffic, something which seemed to be beyond the expertise of Union Pacific management. Gross earnings did increase moderately for the South Park after 1884, but peaked at $1,282,682 in 1887; for the next six years they hovered around an average of a million dollars a year. Operating expenses seem to have settled out at about the same level, resulting in operating ratios of 101% (1885), 97% (1886), 93% (1887), 110% (1888), 116% (1889), 101% (1890), 105% (1891), and 103% (1892). The cumulative unearned bond interest became staggering.

To cap this sorry record came the South Park's disastrous performance in 1893. Thanks to the financial panic of that year — which was to leave a pall over Colorado's economy for decades to come— gross earnings of the line dropped by one third. Omaha tried to cut expenses (the costly Alpine Tunnel operation had already been dispensed with, at the sacrifice of the Gunnison business), but nevertheless the operating ratio rose to a lofty 121%. 1894 offered only slight improvement; the best that seemingly could be hoped for would be a return to the "lower" losses of the early nineties! It's no wonder that the UP receivers decided they would rather have the DL&G be someone else's worry.

Thus Judge Hallett made the worry Frank Trumbull's. Trumbull proceeded to attack the problem from both sides — revenues and expenses. The South Park was in a poor competitive position; the Leadville traffic was as good as lost to the standard gauge Rio Grande and the Colorado Midland, and the Gunnison line was closed down. But Trumbull was a coal man and recognized the potential of the coal mines north of Gunnison as a generator of significant new traffic. One of his first acts, then, was to order the reopening of Alpine Tunnel, so that Baldwin coal could be brought out over DL&G rails both to serve commercial markets such as Leadville and to provide good locomotive fuel. While metal ore traffic had dwindled from a flood to a dribble, Trumbull attempted to build up revenues from such other

With the eighteen nineties receivership came to the South Park — now the Denver, Leadville & Gunnison. The professional photographers frequented the line less often; now, amateur photographers snapped photos of helper engines standing momentarily in the big cut at Rocky Point (left; Lad Arend Coll.). The morning passenger still stopped for little boys at Ferndale station (38 miles from Denver), but the weed-grown track and box of empty milk bottles as "express" seemed indicative of the declining status of the railroad (below; Museum Coll.).

sources as coal, hay and ice. Although he was successful to an extent, it was slow work, and gross revenues in the late 1890's stayed in the three-quarter-million dollar range.

In the area of operating efficiencies Trumbull was clearly successful. Heads-up local management got results that had eluded Omaha, and the operating ratio was soon hovering around 85% — a very creditable performance. This meant that important dollars were left over each year for improvement of the property, rebuilding of the car fleet, and so forth. It also meant that, when the Union Pacific, Denver & Gulf was ready to emerge from its receivership, there was sufficient optimism about the South Park's future to incorporate it into the UPD&G's successor — the new Colorado & Southern Railway.

Plans for reorganizing the UPD&G were being laid as early as 1895. Two important steps were accomplished in 1896, when the Fort Worth & Denver City was rescued from receivership, and the UP agreed to purchase the Julesburg line with the UPD&G bonds it held. The road was doing well under Trumbull's management; traffic was built up, the operating ratio cut from 84% in 1893 to 70% in 1897, and a great deal was invested in upgrading the property. With this improving picture, the Trustee for the Denver, Texas & Gulf and Denver, Texas & Fort Worth mortgages filed foreclosure action in August, 1897, subsequent to the original 1894 foreclosure action on behalf of the UPD&G bondholders. Dodge moved in September to form a Reorganization Committee representing various bondholding interests. There were problems — the UP was balking on the matter of the Julesburg line, to the extent that Dodge threatened to extend it from Julesburg to a connection with the C&NW at O'Neill, Nebraska, and put the UPD&G into the Denver-Chicago trade directly. Morgan Jones, President of the FW&DC, was bitterly opposed to including the South Park in the reorganization plans, and was rather diffident about Trumbull. Nevertheless, Dodge managed to pull all factions together, and by late 1898 plans for the reorganization were completed. A name had even been chosen — after eliminating "Colorado & Texas" and "Colorado & Seaboard", the title "Colorado & Southern" was decided upon for the reborn railroad.

Sale of the DL&G and UPD&G was effected on November 18 and 19, respectively; the C&S in-corporated on December 19, 1898; and the two old roads conveyed to the new C&S on December 28 and 29. Actual operations were not transferred until January 12, 1899, at which time the DL&G (and the UPD&G) followed the DSP&P into history.

Operation of the South Park under the C&S continued in the pattern established during Trumbull's tenure as receiver: local traffic was built up wherever possible, operations kept on as economical a level as possible, and improvements were made to the extent that finances would permit. Many large capital improvements were in fact made during these first years of C&S operation of the (now combined) narrow gauge lines. Hoped-for new motive power did not materialize, but the better existing power was shopped and upgraded, in some cases (such as the Cooke passenger moguls) extensively. The car fleet was added to. It was clear that Trumbull was a friend of the South Park and intended to do as much with it as he could.

In 1902 the C&S came under the financial control of an investing group headed by Edwin T. Hawley. Trumbull worked well with the Hawley group and continued to run the C&S. Then on December 21, 1908, the Hawley group sold their interest in the C&S to the Burlington Road, and at that point Trumbull retired. (Subsequently he joined a group of friends who purchased control of the Chesapeake & Ohio from Kuhn, Loeb & Co., and Trumbull became Chairman of the Board of the C&O.) Following Trumbull's departure the C&S' attitude towards the South Park changed perceptively; Alpine Tunnel was once again closed, this time with finality; even Boreas was "abandoned" for a time. Rumors and half-hearted discussions about abandoning or even giving away the line were to surface at intervals over the next several decades until they would become fact.

After its initial skyrocket of success, the South Park seems to have lapsed into a long and continual decline, interrupted for any length of time only by the semi-recovery realized under the Trumbull administration. It seems possible that the South Park might not have made it intact into the twentieth century but for Frank Trumbull. Some might question whether he should be complimented for his efforts or not, but Colorado railfans certainly owe him a debt of gratitude.

UNION PACIFIC RAILWAY.

GENERAL FREIGHT DEPARTMENT.

CIRCULAR NO. 744.
Supersedes Circular No. 678.
Amends Tariff No. 870.

Omaha, May 30th, 1889.

On and after date hereof,

HANCOCK, ALPINE TUNNEL,

WOODSTOCK and QUARTZ,

Stations in Colorado, on Gunnison branch of the Denver & South Park, between Romley and Pitkin, will be opened for all business.

An agent having been appointed at Pitkin, Colo., freight for that station may be forwarded without prepayment of charges.

Please be governed accordingly.

J. A. MUNROE,
General Freight Agent.

An Alpine Album

Of all the spectacular portions of a spectacular railroad, the greatest spectacle on the South Park was Alpine Pass. The greatest spectacle — and the biggest headache; for its 4% grades seemed unending, and its weather varied from a sometimes balmy summer and fall to a frozen hell of winter that could last until May or June. It became the despair of Union Pacific management, and despite the successful adoption of the rotary snow plow to clearing the line of deep snow, operations in winter (and subsequently even in summer) were given up in surrender to the elements and the economics of operation of a narrow gauge railroad at 11,600 feet altitude. The following pages offer a selection of photographs of the line in operation during the Union Pacific period, from its early DSP&P days to cessation of operations under the DL&G in 1890, reflecting a degree of the atmosphere, intrigue and fascination that surrounded this unique bit of railroad.

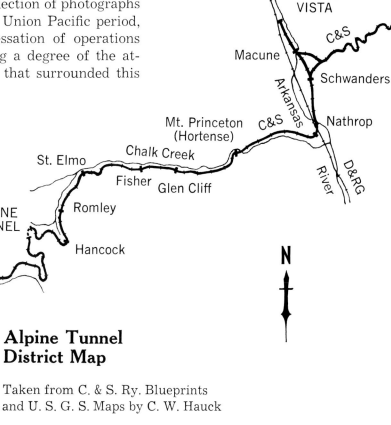

Alpine Tunnel District Map

Taken from C. & S. Ry. Blueprints and U. S. G. S. Maps by C. W. Hauck

The long grade up Chalk Creek Canyon was relieved by only one town of any size, St. Elmo. The view above was taken at Cascade, below St. Elmo, about 1888; two coaches and two 4-wheel cabooses follow DSP&P 200 down the grade (R. H. Kindig Coll.). At right, two DSP&P freights pass at Romley, above St. Elmo, about the same period; the district's biggest producer, the Mary Murphy mine, was located at Romley. (Chase photo from State Hist. Society of Colo. Coll.)

In the upper reaches of the Chalk Creek Canyon the railroad stayed on the north slope, where the mountains blotted out the winter sun. The last station approaching Alpine, and the coldest, iciest, and snowiest of all, was Hancock — shown above in this rare 1884 view (R. H. Kindig Coll.). Just a few miles further near the East Portal of Alpine Tunnel DL&G 112 posed amid snowbanks in June, pulling a special during reopening of the line in 1895. The business cars are UPD&G 1 (left) and DL&G 2 (right) (Museum Coll.).

Above, DL&G 197 has just emerged from the East Portal of Alpine Tunnel (at Atlantic) with a box, coach and combine in this April, 1896, view. Either the mixed was short that day, or this is only the last part. Records do indicate that when freight trains were being run the mixed ran without freight cars as a passenger accommodation. (Dr. Newton photo, Francis and Freda Rizzari Coll.) At left, the same engine (DL&G 197) with identical consist at Hortense, with the Chalk Cliffs in the background. The mob of people would indicate a special party, perhaps a Sunday school group, was riding the train; benches were even set up in the box car (Gary Christopher Coll.).

During early years, most of the track from the West Portal past the stone enginehouse was covered with snowsheds, and snowfences protected the track as it swung around towards the Palisades (right, Litton & Gail Bivans Coll.). Center, removal of the snowsheds revealed the huge size of the enginehouse (Gordon Chappell Coll.). Bottom, a DL&G freight pulled by engines 199 and 196 is dwarfed by the high stone walls; the train is stopped at the miniscule frame telegraph shed, at left. (Lad Arend Coll.)

From Alpine Tunnel, the track swung south, crossing the shear rock face of the mountain on laboriously constructed stone retaining walls at the Palisades, before looping back to reach the Quartz Creek Valley (left, looking downgrade, Denver Public Library Western Hist. Coll.). At right, a westbound freight is in the valley below while a double-headed eastbound freight can be seen on the shelf high above (Denver Public Library Western Hist. Coll.). Above, another photographer (Mellen) posed one of the DSP&P Brooks moguls with a very short train at the same location (Kansas State Hist. Society Coll.).

The Palisades immediately became the place to stop the train and pose for a group picture. The two examples on this page are typical; the one below must have been of an unusually large excursion group, as two of the DSP&P's Brooks moguls were required for the long train. On the page opposite is a less orthodox view; the photographer had carefully picked his way down the slide rock to gain this perspective looking up at the mammoth stone retaining wall and towering cliffs above. (Below, Kansas State Hist. Society Coll.; others, Denver Public Library Western Hist. Coll.)

After negotiating the Palisades and Woodstock Loop, the route down Quartz Creek was fairly easy. These two faded but rare views show DSP&P 217 with a westbound freight at the town of Quartz (above; State Hist. Society of Colorado Coll.), and South Park Brooks mogul No. 30 and passenger train stopped at the coal dock at Pitkin (below; Gunnison Camera Center).

The Snowplow Trials

In the eighteen seventies and eighties the South Park found the task of keeping its line open over the high passes in winter to be almost overwhelming. The little engines and push-plows could cope with light snows in the valleys, but when huge snowstorms and slides buried the tracks on the passes — or when ground blizzards piled up deep drifts in South Park — the railroad had to hire hundreds of laborers to slowly dig out by hand. The answer came in March, 1889, when the DSP&P acquired its first steam-powered snow plow — the revolutionary new Leslie patented rotary plow built by the Cooke Locomotive works. Pushed by locomotives, the rotary incorporated a large, steam-powered "fan wheel", made of many individual blades, which chewed into the snow at a high rate of speed and spewed the snow right or left out of a discharge chute in a huge plume.

The rotary did have one failing — it worked handsomely in pure snow, but working in slides containing boulders and trees, the debris wreaked havoc on the blades. This necessitated sending crews ahead to "prospect" the track for such trouble-spots, and when found they had to be dug out by hand — costly and time-consuming. A mistake in prospecting meant that the rotary would be out of commission for a day or two (or more) for repairs.

A new, competing steam plow was offered that did not seem to have this drawback — the Jull Centrifugal Snow Excavator, which utilized a huge auger or screw; turned by steam power, it bored its way through the snow. The Union Pacific resolved to try the newcomer to see what it could do, and not illogically on the most difficult job at hand — clearing the east side of Alpine Pass. The line had been closed all of the winter of 1889-1890; it had been a terrible winter, and the DSP&P rotary had been kept busy trying to keep the Leadville line open. But with the arrival of better weather in April UP officials decided to send both the rotary and the Jull to St. Elmo to take turns trying to open the line to the Tunnel.

The "trials" began on April 16, 1890, and lasted three days. The rotary had cleared the line up to Romley, and the Jull was then given the opportunity to show what it could do in clearing the packed snow and ice from the South Park's steep grades and sharp curves. It was a flop; the Jull was too heavy, too cumbersome, too inefficient to work under such conditions. For three days the Jull attacked the snow only to derail and become mired down; each time it was withdrawn and the rotary steamed through the trouble-spot like a hot knife through butter.

By the 18th the decision was inescapable, the Jull backers admitted defeat, and the famed Snowplow Trials of Alpine Pass were concluded with the rotary the undisputed winner. The Trials had received National notice and William H. Jackson, the noted Denver photographer, had been retained by the Union Pacific to record the whole affair on film. A selection of his remarkable photos, gathered together by Gordon Chappell, are shown on the following pages.

Curiously, none of the surviving views of the Jull plow show it throwing snow. Above, on the 16th, it is stalled and derailed in shallow snow, while below it is shown on the 18th during its final derailment and conclusive failure.

After the Jull plow failed on the morning of the sixteenth, it was withdrawn and the rotary brought up (right). It promptly chewed into the snow, throwing it out some three hundred feet into the canyon (below).

On these pages are six views of the rotary in triumphant action en route to Atlantic, east portal of Alpine Tunnel. The four locomotives assigned to the rotary, as seen on this page, included two Rhode Island 2-8-0s, a Cooke, and another Rhode Island at the rear. It was slow going even for the rotary in this deep, packed snow and ice.

During the latter years of the South Park's morning departure for Leadville, the crowds on the Denver Union Station platform were not normally this substantial (above). But this bleak April morning in 1937 was not just another day — it was the last day for South Park passenger service to Leadville. The little narrow gauge trains had become an anachronism in the modern, bustling Union Station (below). In this 1930-period view the famed Mizpah arch still welcomed travelers (left), and Denver tastes seemed to be changing from the products of Baldwin and Cooke to those of Henry Ford (nine Fords, two Essex, a Chevrolet and a couple of unidentified marques make up the 14 cars parked in the foreground). (Upper, Lad Arend Coll.; lower, State Hist. Society of Colorado Coll.)

Colorado & Southern:
An Operations Baedecker

Robert W. Richardson

From August 7, 1894, the UPD&G and DL&G were to all practical purposes operated as one system. True they had to keep separate corporate accounts and records, and bill each other back and forth for various items. The Gulf Road rented the South Park roundhouse in Denver for $20 per month, as an example. It also paid the DL&G up to $2,000 or more a month for rental of engines for use on the Gulf narrow gauge (the former Colorado Central).

The roads were dependent on the UP for shops and most of their yards in Denver and the bills for this led to constant wrangles, often between the new Gulf-South Park officials who just previously had been UP people and their former employers. UP officials at Omaha scarcely concealed their anger at some of the disputes. This lessened somewhat when the UP facilities were leased. But it was a year to year lease and it was an uneasy tenancy.

The DL&G had no money to buy new engines, but fortunately had received eight new 2-8-0 Nos. 266-273 in 1890 (to remain in service many years as C&S 63-70). The UPD&G in 1897 received three 2-8-0 (Nos. 9-11, becoming C&S 71-73), and these were the last new engines ever acquired for the narrow gauge. New cars, however, were built at company shops. The old Golden roundhouse was utilized for passenger cars, while new freight cars were built at Trinidad, reaching the narrow gauge via Denver on standard gauge trucks.

The DL&G reported, in its inventory for the year 1892, a nine-stall stone roundhouse at Denver, a four-pocket coal chute at Pine Grove, a 13-stall stone roundhouse at Como, a 50x150 ft. stone engine house at Boreas, an eight-stall wooden house at Leadville, and a six stall stone roundhouse at Gunnison. The line between Romley and Pitkin was not operated and an iron turntable was located at St. Elmo.

In 1892 it reported 61 locomotives (there had been 74 in 1890), 13 coaches, 7 coach and baggage, 3 baggage, mail and express, 2 "Div. Superintendent's" cars, 15 cabooses, 517 box cars, 27 refrigerators, 153 flat cars, 386 coal cars, only 8 stock cars, 2 rotary, 3 "ordinary snowplows", 4 flangers, 5 outfit and 3 "wreck tool cars."

The puzzler in this report was the meager eight stock cars. There is no indication that stock cars were leased from some car company, as often was the case in those times; nor of renting cars from anyone else. Photos do not indicate any foreign

Narrow gauge engines were used to switch the dual gauge yards at Leadville. C&S 62 was used as the regular switcher for many years, and the three-way coupler pocket installed on the pilot to permit handling standard gauge cars is clearly shown here (right). Below, C&S 60 was the switcher when this early photo was made with No. 39 and a large retinue of well-wishers. (Both, State Hist. Society of Colorado Coll.)

92

stock cars. Four years later they still reported only eight such cars. The Gulf Road had seven on its Clear Creek lines, so the total of both lines would provide barely enough for one respectable-size stock train, which would be an absurdly meager equippage for a spring or fall stock rush.

Wooden cars in link and pin days had a short life, so totals would vary slightly as a car would be classified as "worn out", and the numerous wrecks of the times took their toll. By building new box cars, no doubt using parts from 35 flat cars taken off the roster, the DL&G by 1897 had 552 of those cars.

By 1897 the DL&G showed two frame additions to the Como roundhouse of 60 x 60 x 118 and 62 x 95 x 145 feet. At Climax a covered turntable was in use, with a "turntable house 57 x 64 feet." A 29 x 71 foot enginehouse was also located at Climax. Locomotives, though totalling 61, showed 10 as "scrap", 17 as out of service, with 16 First Class and 18 Second Class.

Engine 60 was sold for $1500, for example, to Burns-Biggs Lumber Co. at Chama, N. M. Two more of the Brooks Moguls, 59 and 61, went to the Little Book Cliff RR for less money, and indicative of their condition was their brief life on that road. There was a good market for narrow gauge engines and cars in the 1890s, especially in the latter half of the decade as business nationally began to recover from the 1893 crash. Dozens of small roads were being built, and as most equipment dealers were in the East, the savings in freight expense enabled the Colorado roads to sell most anything that would run to these new shortlines and private roads in the West and Southwest. This enabled the DL&G and UPD&G to clear out their "relics", get some cash and raise their operating departments' hopes of getting new engines — in vain, as it turned out.

Sale of both properties was made late in 1898 to the bondholders, the DL&G at the turntable of the old roundhouse in Denver on a chilly November 18, 1898. The Gulf sale was held with business cars in attendance at Gulf Junction in Pueblo the next day, on November 19, 1898. The new Colorado & Southern Ry. was incorporated on December 19, 1898, and it was agreed that the C&S would take over on January 12, 1899.

On January 11, 1899, Charles Wheeler, Treasurer, wrote a letter to David H. Moffat, President of the First National Bank of Denver, instructing him to close the account of the DL&G at end of the day's business, and to open a new account, the next day, for the C&S Ry. Mr. Wheeler became Treasurer of the new company, and the other officers similarly for the most part stayed with the new company.

Vanished from ticket office plate glass were the Gulf and South Park emblems, and in their place soon came the monogram C&S to last just over a decade. The slogan "The Colorado Road" appeared on the first stationery of the C&S, and this was to last until 1910. An intensive advertising campaign was inaugurated with full page newspaper advertising and folders by the hundreds of thousands.

One thing missing when the C&S was formed was its own general shops. The Union Pacific in 1890 had rebuilt its shop facilities in Denver, adjacent to the Jersey wye, better known in Denver as "40th St." Historically it was the site of ground breaking of the first railroad in Denver, and later UP subsidiary, the Denver Pacific R.R. The new shops, roundhouse, etc. were designed to be the center for the vast Colorado Division, as well as the western end of the Kansas Division. With independence of the UPD&G and DL&G under the 1893-1894 receiverships, these lines became tenants, with the UP doing their repair work on engines and cars, the tenant roads also paying a share of maintenance of the vast Denver yard area, much of it three-rail. This led to frequent disputes over billings, some of them rather acrimonious, as the now-independent officials used that independence.

On May 1, 1898, a new lease went into effect whereby Frank Trumbull, as Receiver of both roads, leased the shop area for $20,000 a year, payable in monthly installments. The situation was now reversed, the Receiver's roads doing work for the UP on same basis as the UP had formerly done for the two roads. Among the terms was that it could be cancelled on 60 days notice (later changed to nine months); that in event of change of receiver, notice must be given to the UP and contract would be reviewed. After negotiations with The Pullman Palace Car Company, the Union Pacific agreed in 1899 to lease the shops to Pullman, so that Denver could be a center of their car fleet maintenance and rebuilding. The UP notified the C&S on December 26, 1899 to vacate not later than January 1, 1901.

Construction of new shops of the C&S was commenced in the spring of 1900, to be ready for use on November 15. These are the buildings located at "7th St." near the Union Depot and their freight yards, buildings now scheduled for demolition as the C&S moves to newer Burlington Northern facilities. It was a large expense for the new railroad, as they had to purchase a great deal of machinery, since most of what they had been using was UP owned. The new site had one unfortunate fault: it was located adjacent to the South Platte River, on a bend of the river, and in times of flood the C&S was inundated and the en-

The Denver roundhouse was a busy spot in narrow gauge days. Top left, No. 68 simmers in front of the 'house (Henry R. Griffiths, Jr.), while the 65 and 8 greet the early morning sun and No. 8 gets a bit of coal (bottom) (Lad Arend). Locomotives for freights moved in multiples; above, the 68, 65 and 73 move through the yards on a May day in 1933 (Gerald M. Best), and the 60 and 58 come off the turntable in 1936 (Richard H. Kindig). At bottom, the 68, 6 and 537 have coaled up and a fourth engine is just moving up (Lad Arend).

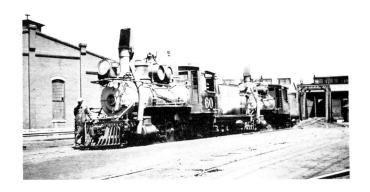

tire area unusable until the river went back into its banks. On November 30, 1900, the C&S ceased to be a tenant of the UP, but not without some final bickering over bills. One last item was the UP bill for a C&S locomotive being run through the brick wall of the roundhouse, and another expense item for a C&S engine knocking down doors of the house. The C&S took the attitude that these incidents were almost normal "wear and tear" of the property, but they paid. Since all roundhouses seem to have suffered these twin afflictions, perhaps there was some merit in their view.

Employed at Denver in 1910 were an average of 300 men in the back shop, about 125 in the roundhouse, 39 just working at coal chutes and the ash pits and sand house; about 340 in the Car Dept. and from 66 to 85 men in the coach yard. The list of occupations is almost a roster of classifications that not only vanished with the steam locomotive but with wooden cars and passenger trains. Total payroll at Denver was $62,641 out of a system total of $94,229. When Railroad Day was observed in 1910 with a parade of employees, the C&S portion of the parade equalled, if not exceeded, that of the D&RG.

In the days of steam engines and before bottled and natural gas use was common, large quantities of coal were used. In 1906, for example, the South Park used these quantities at principal points:

Como	24,933 tons
Pine Grove	9,791 tons
Leadville	3,169 tons
Schwanders	10,288 tons
Dickey	12,772 tons
Pitkin	10,861 tons
	71,814 tons total for those points.

Most of this coal was hand shoveled into docks and chutes and sometimes directly into engines. For this the railroad paid 8 cents per ton.

In 1909, for example, coal cost $3.57 a ton at Como, of which $1.55 was the cost per ton of transporting it from Baldwin to Como. The high cost of bringing coal from Gunnison weighted the decision to discontinue operation of that line. At the same time coal brought to Denver by standard gauge cars, was under $2.00 per ton, plus 10c per ton transfer costs. Moreover coal production in Colorado was approaching the 10,000,000 tons per year production level and there were so many in the business that the market was very competitive.

When the C&S began, with inherited tenancy on the Union Pacific at Denver, freights for that first year or more worked out of Jersey (Pullman) and used the West Side Belt line to get out of town. Later when the C&S moved into the 7th St. yard, and the new shops opened in 1900, these trains

reached the Belt Line by a reverse movement crossing the Platte near the roundhouse. Passenger trains, however, westbound used the C&S main to South Park Jct. and crossed the river just beyond that point, with junction with the Belt Line beyond there. Eastbound passenger trains from South Park Jct. dropped over a couple blocks and often could not be seen by crews on the other track, a factor that contributed to uncertainties as to whether a train had been to the junction one way or the other.

The Denver yard contained many miles of three-rail trackage, but was generally switched by standard gauge engines. The Gulf Route paid the UP under the lease for use of over 40 miles of three-rail track. But not all tracks were dual gauge, and crews therefore were required to maintain care. Not infrequently narrow gauge cars were pushed into standard gauge tracks and vice versa, for some embarassing derailments. The yards being on sharp curves contributed to more than one collision between road crews and switching crews.

The C&S did not require a great deal of three-rail trackage other than in the Denver yard. Unlike the D&RG, it was not standard gauging or three-railing main lines or branch lines. Though there were the usual rumors, nothing was done to standard gauge the narrow gauge lines until near the end, and then such minor changes as standard gauging the orphaned Climax-Leadville section and the few miles of line extending to industries on the outskirts of Denver.

Yet, the D&RG was not unique in running mixed or dual gauge trains, with engines and cars of both gauges in the same train. In the 1930s we find a 63-car double-header narrow gauge South Park freight arriving with a mixed gauge consist in Denver. It had picked up the standard gauge loads after passing Waterton, and sometimes this meant a dozen or more standard gauge gondola loads of sugar beets for example.

How did the two types of equipment couple? It is known that in the sugar beet period there was a standard gauge flat or idler car equipped with dual couplers, much like the idler cars used by the D&RGW. There was also at least one box car, #6305, equipped with three-way couplers in 1907, but equipment records are rather silent on this and these cars were not singled out in listings as special cars for this purpose. Apparently everyone knew which ones they were.

On the Denver end of the South Park one or more yard engines were equipped with dual couplers of the three-position type, a practice dating from the Union Pacific times. One of these engines was assigned to the South Park and so we have the unusual item of a standard gauge engine listed as a "South Park engine" in C&S records. It handled most of the work out as far as Chatfield, end of the third rail for standard gauge, M.P. 14.1. For years engine 455, one of the older and lighter 2-8-0s, was the engine assigned to this work.

Sometimes the yard engine did not use the narrow gauge positions of the coupler for a while and such episodes as the following would happen. The yard crew picked up engines at the Union Station from incoming passenger trains, then would take them to the roundhouse area. On one occasion the coupler pocket had filled with accumulated cinders, jamming the coupler while going thru a switch and derailing the towed narrow gauge engine, tieing up trains trying to leave the station. On another recorded occasion a narrow gauge caboose derailed due to the same cause.

There were frequent derailments due to using the wrong gauge track. For instance, one new brakeman one day in the 1930s swung down from the lead engine of his incoming double-header and lined the switch, not for the dual gauge "South Park freight" track but for the CB&Q transfer track, which lacked a third rail as of course there was never any transfer of narrow gauge to that line. Result, two 2-8-0 engines wallowing in a switch lacking the very necessary third rail. Putting in standard gauge cars onto narrow gauge tracks also required trips to the rip tracks to repair C&S rolling stock.

Things were different at Leadville, where a narrow gauge engine did the switching, much of it standard gauge cars, especially on the extensive Leadville Mineral Belt Ry. There was considerable interchange of standard cars with both the D&RG and Colorado Midland. The narrow gauge engine assigned as switcher was equipped with a three-way coupler on engine and tender, and when an engine had to go to the shop, the tender would be given to another engine. As in March, 1935, when engine 60 was due in Denver for inspection — it was worked on passenger train 71 and the Denver roundhouse instructed to change the three-way coupler and tender to engine 58, and then run that engine thru to Leadville and to stay there as switcher in place of No. 60.

At Leadville the flanger 013, a very necessary item in that high altitude and snowy yard, served also as idler car, or as they termed it "three-way coupler car." This took some of the strain off the engines, whose frames could be damaged as standard gauge cars kept getting larger and heavier, especially when loaded. However, the 013 had a tendency to lift off the track under the strain, especially on the end next to the engine. Eventually

in 1938, after the larger engines were stationed at Leadville, a large casting laying around as unclaimed freight was placed on the engine end of the car.

Another phase of mixed gauge operation was the changing of gauge of a car by simply changing its trucks. When cars were wooden, and standard gauge cars not much larger or heavier than the narrow gauge ones, this practice did not pose too serious a problem, but as standard gauge cars became steel underframed and heavier the weaker narrow gauge cars would sometimes collapse in freight or yard service. Certain special cars, because of their use, were frequently changed under the UP management, especially the business cars, a practice followed by the C&S.

Under the Gulf Route new narrow gauge box cars were built at Trinidad, reaching narrow gauge lines on standard gauge trucks. Narrow gauge coal cars frequently ventured to the southern Colorado fields, some not surviving the trip. In the early 1900s photos show standard gauge box cars under load on the South Park. Non-revenue cars of course changed gauge as required. Among these were scale test cars, B&B cars, and even the rotary. Rotary 99201 now at the Colorado Railroad Museum, although spending most of its life at Cheyenne and working the Northern Division lines, ventured out on the South Park to replace or aid the regularly assigned rotary. Apparently the changing of trucks was not common enough to make special provisions for this activity, as no record of special trackage has yet been noted. Again, in the days of low wages and low costs for car work, it probably was no major item of expense to change trucks.

One interesting item about Leadville switching is the record of using a D&RG engine to fill out in event of problems with the regular switch engine. On December 22, 1905, the yard crew recorded using D&RG #407 for part of their day which normally was 7 A.M. to 6 P.M., noon hour off, a ten-hour working day. On this day they put in 15 hours, and worked thru the noon hour. Perhaps a derailment. Only rarely was another engine used a part of a day. In one typical year of switching, engine 60 was the regular engine there for six months, engines 48 and 43 at other times. The working day of this crew sometimes was long, one day from 7 A.M. to 3 A.M., back on duty again at 7 A.M.! Another time they had a day lasting until 1:15 A.M. because they went to Three Mile Tank to pull #72 out of a snow bank.

It seemed odd to see a dispatcher's lineup in 1939 calling for "Run a work train on South Park using a 600 class engine." The 600s of course were standard gauge 2-8-0 types.

Morrison

Initial objective of the South Park, Morrison was quickly bypassed and by the 1890's was merely the terminus of a country branch line. Above left, DL&G 109 stands at the depot with the accommodation on a wintry day, while in the panorama below the coaches are parked at right and the locomotive is half hidden by the shrubbery at left. The town gives evidence of a devastating fire that destroyed the center of the community. Often used on the branch were the light "cold water" Brooks moguls like UPD&G No. 150 (ex-Colorado Central 8) shown in the two views on this page. (All, Littleton Area Historical Museum.)

Generally the lighter or older engines were used on the Morrison Branch, although in the view above a main-line 2-8-0 (DL&G 204) is posed at the depot. Catastrophes were few on the Branch but minor mishaps more frequent; here (left) DL&G 190, one of the old, light Baldwin 2-8-0's purchased in 1880, has left the iron and nosed into the adjacent embankment. No one seems overly concerned. (Both, Denver Public Library Western Hist. Coll.)

Spills were not unusual on the wobbly branch trackage, and backing with a train always invited a derailed tender. Here (right) DL&G 109 has gone off onto the ice and snow one winter day, while below UPD&G 108 has gone aground with a quarry train, and only a sturdy sprag has kept the tender from spilling over entirely. Both engines are 1884 Cooke moguls, and later became C&S 4 and 13. (Upper, Littleton Area Hist. Museum; lower, Denver Public Library Western Hist. Coll.)

When this photo was taken in 1925 by Richard B. Jackson, both the engine (old Brooks rebuild No. 22) and the train (the Morrison mixed) were about done. Back in 1908, Cooke mogul No. 11 found plenty of snow in Morrison (below) on the fourth of May (R. H. Kindig Coll.).

Passenger Service

The South Park for most of its life had but one passenger train, the day, all-day run between Denver and Leadville. At various times under the UP, DL&G and C&S the night train also was a passenger rather than a mixed, but most of the time the night train was simply a mixed with just a combination car, or a freight. Despite the length of the Leadville run, there were few places of any size en route and traffic from most was meager, a single coach being ample. In summer season one or two extra coaches were added as needed of course, to be cut off at Grant or Como. Head end business varied too, sometimes a full express car, other times a combined baggage and R.P.O. car. When a full express car was needed, then the combination RPO-coach combines were used. The passenger engines seemed able to handle a four-car consist when necessary and keep the time. Unlike the D&RG, which relied on 4-6-0s to handle its passenger runs, the South Park used the Moguls generally and under the C&S almost exclusively, as the 2-8-0 types were classified as "freight."

Excursion business was good on the Denver end of the line. Dome Rock, M.P. 31.7, was the destination of many specials. Crystal Lake, at M.P. 43.1 and less than a mile beyond Pine Grove, was another very popular point. As autos came in this business declined greatly, but even in its last full year extra coaches were being handled to Crystal Lake. The UP General Superintendent stated in 1891 that Crystal Lake was the second most important excursion point on the Colorado Division. First of course was the Georgetown Loop.

There was an intense rivalry among the various roads at Denver for the excursion business. Denver has always been a great place for conventions and this was business eagerly sought. No convention was complete that didn't plan at least one one-day excursion to some point in the mountains. The Denver papers went along with this and invented, for the diversion of their readers, various alleged antics of the rival passenger agents. Military ranks were given the chiefs of the passenger departments, and the C&S' T. E. Fisher was referred to as "Col. Fisher". There was "Major" Hooper of the D&RG, "Lieut." Speer of the Midland, while the new Moffat Road's man was "Sergeant". The press reported their doings as military raids and strategies in carrying off one promotional stunt or another. Hooper undoubtedly flooded the market with the greatest amount of

assorted brochures, booklets, and even ghost-written books like "Crest of the Continent" and "Over the Range." Speer sponsored the most colorful and elaborate timetables, folders, booklets, incorporating many highest quality examples of the lithographer's art. Fisher produced many issues of folders extolling the places along the mountain lines including some oddly-shaped die-cut issues. The D&SL, with fewer attractions, managed quite well promoting the one-day trips to Rollins Pass and Arrow, stressing snowbanks in July, something the others could not offer. It was a colorful rivalry while it lasted and gave not only the conventioners but local residents and casual tourists some bargains in mountain sight seeing. Like the others, C&S had a financial interest in some resort places, but gradually disposed of these within a decade or so. The large fleet of open air coaches were kept very busy summers until the mid-1920s, then rather swiftly they vanished from the rosters, their lessening use not justifying annual overhauls.

Some odd operational things occurred on these lines using train orders and timetables, no block signals. Thus a rotary out of Como might be shown as the first section of the scheduled passenger train, though one wonders if the green flags on the rotary lasted very long under the assaults on snow drifts. The mixed trains, such as those on the Gunnison line, often ran in sections, each section confusingly carrying a combine. During the 1908 fall stock rush, one night #94 came in to Como in four sections. The first section arrived with 18 loads at 9:50 P.M. about seven hours late, with four engines. The second section five minutes later had 16 loads and four engines; the third section arrived at 12:14 A.M. with 16 loads and three engines and right behind it, signing in one minute later, the fourth with two engines and eight loads. Como's night hostlers had some busy times.

The uncertain operation through Alpine Tunnel killed off Railway Post Office operations on the Como-Gunnison line by 1887, though the route existed in fragments into 1889 using postmarks reading "Como & Gunnison R.P.O." and "Buena Vista & Gunnison R.P.O." The original Denver & Leadville RPO route went by way of Buena Vista in the early 1880s, ending when the Boreas Pass route opened in 1884. Then in 1901 the Denver & Leadville RPO was established on Trains 71 and 72, discontinued in 1917 until re-established in 1931. In the period 1917 thru 1931 it operated as the "Denver & Como R.P.O."

Through passenger service between Denver and Leadville was also interrupted briefly when the C&S decided to suspend service over Boreas Pass in the fall of 1910. The mixed train operation after

October 31, 1910 between Breckenridge and Leadville was protested loudly by the communities involved. The railroad said they had access to Denver by the Colorado Midland connection at Leadville, that line being financially controlled at the time by the C&S. But finally their appeals to the Railroad Commissioners had their effect and after two years service was resumed over Boreas. It was, however, just a summer mixed with a combine, operating as Nos. 80-81 through Como until October 14, 1912, thereafter only as an extra. It was resumed again on January 13, 1913, while Nos. 70 and 71 continued to terminate at Como. Even after they were extended on to Leadville, for a long time they ran daily only to Como, six days a week "except Sunday" beyond.

The C&S runs to Leadville were competitive with the D&RG in time but not in service. #71 took 9 hours 15 minutes generally, while the D&RG took ten hours; but as the D&RG offered standard gauge accomodations with such things as diners and Pullmans, they got the business. So considering this competition as well as the combined C&S and Colorado Midland standard gauge service to Buena Vista and Leadville it is easy to see why the narrow gauge had to depend mostly on local business.

C&S was no competition to the D&RG for Gunnison through traffic, as the combination of Trains 81 and 93 took 18 hours and 40 minutes for the 201 miles, while D&RG Nos. 15 and 7 required 12 hours and 50 minutes for their 290-mile route. C&S had briefly tried putting on a Gunnison "passenger", but the lack of intermediate places providing important traffic soon had just the mixed with its single combination car again handling the run.

The D&RG had a regular Pay Car, which covered all its narrow gauge lines. The C&S had none, so generally used Business Car B-2, or if that was unavailable, coach 148 seems to have been favored in the early years. Unlike the D&RG which ran its pay car as a special train, the C&S handled its car on the regular passenger runs. Usually the third week of the month, it would run one day on the train to Leadville, next day back to Como, third day to Gunnison. In 1904 for the briefly run Gunnison passenger trains Nos. 103 and 104, which connected with #72 both directions at Como, the pay car made the run from Leadville to Gunnison in one day, and from Gunnison to Denver in one day. In order to avoid delays to the passenger trains, all station and section employees were alerted in advance to be on hand to quickly pick up their checks, and surprisingly the running of the Pay Car entailed little delay to trains.

The Pacific Express Co. had the express contract on the combined road's trains in the 1890s. The express rates on non-competitive business were to be one and one-half times the rate if the matter were carried by the railroad at its less than carload rates. The railroad was to receive 55% of the gross express earnings. The messengers were paid $70 a month in 1895-1898 of which the DL&G paid up to half at first. Some idea of working conditions in the "good old days" was Division Superintendent S. L. Rainey's report on October 9, 1895, ". . . it is too much to ask two messengers to do the work, as they leave Gunnison at ten o'clock in the morning, and reach Como at ten o'clock in the evening when on time, and leave Como at three o'clock in the morning, arriving at Gunnison 2:50 P.M., leaving them only five hours at Como when the train is on time, and it is frequently late."

Colorado & Southern mogul No. 4 is shown here with the Leadville passenger train in 1903, taking water at Dickey, with fireman Parlin holding the cable for the spout. Passenger business was brisk enough then to warrant using four cars. (Lad Arend Coll.)

A young mother and toddler wait on the Kenosha depot platform, lunch basket resting on the stoop, for the train to carry them to the big city. In the 1890's passengers dressed in style for the occasion. (R. B. Jackson Coll.)

Messenger C. F. Hill had asked to be relieved as soon after October 1st as possible, stating that "when I am required to do 15 to 20 hours work in 24 hours with uncongenial fellow workmen and no extra compensation for extra hours work is more than I can stand . . ." Unable to obtain a satisfactory replacement, the work was turned over to conductors of the mixed train on November 1, 1895, who at least generally obtained some rest between runs and could call on their brakemen to assist in the work. The same arrangement was made for the Morrison run, but messengers continued on the Denver-Leadville train. Their pay was $50 a month, with four days per month off.

Of the Platte Canon District stations, in the year 1907 for example, Como accounted for $2,607 of revenue out of $15,012 total. Leadville District had $22,700, of which nearly a third was Leadville receipts. Gunnison District had $9,264 of which Alma was the source of $3,607 and Fairplay $1,345, while other points ranged from $148 for Ohio City to $940 for Gunnison itself. Conductors collected about one-third of the total passenger revenues in cash fares, as so many of the places had no agent.

With the losses as high as they were it was only natural that the C&S would examine the possibility of using some kind of motor car, with or without trailers. In the 1920s railroads large and small were changing over from steam powered secondary passenger runs to much more economical gasoline or gas-electric trains of one or two

cars. The Burlington system was employing many motor cars in branch line service. The C&S people obtained catalogs and quotes from various manufacturers. Unfortunately almost none of the manufactured cars seemed to meet the requirements, both in capacity of pay load and to operate dependably on the grades of the South Park. Management also investigated building their own motor car, employing a light trailer, as it was clear no single-car unit could have the capacity in mail, express and passengers required. Nothing suitable could be designed, they found.

There arose the possibility, however, that motor cars such as the famous Rio Grande Southern's "Galloping Goose" might replace the steam trains and become the passenger trains on the South Park. Victor Miller, Receiver of the RGS, on learning of the Burlington's offer in the early 1930s to give the South Park to anyone who might operate it, took counsel with Forest White, veteran conductor turned Superintendent of the RGS. So one day, the Leadville train had two extra through passengers, riding on tickets, not passes: Superintendent White and Goose builder Jack Odenbaugh. Their purpose was (without arousing any suspicions) to simply observe the South Park line in its various aspects, traffic, condition, views of the unsuspecting crew, etc. They reported back that the line would be a good one to operate Goose type motor cars, with an immediate drop in high operating costs. They noted little in carload freight, suggesting operations then in vogue on the RGS, of running a freight train only when there was enough traffic. At the time the South Park mustered two freights per week, sometimes rather short trains. They eyed all the idle freight cars and almost drooled at the prospect of moving many of these to the almost car-less RGS, dependent on the D&RGW for all its freight cars. They also noted that by substituting the Goose motors and cutting down on steam runs to whenever they could make a good revenue run, that perhaps a dozen locomotives could be spared to be moved to the RGS. But though Miller made a good presentation, the Burlington people after thinking it over decided not to give the South Park away, professing to believe that he could not operate it successfully in this manner. So the plans and dreams for a South Park Goose died. And while eventually over 100 C&S freight cars purchased by Miller were to be seen on the RGS, the dream of C&S Moguls and Consolidations working the grades of Ophir and Lizard Head was to remain only a dream, except for one engine. Engine 74 did get to the RGS, but only years after the South Park narrow gauge was entirely gone.

The Morrison mixed trains vanished on March

14, 1925, and effective May 31, 1931, the Leadville trains became tri-weekly, the last Sunday trains having been run the previous summer. At first the trains ran on Monday, Wednesday and Friday. For several years the runs fluctuated from those three days to Tuesday-Thursday-Saturday and then back again to Monday-Wednesday-Friday. This last remained the schedule thru the final runs of April 1937.

Freight Traffic

The importance of the South Park, or rather its unimportance, to the freight revenues of the C&S as a whole is best exampled by 1908. In that year the South Park lines originated $350,509.00 of freight, and earned $251,347.00 on incoming freight, for a total of $601,856.00. The same figures for the entire C&S were respectively $6,421,766.00, for originating freight revenues, and exactly the same sum by some rare coincidence for incoming revenues, for a total of $12,843,533.00. In 1908 the Gunnison District originated and received almost half the South Park revenues. Similarly out of a system total of passenger revenues of $1,307,626.00 only $47,559.00 came from the South Park. Total mileage of the C&S then was 1249.64, of which the South Park was 340.36 miles, about one-quarter of the system. Unfortunately South Park operating costs were not in proportion to revenues.

While freight tonnage in 1908 was highest on the Gunnison District, mainly coal from Baldwin, it also was the least profitable. When in 1928 the C&S filed for abandonment of the South Park, it was testified that average revenues 1910 thru 1927 were about $330,000 a year, the average operating expenses about $490,000, the average operating deficit about $167,000 and after taxes was about $240,000. Operating revenues dropped nearly in half from 1920 to 1927, from $444,813 in 1920 to $266,859 in 1927. Operating expenses in those years were $800,715 and $463,650.

As mining accounted for a dwindling revenue, this left the lines with low-revenue items such as livestock, lumber, hay and the like. The livestock was costly to haul, requiring prompt handling and numerous three and four engine trains.

The large proportion of engine mileage "running light" helped account for the line's high operating costs. The eastward runs from Como are examples of this at its costliest no doubt, for helper engines only worked 12 miles to Kenosha, then ran light 76 miles to Denver. Other portions of the Division

On a peaceful summer day in 1935, C&S No. 8 stopped at Frisco, on the Tenmile, with train 71. The depression and the automobile had made inroads on the little train's patronage already, and activity around the station was at a low ebb, even with the train running only on a three-times-a-week basis. (Lad Arend Coll.)

were little better. And though dispatchers worked out some odd runs, turning engines at what to the viewer would be an unusual point, they often were able to reduce the unproductive mileage considerably. Thus the night train No. 81 might pick up a helper at Platte Canyon or Pine Grove that had helped some eastward train from Como to Kenosha. There were many of these odd turn arounds in the busier years, but in the times of twice a week freights there wasn't much opportunity to save engine mileage.

The classic view above was taken by Gerald Best on June 11, 1934, as C&S 5 and 6 left Denver with the Leadville train — an unusual double-header for the thirties. Occasion was a special girls' school group, and the extra cars and helper were dropped about 35 miles out (G. M. Best). The same train was caught by a different photographer at a different location leaving Denver, as shown at right (Lad Arend Coll.).

Ohioan Bruce Triplett made a pilgrimage to Colorado to ride the South Park in September, 1935, and made these photos en route. At top, the passenger pauses to let a double-headed freight storm past. Right, No. 6 stops westbound for water at the Jefferson tank in South Park. Below, a meet with No. 71 and a freight at Long Meadow; the tracks are all but lost in the weeds. Lower right, eastbound No. 8 stops for water at Baker tank on Boreas Pass. (All, Bruce Triplett, Museum Coll.)

In the view above, the Leadville train is shown in its normal consist in the final years — Cooke mogul (No. 9), baggage-mail combine, coach. At right No. 8 pauses with twice the usual consist at Breckenridge in August, 1935. On this day the train seems to have been handling quite a bit of head-end business. Below, No. 6 makes the station stop at Dillon. After abandonment, the railroad attempted to give No. 6 away for historic preservation, but no one would accept the little engine. (Center, Museum Collection; others, Lad Arend.)

C&S No. 10 (left) steams around a sharp bend in the Platte Canyon with the daily passenger in the early years of this century, in a view that graphically shows the frequent proximity of the railroad to the rapid stream. L. C. McClure, who made numerous dramatic photos of C&S trains during these years before the line lapsed into a photographic obscurity only lifted many years later by the coming of amateur railfan photographers, made the view below showing two excursion trains at Dome Rock. (Both, Museum Coll.)

Platte Canyon

The Platte Canyon District for pay purposes was figured as having 42 "Valley Miles" and 46.2 "Mountain Miles." A fireman in 1907 got $2.25 for 100 Valley Miles, and the same amount for 44 Mountain Miles. A ten-hour day was considered a normal day before overtime began. By 1911 the base pay was $2.40 and overtime began after eight hours, but there were numerous exceptions, overtime sometimes not commencing until after 12 to 15 hours.

At Pine Grove, 42.4 miles, almost halfway to Como, there was a coal dock and most engines took coal there, especially westbound, as there was a long pull ahead for freights to reach Como. At first there were some odd runs, freight and helper crews often not running through as would be expected to Como. A crew might go from Denver (Jersey) to Kenosha, back to Platte Canyon, turn and then go through to Como, making what was in effect a doubling of the grade from Platte Canyon to Kenosha. Another time they might go from Como to Pine Grove and back to Como. Since Kenosha Pass had the stiffest grades, as might be expected there was frequent doubling of the pass from both sides.

Most runs westbound in early years were two and three-engine affairs, with much light engine mileage of course east of Kenosha Pass. If it had not been for the need to balance engine locations, a great deal of mileage could have been saved. The many engines running light the 76 miles Kenosha to Denver contributed greatly to operating costs and losses on the South Park, typical of mountain railroads. A great deal of effort, and cost, was used in simply transporting coal for engines. With no mines on the line, except those at Baldwin, and that source lost after 1910, it meant engine coal for Como had to be hauled from Denver, after being transferred from standard gauge cars usually from the Southern Colorado fields. Dickey was supplied with coal transferred from the D&RG at Leadville.

The Platte Canyon was a popular resort area and, in addition to the regular passenger train, the famous "Fish Train" was operated in summer season. Schedules varied slightly, but basically it was a late afternoon departure of a passenger run with a baggage car and several coaches, dropping off people for a weekend at various Canyon resorts and stations. At first the train went on to Como, but eventually it laid over at Grant. The train would then come back to Denver with an early departure on Sunday and/or Monday morning, placing the "fishermen" back in Denver in time to go to work.

Basically the Fish Train provided extra service in the area between Grant and Denver. Even the officials used the service and not infrequently the business car would be spotted on the trestle of the Grant wye. If the train was coming back next day crews would of course lay over. Other combinations of operation would have the engine set out the cars and go on elsewhere, while a freight crew would be sent out from Denver so that they could go to Kenosha, set out their cars, then drop back to Grant in time to take the Fish Train into Denver on time.

Twice at least the Fish Train was involved in a head-on collision at or near the bridge crossing the South Platte at South Park Jct. Today the Junction is obscured by a freeway, but in earlier times it was out in the country. Coming into Denver in the morning there were two opposing trains to meet — the Morrison train and westbound No. 71. On June 11, 1902, Engine 12 of the Fish Train collided with Engine 10 of Train 71, and though officials conceded the Fish Train "had right of track and perfect right to be where they were . . . it was plain they had not kept a proper lookout . . . should have seen #71 at 400 feet." Baggage car 103 was so badly telescoped in this wreck that it was destroyed.

With fatality to the fireman of Train 60, the "Morrison," a similar Fish Train collision of June 1, 1914, was a somewhat more serious affair. The Fish Train (Train 73) with Engine 70, combine 28, coaches 57, 59 and 70, met outgoing #70 passenger at Valverde, then backed out of the siding and proceeded toward Denver on the Morrison train's time. They collided just off the east approach of the bridge, various crew members jumping at the last moment out of engines and baggage car doors to escape. Fireman Hunn on Mogul #12 of the Morrison was killed, literally buried under debris, but the passengers in coaches 26 and 77 apparently had but minor injuries. Conductor T. St. John was just picking up a pass as the brakes went on, throwing him down the aisle. The engineer found himself lying on the ground.

Engine Foreman John C. "Big John" Gstettenbauer played an interesting role in this collision. He and his yard crew were in the chemical works yard when train 70 passed 73. As he saw 73 back out and head for the Junction he commented to his crew that "they must have some time on them." But as he spoke, he looked in that direction and ". . . I saw the smoke in the woods of No. 60 and I said, 'they are going to get together down there, we better cut off the engine and we will go down there and see if we can assist them'" He then sent his men on down and went to a phone to report to the Yardmaster and called City Hall for an ambulance, then going to the wreck, about a block away. He continued: "I met one of my men coming back. I asked him how many was hurt and he told me the fireman was scalded to death on the Morrison train No. 60. Outside of that he did not know of anyone that was hurt bad. I went back to the phone again and called Mr. O'Neil and told him we would need the wrecker and told him what had been done so far as I knew. Then I went back and we cut off the the rear two coaches of 73 and pulled them over Third Ave. Engineer Auers was in one of the coaches. I wanted to load him in the ambulance at the crossing, figuring the ambulance would come to that crossing. I then went to see if there was any passengers who needed anything or sent to the hospital and was informed there was none killed. Mr. Skinner, Superintendent of the Chemical Works, volunteered to send his automobile down at once. In fact he sent for it. The ambulance not arriving, we put engineer Auers in the automobile

and took him to the address he wanted to go. After that I found out the conductor was getting the names of the injured and everybody was being taken care of. I could not get across to the other side of the bridge."

Engineer Auers of the "Morrison" said in his report: "We have a straight track there for half a mile. Everything looked clear and when I got down close to the end of this straight track I still looked ahead. Then I saw coming off the bridge an engine and two coaches was all I could distinguish. There is a bunch of trees there to obstruct the view all the way along and I do not think you can see too far onto the bridge, but when I saw them I hollered to the fireman The Fish Train is coming. I applied the emergency brake first. And then I started to straighten myself up. I realized we were going to strike, because we were too close together to prevent it. We were not going I presume, over 15 miles per hour. So in applying the brakes I must have straightened up as I was standing up in the cab and when the engines came together the contact knocked me out of the cab."

On the page opposite is another L. C. McClure view, showing C&S No. 6 storming up the Platte Canyon with a regular passenger run. On this page, an assortment of people and dogs await arrival of the daily train at the South Platte depot, while a very capable-looking lady baggage-smasher unloads a large trunk from a wagon (Lad Arend Coll.).

Officials were so concerned over the fact that even though No. 73 was on 60's time, each crew should have been able to see the other train in time to avoid a collision, that a week later on June 8 a test was made with two trains made up with the same number of cars as the two trains in the collision. The test report read:

MEMORANDUM

On June 8th a test was made with two trains made up with the same number of cars as in trains Nos. 60 and 73 on the date of collision.

The train representing No. 60 had two cars and the train representing No. 73 had four cars.

It was determined that the enginemen of both trains were in sight of each other 250 feet from the point of collision.

Engine No. 68 with four coaches was run from a point at Valverde siding on the main line where train would stop after backing out of side track. Required two minutes to make the run to point of collision, rate of speed about thirty miles per hour.

The same engine and four coaches made a run, reaching a speed of about thirty miles an hour and set air in emergency 250 feet from place of accident. The pilot of engine when stopped was 85 feet beyond point of accident.

Engine No. 38 with narrow gauge business car 910 was started from South Park Junction with instructions to make a fast run to point of accident, which was 1860 feet from the starting point and made the run in one minute and fifteen seconds.

A running and stop test was then made, air set in emergency 250 feet from point of accident and when stopped the pilot was 40 feet beyond point of collision.

The train was then taken back to South Park Junction, another coach coupled on, giving them two cars, starting from South Park Junction and run made to west end of Valverde side track in three minutes flat.

These tests were made to demonstrate whether the engineer on train No. 60, who was on the inside of the curve, could have seen train No. 73 in time to have stopped before collision occurred. The tests made exonerated the engine and trainmen of train No. 60 from all blame and placed full responsibility for the collision upon the engineer, fireman, conductor and two brakemen of train No. 73. Train No. 60 having superior right by direction over No. 73, both being passenger trains.

The railroad owned two hotels, Kiowa Lodge at Bailey and the Shawnee Lodge at Shawnee. Generally the hotels were operated each summer under lease by either individuals or companies specializing in this type of operation. The railroad was to be repaid for furnishing supplies and had a man at each place to maintain electricity; net profits were to be split. However, there seldom was any net, and when all costs were tallied the railroad usually was out of pocket for maintenance. Rates charged in 1912, for example, were $15 per week when two persons occupied a room, or $17.50 per week if one person occupied a room. For overflow crowds, such as frequently occurred when handling small conventions, tents were supplied and the rate then became $12.50 per person. 1912 by the way was a "heavy loss" to the railroad on the various hotels and eating houses. Reform legislation in the Colorado Legislature in 1913 limiting the issuance of passes compounded the contractor's problems, as no longer could employees travel free, nor much of the supplies be handled free or at special rates. Reluctantly the contracts were canceled and the C&S Dining Car Department took over operation of the Canyon hotels.

Bailey had a station agent year around, but Shawnee was a typical summer office, with an agent reopening the office each June. For four months it was a fairly busy place. In addition to passengers, there were all manner of supplies for the company hotel and others. Among the first freight of each season would be a car with ten tons of ice, brought from ice houses at South Platte, Haviland or Denver. Ten tons of coal for the power plant also was among the first shipments. The season generally ended with closing of the hotels on or about September 30th.

There wasn't much freight traffic in the Platte Canyon. Some stone quarrying at times; feldspar at South Platte and on the Night Hawk Branch. Various tie contractors loaded ties all along the route to Leadville. Once, in 1902, about 35,000 tons of sand for use in filters of the Denver Union Water Co. was handled to Platte Canyon (later "Waterton"). This unusual movement was from a point on the old standard gauge main line, where the sand was dug from Cherry Creek, and transferred to narrow gauge cars at Denver. For all this the C&S received 75 cents a ton.

For a while around 1900 it looked as if a major change in railroads was in the making, using the first 29 miles of the South Park as a part of a standard gauge route to Cripple Creek. In February, 1896, the Gulf-DL&G people put surveyors into the field to find the best route to Cripple Creek. The matter was urgent and despite very bad weather, was pushed. One of the men was sent to Denver with a severe case of snowblindness. By March 3rd they had 55 miles of the line run and were heading for the valley of the South Fork, working from direction of Cripple Creek. The new road was to be named the Denver, Cripple Creek & Southwestern. Some idea of the speed with which such work was accomplished was that the first ten miles from South Platte was done between January 29 and February 6. Grades would have been heavy, at one point three miles of 4%. Real estate speculation entered into the selection of a route, one promoter complaining the line was one mile too far to the east of his

townsite, to which a surveyor retorted his townsite was one mile too far to the west! One townsite was named for Trumbull.

A 4.1-mile piece of this line, which was later called the Night Hawk Branch, was built from South Platte to the site of some feldspar mines, and though surveyed on through Deckers and beyond, tracks went no further. Known at first as the "South Platte Extension", further construction was blocked by construction of the Cheesman Dam on the stream, the South Fork of the South Platte. Track was lifted in 1916. The clearances on this branch were so close that crews were warned that only Business Car B-3 of the passenger stock could be handled on the branch. Only 26 feet over sills, the car could go anywhere a freight car could. The grade is now a county road.

Como

Como was a natural center for South Park operations. Junction point of three lines, it was an important railroad center with reports at times of as many as "350 railroad families" comprising the bulk of its population. Its nearly 10,000-foot altitude (9,775 ft.) made it an unpopular place to live and wives complained. Winters were long and South Park's winds made for miserable conditions, drifts enveloping the entire side of a home. Many a railroader had to use the back door of his home, the front door being drift blocked. From Como radiated the three operating "Districts" — Platte Canyon, the 88.2 miles to Denver; High Line, the 62.9 miles over Boreas to Leadville; and Gunnison, 131.1 miles of main line to Baldwin plus branches to Alma, Leavick and Buena Vista.

C&S operations in the early 1900s were about the same as under the DL&G. In addition to the daily passenger Denver to Leadville, the night mixed operated on same route, with extras additionally as needed. On the Gunnison District there was the daily mixed to Gunnison, the daily mixed to Alma, and an occasional run to Leavick, which at first had its scheduled mixed as well. There were frequent extras to Buena Vista. A switch engine was on duty at Como.

The Gunnison mixed (Trains 93 and 94, later renumbered 94 and 95) were generally double-headed, and often had three engines. Coming into Como it was not unusual to have four engines on the train, but two of these had been sent out from Como light only a few hours earlier to help the train in from Garos. The Alma train laid overnight there, and for ten years invariably had engine 30, oldest South Park relic. Usually it had

In September, 1935, Bruce Triplett made this panoramic view, above, of No. 8 with the eastbound passenger making the station stop at Como. At the same time he found 2-8-0 No. 72 standing alongside the stone enginehouse, with a typical railroad official ready to pose by the engine for a picture. (Bruce Triplett, Museum Coll.) Below, this 1905 view of the Como roundhouse area indicates quite a bit of activity; there are six locomotives visible outside, and four in stalls in the wooden section of the roundhouse. (C. O. David photo from Lad Arend.)

The rail's-eye view above of the center of the Como yards, showing the roundhouse and water towers, indicates graphically that the layout was not entirely flat. The diagram below, taken from an old C&S blueprint, shows the odd track arrangement that required turning the Leadville passenger train on the wye east of town on each trip. (Museum Coll.)

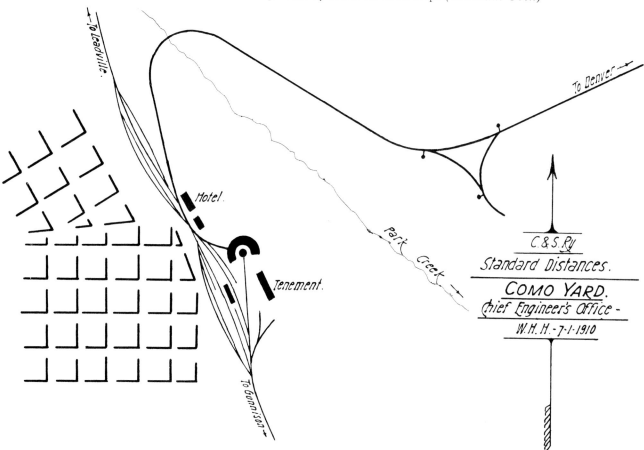

To Leadville.

To Denver.

Hotel.

Tenement.

Park Creek

To Gunnison.

C.&S. Ry
Standard Distances.
COMO YARD.
Chief Engineer's Office -
W.H.H. - 7-1-1910

one or two freight cars and the combine, but sometimes would fill out to five or six cars.

To take care of this multitude of comings and goings, Como had a 19-stall roundhouse, six of them the stone section still standing. There was a large brick hotel, a rather small depot, dispatcher's office, reading room, Superintendent's house, Master Mechanic's office, coal dock and the numerous outbuildings and old car bodies usual to a railroad center. The monthly payroll for the mechanical department alone, not including enginemen, was over $4,000.00 a month. It took a considerable number of roundhouse and car employees to keep things moving.

The railroad had to offer extra inducements to obtain employees at Como. As mentioned, it was somewhat of a hardship place to live year around. Living costs were higher too. Coal, which was used in large quantities and virtually year around for heating, as well as cooking, cost more at Como than in Denver. A group of enginemen got together and purchased two carloads of Baldwin coal; when the cars arrived at Como they were confiscated by the local agent of the Rocky Mountain Fuel Co. on grounds he had the sole sales authority at Como. Master Mechanic J. C. Lord, having enough troubles keeping good men on hand, entered the fray and succeeded in swaying Denver officials to make an exception to policy and sell coal to employees at Como for $3.00 a ton. The coal cost the C&S $1.35 a ton at the mine, and $1.65 to get it to Como. That was in 1909. The coal company's agent had charged $2.75 a ton, plus $2.75 shipping, plus 75c drayage, total of $6.25 a ton, a big bite of 1909 wages. As one official declared: "Como is an out of the way place and is not a desirable place for men in the railroad service; and I believe we will be justified in smoothing the rough spots for them to some extent by reducing the cost of coal. We favor them in other ways, such as supplying a club house, library, bathroom, etc. which we do not provide for our employees at other stations." So opined General Superintendent J. D. Welsh.

The library building at Como had a reading room, library, barber shop and bathroom. The barber shop and bathroom were operated by a barber, induced by attractive low rental to maintain the shop, and at same time look after the building. He pocketed the proceeds from the bathroom, which in 1903 averaged about two baths a day at 25c per bath. Baths in the "good old days" were not indulged in as frequently as in present times. Six days a week from 8 A.M. to 8 P.M. the barber was on duty, and his contract stipulated that he was to assume the duties of janitor and "librarian", and be responsible for all property of the "Library Association of Como."

The South Park Hotel, another railroad property, had its problems — chiefly not enough business. Yet accommodations for lodging and restaurant were a must. The company gave passes to and from Denver for the proprietor and his family, and also hauled coal free from Baldwin. The lessees paid $300 rental per year and obviously made little profit.

Another service supplied by The South Park Hotel operators was to provide quick supplies for the wrecker. A typical bill of supplies is exampled by one submitted by C. C. Stebbins, Proprietor, on August 24, 1908. Two loaves of bread, a pound of butter, a dozen eggs, 3 pounds of beef, one pound of ham, a can of cream, a can of tomatoes, a can of corn, a pie, a pound of coffee and five pounds of potatoes, came to exactly $2.00. For such a heavy (?) expenditure, the "O.K." signatures were affixed of Pat Gibbony, J. C. Lord, Master Mechanic and Supt. of Motive Power H. C. Van Buskirk. No one could accuse the South Park people of reckless and extravagant expenditures.

The rotary was kept at Como. Generally it was used over Boreas, often going on to Leadville. Occasionally it would go out on the Gunnison district, needed for the especially troublesome Alpine Tunnel area. With ample engines and employees handy, Como was a good point to outfit a rotary or a wrecker train. The rotary seldom was needed east of Como. C&S rotary operations were somewhat different from the D&RG, who took along all manner of supply cars, extra coal, tool, living quarters, cook, etc. C&S normally sent out three engines pushing the rotary and tender and trailing a combine, making a light tonnage train that seemed to do well in getting over the line. On a couple occasions it even took along a couple of pay loads. On other occasions it would be run as first section of the passenger train or even coupled on ahead of it. Trips to Boreas could be rather short, returning same day or next day. Trips to Alpine Tunnel were another matter, and a trip departing with four engines and caboose on February 21, 1907, was not completed until March 3. C&S had three snowplows, but two of these were stationed on the standard gauge — a rotary at Cheyenne, and the ill-fated Jull plow of the 1890 Alpine tests lived out its life at Trinidad. Some locomotives were equipped with a Butterfly plow on which the railroad paid an annual royalty of $50, and the effective use of these engines often bucked a line open. A flanger was kept at Como, another at Leadville, a third one west of the Tunnel, at Pitkin or Gunnison.

Trains 70 and 71 varied little in length over the years, generally three cars. The two head end cars varied, sometimes a baggage car and a combination R.P.O.-smoker combine, other times a full R.P.O.-baggage car. The night mixed train had only a combine on the rear. The mixed was generally double-headed and tonnage kept down to what the train could handle and keep on time. As the passenger train carried the "Denver & Leadville Railway Post Office" with mail schedules to be met, these trains were given priority and maintained a good on time record. Today in postmark collections are to be found covers bearing this postmark, a highly prized item, representing the highest altitude route in North America.

The Alma train (91-92) had an uneventful life, considering its entire run stayed at an altitude around 10,000 ft. Its engineer, W. E. Gallagher, was a 24-year veteran of the South Park in 1906 when, on September 24, 2½ miles west of Fairplay his Engine 30 dropped its crown sheet without an explosion, or injuries to the crew. When word reached Como, Engine 43 was sent out and got No. 91 into Alma three hours late. Next day No. 92 was on time into Como, the consist of four cars and dead No. 30 behind No. 43. Eventually No. 30 came back from the Denver shop; Gallagher was forgiven and reinstated and returned to his old run.

The Alma mixed was cut to a twice a week run in 1928, but some increase in gold mining brought it up to tri-weekly in 1931. But when the South Park operations ended in 1937, it was down to a twice a week run again.

The closing of Alpine Tunnel in October, 1910, was a heavy blow to Como. The washouts that fall in Trout Creek were not repaired, and on October 31 service over Boreas Pass was discontinued also, leaving the C&S South Park lines in four disconnected segments — Denver to Como and Alma, Breckenridge to Leadville, Buena Vista to Hancock, and Quartz to Baldwin. The final run of 93 took place on October 30, 1910, departing for Buena Vista at 2:25 AM with Engines 45, 63, 61, and 64, 6 loads, 3 empty stock, an empty box, 16 empty coal cars and combine 27 — 390 tons. The last 95 arrived that day at 1:10 PM — engines 73 and 38, 12 loads, a deadhead coach, and combine 21.

By the end of November most of the force at Como had been laid off, discharged, or gone elsewhere to work, most of them never to return to the South Park. Less than 50 families remained in town. The August payroll was $4,074.00, in September it was $4,900.00, in October it dropped to $3,330.00, in November to $2,711.00, and in December to $254.95! The 1909 payroll had been $53,084.00, and Como was never again to see anything like it. The total payroll in 1911 was but $2,033.95, about half of what the minimum per month had been for a decade. True, the round-

house was far from empty, but unfortunately 11 of the stalls now had dead engines stored in them. Most would never operate again on the C&S, although some of them were to stay there for a decade until sold. Among them was #30, which had been one of the first seven 2-8-0s obtained by the DSP&P, in 1880.

After Como's railroad population shrank to a very few in late 1910, most business houses closed. Railroad employees were able to get coal through the company, but the local doctor could get none. The railroad finally supplied him, as he was their Local Surgeon. A watchman was on duty at night, but was unable to prevent much pilfering of coal, for while he was in one part of the mostly deserted railroad buildings, various parties would be busy hauling coal away from cars or storage bins. By January 1912 there were only about 12 families left in Como, and in the words of Supt. John Dwyer one lady "runs sort of an eating house at Como and furnishes meals to our trainmen when necessary for them to eat in Como; in fact it is the only place you can get a meal in Como." The remaining storekeeper declined to stock coal. While the company avoided sale of coal to non-railroad people, viewing the obvious shrinkage of its supplies overnite, it is assumed from the record that enough coal was sold to the railroaders so that they could in turn supply the non-railroad portion of the population. It might be mentioned that in Colorado there was a constant loss of coal in transit on the railroads. If a coal car had to be "set out" on a siding on account of some defect, by the time it was picked up again after car men had reached it and effected repairs, in the words of more than one conductor it would be "nearly empty." Country folk for miles around would often simply strip such a car of as much of its load as they could carry away in buggies and buckboards. The coal companies often acted as monopolies and this, coupled with their labor trouble of the pre-World War I period, made them targets for dislike, and stealing coal was not really looked upon by many people as a crime.

By 1914, time of the famous Ludlow incident, coal coming from the Southern Colorado fields cost $1.75 per ton at the mines, $1.85 to get it to Denver, then 10c per ton to transfer to narrow gauge cars. So the railroad sold this coal to Como employees for $4.00 per ton. During labor troubles in the southern fields, coal for the South Park had to come from Wyoming, and by time it was transferred at Denver it cost about $5.00 per ton. At that time this was a much greater expense for coal than on the D&RG's Colorado narrow gauge lines, which were fortunate in having short hauls from mines on the various lines.

Above, Red Hill was a desolate passing siding 5 miles beyond Como on the Gunnison line. In later years this stretch of track served only the Alma and Fairplay branch. 2-8-0 No. 30 was the branch engine for many years, and is shown at left with the train's combine at Alma in 1910. Below, a two-car passenger special at Garos on a cold winter day in 1929; the train is just entering the wye from Fairplay, and will proceed towards Como to the right of the picture. (Museum Coll.)

Two C&S officials stand on the track about a mile north of Como, on the High Line to Leadville, and watch No. 9 and a two car special train climb out of the Park some two track-miles further on (left). About three miles further, and some 4½ miles from the summit of Boreas Pass, the line skirted a rocky point high above the valley below (both, museum Coll.)

High Line

The High Line District to Leadville required the most engines and crews, and had the most difficult operating problems of the three Districts. At Dickey the C&S built a new engine house in 1902, the better to service the many engines in and out of that point for trains over Boreas Pass, or for those heading up the long grades of the Ten Mile Canyon for Leadville. The latter had miles of track plagued by frequent slides.

The passenger trains ran out on the 2.7 mile branch to Dillon, but only occasional freights ventured on to Keystone, another 6.2 miles. Though this line had been graded a little beyond Keystone to reach the Montezuma mining district, it was left unfinished by the U.P.

Some incidents in operating the High Line sound as if today's careless motorists were at the throttles. At 1 A.M. November 17, 1902, No. 43's engineer was going to put the engine into the new Dickey engine house. He opened the doors, examined the track inside, as his was to be the first engine to use the building. Back on the engine, he opened the throttle and just as he reached the doors, a gust of wind blew one in front of him, the 43 reducing it to kindling. He had forgotten to hook the door! Superintendent Bacon had him on the carpet for that.

When Extra East, Engines 22 and 52 stopped at Climax at 1:35 A.M. March 8, 1908, engine 22 was cut off to run ahead to Kokomo. Wanting to do some tinkering on his engine, thinking he had plenty of time, the engineer stopped the 22 just inside the east end of the snowshed. Along came No. 52 sooner than expected with its six-car train and in the gloom of smoke and steam the engineer was unable to see anything, so hit No. 22, breaking the 52's pilot beam. The 22's engineer received 20 brownies for "stopping in a place where his engine could not be seen and not seeing that same was protected."

In a howling snowstorm, with drifts so deep a flagman could not get out and do any good, the January 28, 1909 night mixed from Leadville, No. 82, collided head-on with the rear portion of a stalled westbound freight at Johnson's Spur, east of Kokomo. A two-engine freight had left Dickey for Leadville at 3:10 A.M. with Engine 58 on the point and No. 69 back in the train and made good time to Wheeler as they had a light train. There they lost "three or four hours" because the cars they picked up were frozen in ice and had to be picked out. They were now on 82's time, but

westbound 81 had orders to Kokomo and the freight tried to follow 81 into Kokomo, stalling about four miles short of there. Conductor J. F. Snee cut off the head engine 58 and with four loads followed 81 and left the rest of his train sitting on the main, intending to come back with the engine and double into Kokomo. But at Kokomo some misunderstanding occurred, partly due to confusion in the storm. Engine 41 with 82 was nearly out of coal, the engineer sure he could not make Dickey without help and misunderstanding just where the rear portion of the Extra was, took off with ten cars, engine 71 cut in behind the third car and the combine on rear, with No. 58 following to help. The rear brakeman "with snow and ice up to his waist" saw them coming, and at first both he and Engineer Aichele on the 69 thought it was their own engine coming back. To late they realized it was 82, and coming so fast that it would be unable to stop in time. Aichele desperately tried to back up, blowing his whistle also in frantic stop signals, but the four cars of logs ahead of his engine were frozen down and 82 hit hard, tieing up the line at a most miserable time to do so.

The line over Boreas, of course, was the scene of many misfortunes. One engineer, helping a freight west, broke the drawbar between the engine and tender when he cut off at the top. He was advised by the crew to chain up the tender, couple on behind the caboose or else follow them down. He tried the latter and when the brakes were applied tender would stop first, so he decided to return to Como. First he went into the Boreas telegraph office and wired his resignation to the Master Mechanic. Then he did the hard-to-believe of backing down from Boreas, tender first, held to the engine by tank hose and a chain, and made it to Como, where an outraged Master Mechanic refused to let him take back his resignation, instead insisting that it was indeed accepted December 18, 1907, refusing to accept the excuse he couldn't turn on the turntable at Boreas, and thereby risked losing the tender.

Carelessness in testing brakes caused many a runaway. One with engine 49 on June 2, 1901, ran away so quickly that the combine drifting down onto the train never got coupled and the train piled up just beyond the snowshed. Another train of nine cars and combine with four engines had come up from Dickey on March 9, 1909, set out two Bad Order cars at Boreas, and picked up six more cars. One engine went on ahead to Como, another turned back to Dickey, while the third was to follow down. Engine 41 and the entire train ran away and all except the combine derailed and turned over down a 50-foot embankment at M.P. 93, on a big curve just east of Halfway. Apparently no accurate test was made of air in the train after being coupled up again. The fireman jumped just east of Selkirk as speed picked up over 15 m.p.h. and it was estimated at 40 to 45 m.p.h. or more at the time of derailment. The conductor earlier had told a brakeman "We are gone", and the three trainmen cut the combine off, coasting down to the wreck. Apparently this No. 82 had no passengers that night.

There was no 16-hour law for many years and one engine crew was discharged for delaying a freight, because after making a trip from Dickey to Climax they stopped to dry their clothes at the bunk house at Dickey. They had left Como at 3:30 A.M. January 11, having been called for 1:30 A.M.; got to Halfway with one train, went back to Como for another, coupled up and stuck in the snow at Selkirk, shoveled snow and got stuck two or three times, finally doubling into Boreas. They tied up at Dickey at 2:55 P.M. and worked on their engine until 6 P.M. Called at 12:30 A.M. and did switching, left for Climax at 2 A.M. with three engines (68, 47, 49), turned at Climax using the covered turntable, arrived Dickey at 1 P.M., where they were expected to go on to Como with another three-engine train. They had gotten soaking wet as their engine 68 had gone into Wilfley's spur, derailed and broke a rail. The engineer said he spent "50 minutes wallowing under that tank and that's where I got wet." The Conductor said "the man was worn out soul and body." That was mountain railroading back in 1904.

Halfway siding and tank on the east side of Boreas were only 5.7 miles west of Como. As usual a three-engine westbound extra stopped for water there on April 18, 1906, with engines 48 and 61 on the head end of seven loads and engine 37 and caboose on the rear. They backed into the siding to clear Train 72, but in doing so nudged six empties there enough so that they did not quite clear the east switch. The 37 cut off and went down to pull them into the clear but a fireman called a signal to back to the head engineer who did so, hitting the 37 and pushing the empties out onto the main. Interestingly the crew said the seven loads were a "hard pull" for the three engines, giving an idea of size of trains, and also why so often four-engine trains were used.

At the same time that Alpine Tunnel was closed, and Trout Creek canyon line also shut down, management closed operations over Boreas Pass, with final trains through to Leadville from Como on October 31, 1910. There was quite an outcry, but there was so little revenue traffic in Breckenridge and the line on to Leadville that the losses were all too clear to anyone. Leadville had ample and

very competitive rail service, standard gauge to boot, by both D&RG and Colorado Midland. Boreas stayed closed down that winter, but passenger service resumed in May, 1911, for that summer only. There wasn't any summer service in 1912. Finally on January 20, 1913, service was resumed and continued except for occasional operational problems until the 1937 abandonment.

Some mining continued between Boreas and Breckenridge. The Blue Flag Gold Mining Co. had been loading at Bacon (M.P. 103.7) and the Chamberlain Dillingham Ore Co. had occasional loadings at Washington Spur (M.P. 105.9). Management in the summer of 1912 agreed to serve these mines on a special train basis, for a minimum charge of $30.00 for the round trip of an engine and one to six cars from Breckenridge. They figured actual costs were $30, so to move one car would be $30. The same minimum rate was to apply to a passenger extra of one engine and a coach. So on June 20, for example, Engine 67 moved three empty box and some l.c.l. up to Bacon Spur. Intermittently thereafter similar trips were made, including one Passenger Special on June 25, with one coach. During July one trip was made with two cars. In August three trips were made, one with a coach, the other trips taking two empty box cars to Mayo Spur (M.P. 106.5, a mere 3½ miles from Breckenridge depot), and picking up those two loads on another trip three days later. One trip each was made to Bacon Spur in October, November and December, and then the special service ended.

One of the items that kept train crews on their toes was the matter of the doors on the Boreas snowshed. To keep snow, blown by wind from the west, from packing the inside of shed, the doors at the west end were kept closed at some periods in the winter, usually after Christmas when the weather was at its worst. The effective date of "keeping doors at West End closed" would be bulletined and hopefully everyone read and remembered that! Along with that season of the year a Bulletin would appear advising that trains moving up grade "will go 15% lighter than full tonnage . . ." listing then the various 4% or similar grades. Boreas lost some of its importance when its post office closed January 31, 1905.

For a brief period in 1911, the C&S scheduled trains on two closely paralleling lines in the Leadville-Dillon area. Under the agreement of February 13, 1911, the D&RG assumed operations of all lines of both companies in the Gunnison area, while the C&S took over the D&RG Blue River Branch, 37 miles of meager traffic, between Leadville and Dillon. With closure of operations over Boreas Pass November 1, 1910, between Como and

Breckenridge, the C&S was operating a daily round trip passenger from Leadville to Breckenridge and return with a side trip to Dillon. Now it was scheduling as well but not operating over the D&RG its version of that road's mixed train, tri-weekly on Monday, Wednesday and Friday, and for operating reasons still bearing the D&RG train numbers 263 and 264. The exchange agreement went into effect on February 15, and in deep snows, Supt. Bacon checked the line three days later. He found very little in traffic, and up to five feet of snow. The D&RG had run their final train on the 14th, and at the Wilson Mill spur at Robinson the cuts had already drifted full of snow and he estimated labor to move each loaded car from the mill in winter would cost $8.00 to $12.00. He put a section crew to work making a connection from the C&S to the D&RG at this point, but estimated 15 men working two days might be needed to open and make the line operable at this one point. At Wheeler and Uneva he found cars being loaded with mine props, and other carloads being accumulated, informing the shippers that after these were moved they must load at the nearest C&S siding. At Frisco about 40 carloads of props were waiting for cars, and he promised those shippers the needed cars. He suggested management might connect the two lines just west of Frisco, then abandon the C&S line between Frisco and Dickey and use the D&RG line Frisco to Dillon and then C&S to Dickey. Eventually all that was done was to use a connection to the Dillon stock yard. He also found an empty gondola at Kokomo and figured it would cost about $30 to reach this car account of so much snow and recommended it be left there until spring.

On June 7, 1911, the C&S informed D&RG they would "not use" the Leadville-Frisco line, nor any of the depots or other structures, all the way to Dillon. Despite this, the D&RG track lay in place until finally, on October 3, 1923, the D&RG applied to abandon the entire branch. This was routinely approved by the ICC on December 1, 1923, and track was removed. Much of the grade has vanished in recent years due to highway changes, not to mention the lake behind Dillon Dam.

Strangely, in the *Official Guide* dated "March, 1911", a schedule is found under the C&S for the D&RG's Blue River Branch, under the heading "Between Leadville and Dillon." From February thru the end of April the Superintendent in his references to this trackage plainly indicates not only are no trains operating, but that no operations are intended ever, saying that the only part they will use will be between Dillon and Frisco and the siding leading to the Wilson Mill at Robinson.

The movement of molybdenum ore, or concentrates, became an increasingly important item in the late 1920s. It came in sacks in gondolas to Denver, there to be transferred to box cars for the trip to Langloth, Pa. In the 1930 abandonment case the C&S contemplated abandoning the line all the way through Como to Leadville, but in 1935 the realization of the revenue traffic to and from Climax forced a change, and the application this time did not include the Climax-Leadville trackage.

On March 20, 1937, a circular notice went to all agents advising them of what equipment would be assigned to "Leadville-Climax service", directing that these cars were to be moved to either Leadville or Climax without delay, and must not be loaded for other points. And after they reached the Climax portion, they were not to be sent east of Climax, either loaded or empty. Engines 74-75-76 were assigned; combine #26 and caboose 1009. Rotary 99200 and flanger 015 also were assigned. 57 box cars, 26 coal cars, two refrigerator cars and 12 flat cars were initially assigned. It was intended to send additional cars to the line as follows: 3 box, 9 coal, and 3 flat.

By the summer of 1938, as dismantling was underway and cars could no longer be moved through on C&S rails, they had collected at Leadville another caboose, #1003, 66 box cars, 2 refrigerators, 1 flat car (#1098, a steel underframe car), 15 other flat cars (carrying their coal car numbers as they were made by removing the sides), 36 coal cars, 2 combination cars (Nos. 26 and 30), flanger 015, 1 cinder dump non-revenue, 4 side dump non-revenue and three-way coupler car 013 which doubled as flanger. Engine 60 was assigned for awhile to Leadville.

The cars on the Climax line were often strained to their limits and beyond by heavy inbound shipments of machinery and material as the mine and mill expanded. Some cars just simply collapsed, the weight going through the floors. Outbound the concentrates from Leadville on the standard gauge had to be in at least 56,000 lb. lots to get the minimum carload rate. The C&S cars, with their steel underframes, had a capacity of 50,000 lbs. with a permissable increase of 10%, making a 55,000 lb. limit. Because of the short haul, the road permitted loading per car to be the 56,000 lbs.

One of the heaviest traffic periods for the line, while still intact all the way from Denver, was in June 1936, when about 2,000,000 pounds of structural steel, lumber, sand, cement and other building materials bound for Climax taxed the ability of the railroad. It figured out to about 800 carloads and the Climax officials stated plainly the deliveries must be promptly done, or else they would have to look to trucks to keep the work supplied. All the available power including the three

D&RGW engines was needed to keep this freight rolling, and the activity belied a line already under the sentence of abandonment.

The moly concentrates kept coming into Denver up to abandonment in April, 1937, as much as 17 carloads per train being recorded. After abandonment this was transferred to standard gauge at Leadville, a costly process. By the summer of 1938 management was looking into standard gauging the Climax line, and this was done in 1943.

Even this little branch, remote from the balance of the C&S, had its problems. One was moving of equipment to Denver shops. It had to be hauled back and forth over the D&RGW on standard gauge cars, and of course because of the cost this was avoided as much as possible.

The cars' need of repairs did not always stem from their being too small for the loads. On one occasion Climax received some machinery, which was unloaded beside the track at the plant. Later it was decided to place the machinery some distance away. Someone eyeing the paralleling railroad track had a bright idea: they would use the rails as a sort of greased steel slide on a day when

no train ran. Nothing was said to the railroad people of the idea. The machinery was skidded onto the track, the rails greased heavily, and the machinery skidded downgrade to the desired location. On the next trip of the train, the brakeman climbed onto the empty flats and let off the hand brakes to drop them down to the main, unaware of the skidding episode. When his practiced hands tried tightening the brakes, nothing seemed to happen, the cars just took off out of control, and he jumped. The cars ended up badly smashed off the track. The carmen at Leadville came up to take a look, found all brakes seemed to be working as near as they could determine. One, suspicious, walked up the track, and noted the extra grease on the rails. No detective, and despite the fact that no one "knew nothing", he soon pieced the story together. Then there ensued a wrangle to get the mine people to pay for the damage.

Once in a while, every few years, a rotary was needed on the Climax line, so 99200 stayed in the enginehouse, checked every summer to make certain it was ready. It lasted into the standard gauge period for many years.

No. 9 crests Boreas Pass with the Leadville passenger a little more than a month before service was abandoned. The snowsheds had burned a few years before, and the stone enginehouse had gone up in flames many decades earlier; only scattered ruins remained. (Lad Arend Coll.) Page opposite, looking back upgrade east towards the summit from Baker's Tank provided this bleak, windswept view (top) in winter. (Museum Coll.) In summer the west side of Boreas was a mass of aspen and evergreens that almost enveloped No. 69 with a clean-up train in 1938. (Bottom opp., Richard H. Kindig.)

At left, a South Park passenger train can be seen dropping down the west side of Boreas Pass in 1929, crossing the curved trestle some 2½ miles east of Breckenridge. The photo was taken from a higher point on the line, about 1½ track miles east. Below, in a reverse view, a three-engine freight is shown battling upgrade towards Boreas near the location from which the first photo was taken. (Museum Coll.) Page opposite, two interesting Lad Arend views show a meet at Bacon in August, 1936. Eastbound train 71 with engine 6 has taken the siding to let westbound extra 72 drift by, followed by helper engine 75. (Lad Arend Coll.)

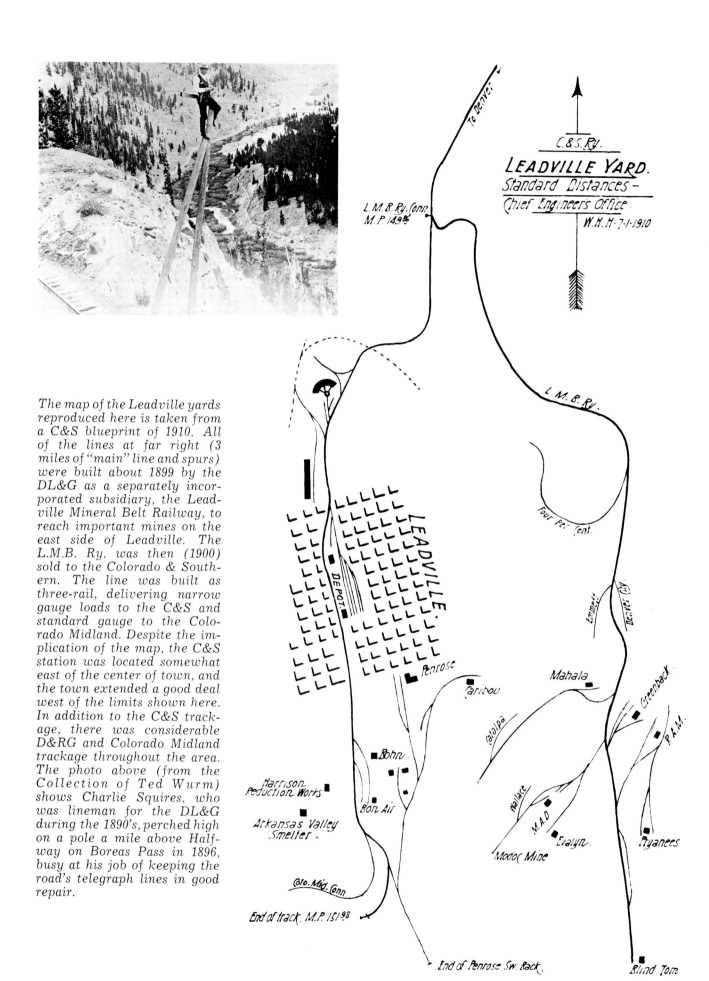

The map of the Leadville yards reproduced here is taken from a C&S blueprint of 1910. All of the lines at far right (3 miles of "main" line and spurs) were built about 1899 by the DL&G as a separately incorporated subsidiary, the Leadville Mineral Belt Railway, to reach important mines on the east side of Leadville. The L.M.B. Ry. was then (1900) sold to the Colorado & Southern. The line was built as three-rail, delivering narrow gauge loads to the C&S and standard gauge to the Colorado Midland. Despite the implication of the map, the C&S station was located somewhat east of the center of town, and the town extended a good deal west of the limits shown here. In addition to the C&S trackage, there was considerable D&RG and Colorado Midland trackage throughout the area. The photo above (from the Collection of Ted Wurm) shows Charlie Squires, who was lineman for the DL&G during the 1890's, perched high on a pole a mile above Halfway on Boreas Pass in 1896, busy at his job of keeping the road's telegraph lines in good repair.

C.&S.Ry.
LEADVILLE YARD.
Standard Distances—
Chief Engineers Office.
W.H.H-7-1-1910

To Denver

L.M.B.Ry.Conn.
M.P.149.86

L.M.B.Ry.

Four Peak Cent.

Emmett

Denver City

LEADVILLE.

DEPOT

Penrose
Caribou
Mahala
Jalalpa
Greenback
P.A.M.
Bohn
Wallace
Harrison Reduction Works
Bon Air
M.A.D
Evalyn
Pyanees
Arkansas Valley Smelter.
Modoc Mine
Colo. Mid. Conn
End of track. M.P. 151.98
End of Penrose Sw. Back.
Blind Tom

128

These views show the last freight on the High Line east of Climax. In July, 1937, nos. 76 and 74 made a trip from Leadville to pick up cars at Breckenridge, Dickey and Dillon. The upper view shows them working uphill from Dickey, while the lower view shows them stopped for water at Solitude. (Oscar Perschbacker photos from Lad Arend.)

Trout Creek

One stretch of line that seemed to give continuous trouble over the years was that in Trout Creek Canyon, on the Gunnison District, leading from the exit to South Park at Trout Creek Pass down to the Arkansas River near Buena Vista. The line had been built in the bottom of the narrow little valley of Trout Creek, and after the protective timber had been cut over the barren watershed became subject to severe flash floods, which played havoc with the railroad line.

The C&S on occasion was able to use the Buena Vista — Leadville trackage of the D&RG to keep things moving while Trout Creek Canyon was washed out. For example, in August, 1901, there occurred, as Pres. Frank Trumbull described it, "unfortunate and almost unprecedented floods between Newett and Schwanders." He contacted the D&RG's General Manager Metcalf and stated "we would like to run a few freight trains over your line from Buena Vista to Leadville and back, between now (August 12) and the 20th or 25th . . ." He asked for the usual 50c per mile emergency trackage rate per train. Metcalf not only declined to handle the narrow gauge trains, but also demurred at the 50c rate. He pointed out it "is not our custom to permit even our own narrow gauge engines to run on the main line between Buena Vista and Leadville" and would prefer to handle the freight with their own engines and crews. After some discussion back and forth, and the summer coal traffic from Baldwin piling up on the C&S meanwhile, the C&S finally agreed to pay the D&RG 56 cents per ton to handle the coal to Leadville and to return the empties free of charge to Buena Vista. This particular happening occurred during the time the C&S was transferring coal from its cars to standard gauge Colorado Midland cars at Newett for the Leadville business.

The washout, the reluctance of the D&RG, etc. brought on a study of the matters involved, and on September 25, 1901, Mr. Dyer wrote Pres. Trumbull as follows. Something to ponder is what might have happened if the C&S and Midland had acted on the proposal, which they didn't.

Denver, Colo., Sept. 25, 1901
Mr. Trumbull: —
Referring to the attached blue print and letter from General Auditor Parker. I have read Mr. Parker's letter with a great deal of interest; certainly contains a great deal of information and I feel quite confident that his computations are correct.

From an operating stand point I predict increased net earnings if we make the connection from Buena Vista to Wild Horse, also at Bath with third rail from Bath to Leadville. The lighter grade and less distance from Schwanders to Leadville will warrant paying the Midland a very liberal amount for trackage, and as Mr. Parker has stated the grade from Buena Vista to Leadville will only be 1.6%, except 5 miles from Arkansas Junction into Leadville, as against 4% around over Bath, Boreas and Climax divides.

The principal tonnage from off the Gunnison Branch is coal from Alpine mine and I judge quite a large percentage of this coal finds a ready market in Leadville; nearly all that we do not need for our engine supply. The distance from Schwanders to Leadville via Bath, Wild Horse and Colorado Midland Road is 37 miles. The distance from Schwanders to Leadville via our own line is 117.3 miles, or a saving of 80 miles, and via the shorter line we have 1.6% grade over the entire line, with the exception of 3 miles, as against a large percentage of 3 and 4% grade over the longer line. The amount of coal or other tonnage coming from Gunnison District to Denver, which would have to make the extra mileage from Schwanders to Wild Horse and back to Bath, is very small, and even with this extra mileage, I do not think it would cost us more to handle a ton of freight over that longer mileage, because the grade line would be so much less than the short 13 miles from Schwanders up Trout Creek to Bath.

The question of delay to our trains during the winter between Denver and Leadville over Boreas and Climax Divide would be entirely eliminated with this new line, because there is never any snow trouble between Como and Leadville via Bath, Wild Horse and Arkansas Junction. Whenever we had extremely heavy storms over Boreas Divide we could even do our business by way of Breckenridge running via Leadville. We do have some considerable trouble on the Climax Divide in the spring on account of slides and that expense we could not eliminate without making some arrangement with the D. & R. G., but it would only affect Breckenridge business, which is not heavy at that time of the year.

I assume that we want to increase our business between Denver and Leadville so as to get an increased percentage in the pool; we also want to be able to handle the Baldwin coal into Leadville. This arrangement via the Midland I think is going to very materially benefit both propositions. According to Mr. Parker's figures we can pay the Colorado Midland about 15% on their investment, which will enable them to renew their rail within 20 years and still leave them 10% on the cost of their investment. It will also enable us to reduce our operating expenses very materially, both in conducting transportation and maintenance of way. Considering the fact that the Midland people now have sufficient second hand 60 pound steel to lay this I believe it is an opportune time to take the matter up with them. The increased cost of maintenance of way expense to them on account of third rail is going to be very light indeed; it will not increase their supervision: i.e. Roadmasters, Section Foremen and Track Walkers' wages one cent, and this constitutes a large proportion of track rolls.

The Colorado & Southern and the Rio Grande Western had jointly purchased the Colorado Midland just the year before, which might have made such a joint operation easy to arrange, and the Midland's higher line and superior grade would have relieved the C&S of a nasty maintenance problem. Nevertheless no agreement was reached, and the persistent Trout Creek problems were reviewed again in a letter from Superintendent J. A. Rasbach to General Superintendent Charles Dyer in the spring of 1902:

Denver, Colo., March 26, 1902
Mr. Charles Dyer,
General Superintendent, Denver

Dear Sir: —

In regard to the water question at Schwanders: It is getting to be a very serious matter, and we must decide upon some plan before a great while, to carry this water from the west opening of the canon across our Buena Vista track; and as it appears to me, we should do a job there that will be of some permanency so that it will not be continually costing us an extra amount to handle the water in protecting our yard and tracks at Schwanders.

I have been there and looked the matter over, have also had Nolan there to look at it. Nolan mentions three ways to protect ourselves there: First, to dig a deep ditch, say 30 feet wide on top and 8 feet deep, for about one mile. Second, to put in a large box flume. Third, to build a stone wall on our track side, three or four feet high, to protect the track only, figuring on the ranchmen to take care of themselves.

The wide and deep ditch and the flume do not look practicable to me, for the reason that I believe either would soon fill up with sand. While the ground next to the 3 or 4 foot wall might fill in with sand, and if it did so we could build the wall higher; but I do not think it would fill in for the reason that the water and sand would have a larger space to operate in; and the idea would be to build this wall with as slight a curve in it, following our

The proposed connection with the Colorado Midland is shown on the adjacent map. The Midland, coming from Colorado Springs, crossed over the South Park on a bridge at Bath, at the top of Trout Creek Pass; the two roads had no connection there. The South Park dropped straight down the Trout Creek valley, while the Midland looped around on a side valley, reaching Newett at about the same elevation as the South Park, and transfer facilities were maintained there for a time. The South Park then dropped down along Trout Creek while the Midland skirted the sides of the hills on a gentler grade; at Buena Vista the Midland was still high above the town, making a connection there impossible. The closest point for a connection was Wild Horse, some 2½ miles north; but this required building a bridge across the Arkansas as well as constructing new track for the South Park to reach the Midland. Despite its promised advantages, the C&S could not find the money to effect this change. (Map taken from railroad blueprints, U.S.G.S. and other old maps by C. W. Hauck.)

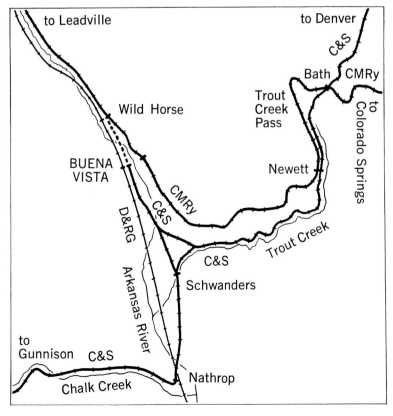

wye over to the Buena Vista track, as possible. If we can be compelled to protect the ranchmen in that vicinity, it would then appear that we would have to construct this wall on both sides of the channel, but I do not know or understand that we will be compelled to give this protection, for the reason that it is a natural outlet of the water from the canon.

The wall mentioned will have to be carried about 2600 feet, and I would say would cost close to $1,000.00. As it is now, and has been for some time, it is costing us a daily expense, account being compelled to keep more men on that section all the while, in order to keep the water within bounds.

In connection with this matter, resulting from last Summer's flood in that district, we must also very soon look after the water question in the Trout Creek canon, from Schwanders as far east as Newett, as the high fills along the line in that territory are being washed continually, and we must necessarily protect them from getting out entirely. A great deal of rip-rapping and rock embankment work should be done between Newett and Schwanders to put that track in a safe way from being seriously washed out again this Spring and Summer.

I would be glad if you can make it convenient to look over the situation yourself very soon.

This to you for your information.

Yours truly,
J. A. RASBACH
Superintendent

Shortly afterward General Superintendent Dyer journeyed with H. W. Cowan, Chief Engineer, to look over the scene. Dyer commented to Cowan on March 27 that in the previous year they had "then expected to make some connection with the Midland road at Bath or Wild Horse. That scheme appears to have been abandoned. If we are going to operate Trout Creek canon this summer a great deal of protection work will have to be done." One reason the use of the Colorado Midland line was not very practical was that line passed Buena Vista rather high above the town and north of the Arkansas River. By the time the CM got down close to the river it was near Wild Horse, two miles west of Buena Vista, involving, aside from the tracks of the D&RG closer to the river, a crossing of the river to connect to the C&S. Dyer and Cowan made their report to Pres. Trumbull but apparently it was decided at the time not to make any major changes in the line. It was to be 1908 before the worst part of the line was abandoned, and operation diverted over the original line of 1880 via Macune. Schwanders lost its importance after closing of Alpine Tunnel and the structures were eventually sold for small sums

in 1915. But in the early 1900s it had been an important service point at the mouth of the canyon.

The canyon had its share of wrecks and misfortunes, one being blamed on a fire destroying the trestle at McGees on June 4, 1908. Train 93 with Engine 61 ran into the burned bridge despite 760 feet of "clear view", according to the Superintendent. However, the engineer, T. W. Hayes, went to within 75 to 100 feet of the bridge before being satisfied it was gone, as rails still spanned the site, the fire being over and there being no smoke for the crew to see. The engine, tender and one coal car went into the "river." The odd manner of running the train is shown by the fact that at the time of the accident Train 93 was in two sections. Engine 61 had 13 cars and the head brakeman was riding on a coal car behind some stock cars, so saw nothing ahead. The rear portion of the train with the helper engine was following close behind with three more freight cars and the combine.

For turning helper engines there was a wye at Newett where the C&S was very close to the Midland, and another wye at the summit, Bath. The Newett wye was also useful for turning snow bucking trains, as snow was not a problem down the canyon.

From U. S. Highway 285 one can today view the whole of Newett, one empty building, and the closely parallel long abandoned grades of both the Colorado Midland and the South Park, with the big scars on the low mountain ridge behind the town site indicating a once busy limestone mine, source of many carloads of freight. For several years this place, unlikely as it may appear, was the scene of considerable transfer business between the two railroads. The South Park got into the booming Cripple Creek trade by bringing many carloads of Baldwin coal and many other cars of hay to this point from the Gunnison region. In the summer of 1900 additional trackage for transfer purposes was installed to a total of 3108 feet. The C&S made it a joint station and paid half the agent's salary of $75 per month. A Charles Schultz made contract to transfer loads at a rate of 9c per ton for coal cars, 10c per ton for loads in covered cars, 15c a ton for hay. In October, for example, he transferred 17 cars of hay from points on the Baldwin Branch, total weight 229,300 lbs. Some of these cars had to be transferred again when they reached the District as they were consigned to points on the narrow gauge Florence & Cripple Creek R.R.

Among railroad employees who go unsung for their long hours and uncomfortable trials is the Traveling Auditor. He is the man who has to check out and "transfer" a station when an agent leaves or arrives, even if only for a trip or vacation. On August 4th this gentleman endured the three A.M. departure from Como to check in the Midland's agent at Newett that day as joint agent. There was an extra problem too, for the C&S name for the point was "Divide" and the name had to be changed to "Newett."

The demand for hay was so great that additional transfer traffic was obtained by hauling it from points between Jefferson and Michigan Spur and other stations. The Gunnison mixed enjoyed considerable traffic to and from Newett. Still further transfer work was coal destined for Leadville. But this traffic faced the almost annual closing of Alpine Tunnel. Superintendent J. A. Rasbach on February 12, 1901, asked if they could be relieved of paying half the agent's salary "now that we will abandon the line through the Alpine Tunnel." Just as the Tunnel closed the two roads' traffic departments finally agreed on a rate.

In the spring of 1901 the Alpine Tunnel line was readied for opening. On the morning of June 1st, Superintendent Rasbach boarded the mixed at Como for this purpose, enroute re-opening the stations of St. Elmo and Pitkin, taking along the agents. The Traveling Auditor too joined the trip, but he didn't get back to Newett to check in the agent until the 9th. The Alpine Coal Co. mine at Mt. Carbon became busy. The rate was $3.00 a ton to Leadville, and as the Midland received $1.00 per ton of this, the South Park people decided if it would haul their engine coal at same rate, they would ship it that route, avoiding the long roundabout trip on their own line via Boreas and Climax divides. The Superintendent was happy, as this would spare engines and crews at a time when he was short of power. On June 6 Alpine commenced to load two cars a day of company coal for the C&S. General Superintendent Charles Dyer of C&S had some other thoughts and stated a week later to the Traffic Manager, "If we had sufficient power and cars I am quite sure I could haul it for less than that amount, although I should have to haul it at least three times as far as the Midland and over a 4% grade." However, the transfer continued until October 14 when, due to a shortage of standard gauge cars, the Midland ordered no more cars be spotted at Newett for coal loading. When the C&S protested, they pled shortage and asked if the C&S could spare some standard gauge cars for the traffic pending arrival of 100 40-ton capacity cars then under construction at a car builder in the East.

Nearly a year went by before transfer resumed, then once more a joint agent was checked in on September 9, 1902. This lasted just 14 days as

transfer was again, and for all time apparently, stopped on orders of September 18. A large commercial buyer, Hamm, at Leadville had refused 10 cars of transferred coal, claiming too much breakage was done at Newett. Also the South Park was suffering a serious decline in traffic with ample crews, cars and engines, and when the Newett transfer had been ordered again, some crews were laid off. So, as long as the Tunnel remained open, Baldwin coal continued to be burned by South Park engines hauling more Baldwin coal to Leadville. Newett continued as a limestone loading spot, until the Midland suspended operations in 1918, quickly reverting to the ghost town site it appears today.

At least once every year Trout Creek seemed to become a raging and destructive torrent, as it drained a large area subject to occasionally heavy rains and cloudbursts. Trout Creek played an important part in management's decision to give up on through operations from Como to Gunnison. So, when service beyond Hancock through the Tunnel ceased in October, 1910, it was only a few days before scheduled operations between Como and Buena Vista also ceased. Some washouts occurring that fall were left unrepaired.

As the summer of 1911 approached, C&S officials discussed what to do with over 200 surplus cars, chiefly coal cars, in the Buena Vista area. Should they go to the expense of re-opening the Trout Creek line; or pay the D&RG to haul them to Leadville? Superintendent Bacon in June made a trip over the line from Schwanders to Bath; probably a combination of walking and hand cars for transportation. Six of the bridges needed repairs, but he felt certain there was enough material at the locations for repairs if three or four bridge carpenters and their tools could be spared. Further, a work train of ten men and four or five carloads of rock could make all that type of repair necessary in two or three days. Total cost was estimated at $300.

No sooner had Bacon made his report, on July 1st, than heavy rains hit the area again. On July 5th he suggested, without looking the line over, that it was probably going to cost more than his earlier estimate to put the track in shape for service. Those rains of the first week of July might be described as the deciding factor against reopening Trout Creek canyon, and the line was to remain abandoned to operation until dismantled 11 years later. Almost total destruction of the canyon line occurred in floods in July, 1914, so extensive that some bridges vanished and much of the track also vanished under washed down debris. When the line was dismantled much of the rail was not found. It is still there, often deeply buried.

133

Alpine Tunnel

The Alpine Tunnel line was from the beginning an operational nightmare in the winter months — and at that altitude winter lasts a long time! The troubles were almost entirely along the east approaches, where for many miles of 4% grade the track lay on the south slope, out of reach of the winter sun. Worse, the sun could reach the slopes way above the track, resulting in melting slush and slides trickling — or roaring — onto the track below, to become an ice problem. In Colorado above 9,000 feet altitude the snows generally stay put and pile up in winter, and the dryness of the snow tends to build drifts quickly. So from below St. Elmo (10,047 ft.) through Romley (10,512 ft.) and Hancock (11,524 ft.) crews had slippery track both directions, running up operating expenses in delays upgrade, with slippery conditions contributing to frequent runaways and wrecks eastbound.

The west side was like another world. Here the wind and sun combined to leave stretches of track bare and dry ("summer rail" the crews called it) much of the time. This characteristic of Colorado often amazes and surprises the easterner, for in much of the eastern U. S. a location on one side or the other of a valley meant little insofar as it affected snow problems. But locating the South Park on the shady side of the valley approaching the Tunnel from the east was a mistake that helped account for the erratic operations and short life of the route.

The Union Pacific management started giving up on the line by closing down during the winter of 1887. The Post Office Department had no choice but to discontinue the Como & Gunnison Railway Post Office and it never was put back on, losing a steady item of revenue to the South Park. Other mail routes were set up to serve the communities on a year around basis. So from 1887 onward the pattern of operations was erratic, with mixed train service reaching to the mining communities up Chalk Creek, and on the west side similar service between Pitkin and Baldwin. The coal mines at Baldwin, principal freight shippers, therefore led an erratic operational life too.

Each spring the UP would re-open the line, but in 1890, after re-opening the Tunnel, they failed to resume operations. And it stayed closed with no attempt to reopen from 1891 until the spring of 1895. The DL&G placed a turntable at St. Elmo and some schedules show trains working past St. Elmo to Romley, then coming back to St. Elmo, to spend the night, returning eastward the next day.

Perhaps the best example of the problems of Alpine Tunnel is the summary given by Superintendent P. Touhy in a report in the form of a letter on June 26, 1891, to General Superintendent R. J. Duncan of the Gulf Division of the Union Pacific System.

> Referring to the question of opening the Gunnison line for business. The cost Hancock to Quartz will depend on the condition Tunnel is in which can not be determined until the cuts at either end are opened.
>
> For a short distance above Hancock to the tunnel the snow is from one to 12 feet deep, and from the shed at West end of tunnel to Quartz there is no snow to speak of, but, there are quite a number of rock and land slides, much of the rock will have to be blasted. There are also a few broken rails and a washout or two, but nothing serious.
>
> The Rotary I think will open the line from Hancock to the tunnel in two days, and work train with twenty-five men from tunnel to Quartz, so we can get over it in ten days, if there is not too much ice in the tunnel.
>
> The distance from Hancock to Quartz is about 14 miles, track is not in very bad shape, but the ties have been in use eight years and many of them will give out as soon as we commence running over them. It will take three hundred ties to the mile to hold the track together, and balance of the season, and a great many more next year.
>
> In my opinion the line cannot be operated at a profit and I would advise against opening it up, at least this season.
>
> Below I hand you an approximation of cost of opening, and an estimate of some of the most prominent items of expense of operating the line.

Cost of Opening line	
Rotary two days	$ 280.00
25 men ten days	375.00
Foreman ten days	25.00
Engine and crew ten days	250.00
4200 cross ties at 40 cents	1680.00

Partial estimate of expense of operation
(per train mile)

Wages engineers and firemen	17.60 cents
Repairs of engines	12.22
Fuel	27.68
Wiping	2.20
Oil tallow and waste	.65
Repairs freight and caboose cars	10.77
Repairs air brake	1.00
Wages conductors and brakemen	8.90
Total train expense per train mile	81.02 cents

Operators, Section men, etc.

One operator at Tunnel	$ 60.00 per month

One operator at Schwanders	60.00	"	"
One engine watchman Pitkin	60.00	"	"
One car inspector St. Elmo	70.00	"	"
Three section foremen between Romley and Pitkin	186.00	"	"
10 section laborers between Romley and Pitkin	450.00	"	"
Increase of force 25% west of Pitkin	400.00	"	"
	$1286.00	"	"

(or 43.00 per day)

To handle 20 cars of coal from Baldwin mine per day, will require a train mileage of 510 miles at 81.2 cents.

for train expense	$459.00 per day
add increase in payrolls	43.00 " "
	$502.00 per day

Estimate of earnings on 20 cars of coal

20 cars at 13 tons per car	260 tons
Less 15% to be used for locomotives	39 tons
	221 tons

221 tons at $2.75 (Rate Baldwin to Denver)	$607.75
Train expense and daily increase in payroll	502.00
	$105.75

This $105.75 per day will not cover the cost of material, maintenance of track, bridges and other unavoidable expenses not included in above estimate.

Two days later Duncan wrote to his superior, E. Dickenson, Assistant General Manager of the System at Omaha, Nebraska:

It has been our intention, when the snow was off the ground, or about July 1st, to open the line through the Alpine Tunnel, so that the mines at Baldwin might be operated to the extent of stocking up the company's platforms at Hortense and Schwanders, and to furnish the Mary Murphy Mines with about 1,000 tons of coal, and to otherwise take care of the local business in that territory, to the extent of the capacity of the one engine and crew now working between Pitkin and Baldwin, thus utilizing to the best advantage the fixed operating expense of the Gunnison end — but it so happens that the unusual snows and heavy rain storms have resulted in considerable damage to the track, and a number of rock and land slides, would make the opening of the line, even if the snow is off, quite expensive, and I beg to call your attention to some statements and figures, herewith, showing the difficulty of operating the Gunnison district, and in view of the fact, that it would cost more to open the line than it is possible for the one engine and crew to

earn, and the impossibility of our doing either a large or a small business from the Baldwin mines without loss, I would suggest the consideration of allowing the line to remain closed this year.

Mr. Duncan usually wrote one-sentence replies, whether they be short or long!

So the clerk in Duncan's office made a letter-press copy of Touhy's report, to join all the other bad news of high expenses, losses, etc. that had become almost routine from Colorado to the financially hard-pressed officials at Omaha. At this time the UP was in one word, poor. As it extended its lines, it had to add still more lines to hold the traffic of the territories reached, as competitors sprang up. The company was pinch-pennying in all directions, but bankruptcy was looming. There wasn't any money to lose on local lines in the depths of the Colorado mountains.

Thus it was probably no surprise to anyone that Superintendent Duncan wrote the Superintendent of the Mary Murphy Mining Co. on July 12 advising that no decision had yet been made to reopen the Tunnel, but that if the Tunnel remained closed ". . . an arrangement will be made, as I understand it, with the D&RG for the movement of Baldwin coal, so that you can get your supply from that mine, but the delivered price will be, of course, some higher. I do not know how much, but it cannot reach you as cheaply as if it were hauled over our own line." On July 8 Duncan had his business car 06 placed on D&RG Train #5 at Denver and traveled to Gunnison. The car was on narrow gauge trucks for the journey. Evidently his findings on this trip confirmed previous reports and his first written act on return was to issue a Bulletin to all concerned to keep a close watch for "water spouts." It was a bad summer for this type of trouble. He admonished all that "it is better to lay trains up than to have them in the ditch." Omaha frowned on the Bulletin and it was withdrawn, to be replaced by verbal cautions.

In May 1895 Receiver Trumbull of the DL&G started the re-opening of the tunnel. Trumbull and associates had coal interests at Baldwin. When all the bills were paid by late fall, the cost of re-opening totalled $16,190.90, of which $500 was in settlement of tragic deaths of a crew during the work. But it was still a mixed train operation with three and four-engine trains from the Gunnison side, burning a lot of good Baldwin coal to get the revenue loads to market. There has been speculation that it was not profitable to haul the coal to Denver, considering the long grades involved up Trout Creek, Red Hill and Kenosha, and the wasteful light mileage of returning helper engines. But the Baldwin coal was the only coal

This (page opposite) is what *Alpine Pass* looked like when the C&S assumed ownership. Doors still guarded the entrance to the east portal (left), but the snowsheds had been almost entirely removed from the west portal (right, opposite). The stone enginehouse still dominated the scene at *Alpine Tunnel Station* (bottom). (Three photos, Museum of New Mexico.) Years after the line was closed, many evidences remained. On this page, top, the little stone depot in *Gunnison* served as a home for years until destroyed in a highway relocation (R. B. Jackson). Center, the old turntable frame at *Romley* looked like this in 1940 (John W. Maxwell). At bottom, the frame boarding-house erected after the 1906 fire leaned crazily in the 1940's, as seen through the portal of one end of the enginehouse ruins (R. W. Richardson).

mined on the South Park, except for the King mines near Como, which closed in the 1890s, never a good source.

As the 2:15 A.M. mixed out of Como for Gunnison was not the type of schedule to entice much tourist travel, the DL&G and the C&S tried $10 excursions from Denver, using the night train as far as Como, then often a special from Como. Though these are something to dream about today, they obviously did not attract any great turnouts and by 1905 the two remaining Pullmans were in storage.

Most of the accidents in and around the Tunnel involved eastbound trains. From the station stop to the tunnel apex was a stiff grade. Rules required train crews to be out on the cars setting retainers and ready to set hand brakes after the train passed the apex, in either direction. The tunnel had the closest clearances on the South Park, 14 feet in height above rails, 11 feet extreme width. This was two to two and a half feet less than snowsheds and bridges elsewhere in height, and two and a half feet less width than any other restricted points and structures. This meant that the tunnel roof was a mere 14 inches above some stacks of locomotives, and barely two feet above brake wheels on box and stock cars. Brakemen of course could not be on top of high cars in the smoky inkiness but would select a spot in the train where brakestaff ends of gondolas were adjacent (setting "double brakes" it was called). The gassy condition of the tunnel during and after passage of a three-engine freight can be imagined! Trains were frequently out of control (exceeding 15 m.p.h.) as they emerged eastbound on the 24-degree curve that started inside, the crew often unable to get the train under control and stop until reaching Hancock, three miles away. Some never made it, as debris found to this day testifies. Before leaving the station at Alpine Tunnel, trainmen were required to go under cars and adjust the brakes, making sure that the pistons of the eight-inch cylinders were set for not more than 4″ of travel. An unpleasant task most of the year.

At Hancock brakes were again checked, helpers cut off and wyed sometimes for return to Pitkin. One of the first things the C&S did was to remove the St. Elmo turntable and place this 50-foot iron table at west side of the Tunnel, in 1899. Though built above ground, thus less likely to get snowed in, it sometimes was not operable for that reason and engines would have to back to Pitkin, or Hancock.

Westbound trains generally were three-engine affairs, two engines on head end, one cut ahead of the combine. As they would have to work quite a ways into the bore, the smoke conditions were bad for the brakemen out on the cars and the third engine crew, who often got down on the deck with wet handkerchiefs over their faces.

Oasis to all was the boarding house and its excellent meals, and the frequent meets there of Trains 93 and 94, the scheduled mixeds, made it a popular meal stop. The $3.00 meal ticket sold by the proprietor was one of the most popular "pie tickets" on the South Park.

Can you imagine a head-on collision at Alpine Tunnel between two three-engine trains? It happened, a three-engine westbound freight coming out of the Tunnel and running into the eastbound mixed standing on the main! On November 25, 1904 the mixed had arrived at 1:40 P.M. with engine 41 on the point, stopping 73 feet short of the head block of the east switch. Engineer Simpson and Fireman Thady got under the engine "to take slack up on tank" while Conductor J. R. Wilson went to the telegraph office to get his orders. His words ". . . then went to east switch to throw switch and let Extra pass, but about time I got close to switch the extra came up and ran into No. 94."

Engineer Simpson said he heard a whistle and fireman said "train is coming and switch is for the main line!" The men scrambled out and the engineer ran ahead of his engine attempting to flag the oncoming freight "but I saw they would not stop, then I got farther away from engine." The Extra West composed of engines 72, 61, 23 cars, engine 37 and caboose had received orders for the meet at St. Elmo, stopping at Hancock to take water. Engineer S. Andrews was on the 72 and brakeman F. M. Wilson was riding his engine, while the rear brakeman and Conductor G. W. Miller were riding the caboose.

Although Superintendent Bacon testified that from the west portal he could see 700 to 800 feet to the switch and 30 to 40 feet beyond, none of the persons on the two head engines admitted they saw the mixed until several car lengths from the east switch. The fireman of No. 72 jumped ("stepped") off, while Engineer Haight of No. 61 called to his fireman to get off and "did the same myself" but he struck the ground only 15 feet before the collision occurred. He admitted seeing a smokestack when only about three car lengths from switch and at same time heard the head engineer whistle for brakes, a futile call, as no one was on top.

No. 72's pilot was broken off as well as other front end damage, the pilot truck having to be removed. The engineer admitted brakes seemed O.K. and he could not explain the accident. Speed he estimated at 4 to 10 m.p.h. He said that he had applied a reduction as they emerged from the

Tunnel, and as the collision loomed, he reversed the engine as did the engineer on 61. Two damaged cars were set out at the Tunnel, and 61 took the train on to Pitkin with no problems. Engineer Andrews and Conductor Miller were discharged, the brakemen given 15 to 20 demerits. Master Mechanic Patterson felt the engineer was without excuse as he had "failed to stop an ordinary train under ordinary circumstances with brakes in good condition." The Conductor was held at fault for not insisting that his brakemen be on top of the cars. No. 94 was somewhat late in Como that day.

The winter of 1904-05 required use of the rotary through the tunnel and on February 6, 1905, a telegram from Alpine Tunnel reported timbers had come in from the sides, as a result of cutting three inches off of them in order to get the rotary back through the tunnel — this in addition to several inches taken off for same reason earlier. Three days later the night freight out of Denver had four carloads of timbers and material for 93 to forward from Como that same night. It took 50 12x12x24 and 120 3x10x20 and the B&B Foreman estimated would take 43 days work if no trains were run. On April 10th the job was completed at a cost of $1,229.84, but two months later they had to come back to replace four timbers that had split and were "kicking in." To illuminate their work, old locomotive kerosene headlights had been used and a telegram of February 9th had urgently requested a barrel of headlight oil. Presumably the rusted pieces of headlights found outside the east portal came from these used in repair work.

An inspection of the tunnel in the summer of 1906 indicated some major replacement of timbers was necessary and immediately, and the Vice-President signed an authorization for an estimated $2,960.00 of work on September 20th. Work was to commence as soon as grade in the tunnel was frozen. The B&B foreman had wired after his inspection on September 15: ". . . have made repairs often, but conditions grow worse as the mountain crowds the timbers." A week earlier he had estimated "about 600' of timbers to be taken down on the north side near east end and timbers set back. Also on the south side there is about 300' to be taken down and set back." He used 16,000 feet of 3x12 and 10,000 ft. of 12x12, this larger size for posts and segments. That the trouble never ended is shown by a telegram of November 16, 1907, from the crew of No. 94 reporting a gondola had "bulged about 12 inches and had rubbed timbers", "timbers in Alpine Tunnel crowding in." One problem as well was formation of ice on the timbers which had the same effect,

giving crews some bad moments as cars passing through tore at these obstructions.

Small cave-ins that occurred were matters for the section men, but were always on crews' minds as shown by a collision inside the tunnel on February 9, 1906. Engines 67 and 68 had been on an eastward freight, cut off and turned at Hancock and while 67 was still in the west end of tunnel, engine 68 came along in the gloom, so smoky the red lantern on rear of 67's tender was not to be seen, and the 68 hit the tender of the 67. The fireman on the 68 said he "thought we had hit a cave-in in the tunnel." He ran back and managed to flag engine 59 which with a short freight was just entering the tunnel. 67's tender was derailed, providing a most unpleasant rerailing task inside the tunnel.

Due to the low speeds involved most accidents resulted in little in the way of injuries, but that of eastward mixed No. 94 on November 17, 1906, near St. Elmo was an exception. Conductor Frank Land and Brakeman C. E. Burnside died when two cars of their train on which they were attempting to set brakes went down the mountainside. The engineer was dismissed "for improper handling of train."

It was dark at Hancock as Engine 71 was cut off and helper engine No. 54 brought from rear end and put on the head end. But air could not be pumped above 70 pounds and despite careful checking of the train no leaks could be located. The engineer asked the conductor: "Frank, what will we do about this?" to which he got the reply "Billy, hand brakes are in first class shape and if you get short of air let me know and we can stop with hand brakes." They made stops with no problems at both Romley and the Lady Murphy Mine spur, even having to work steam leaving the latter point. But when the train got to about 7 m.p.h. neither the first or subsequent applications of air seemed to check it, at which time he threw engine into reverse and whistled for brakes. The crew already was setting hand brakes, but as the speed increased the conductor told the surviving brakeman as he passed him "I guess it is goodby" and said something about cutting off the rear portion of the train and saving the combine. After the two cars carrying the two men crashed down the mountainside, the rear did coast to a stop and the four children of the dead brakeman in the combine escaped unharmed. The first part of the train passed St. Elmo at 30 to 40 m.p.h. and piled up in a cut beyond there, the engine crew having jumped and received minor injuries.

A derailment of a gondola in another train on July 5, 1909, almost got both engineer and conductor fired, receiving 40 demerits each for "fast

A C&S freight leaves Pitkin (left) for the tough climb to Alpine Pass; 10 loads of coal, 4 box, and the combine are in the hands of four 2-8-0s. Below, a similar three-engine train further along at Midway tank, with engineer Walt Parlin hanging out of the 57's cab. (Both, H. L. Curtis photos from Mal Ferrell.) Right: top, a three-engine C&S freight pauses near the Palisades (Otto Westerman photo from State Hist. Society of Colo.) and below, DL&G 206 pushes the mixed past the Alpine enginehouse (Dr. C. H. Scott photo, Mal Ferrell).

The long climb over Alpine eastbound began at Pitkin, and helper engines were turned and serviced there. It was no vacation spot for enginemen in winter, as a glance at C&S 65 at the depot in 1902 will attest. (H. L. Curtis photo from R. H. Kindig.) The same engine is pictured below on a summer day in Pitkin, waiting to help an eastbound train, and affording a pleasanter appraisal of duty there. (State Hist. Society of Colorado.)

running." They had run through a slow order of 4 m.p.h. at 18 m.p.h. and the conductor's record showed he had 15 derailments between May 3rd and June 28th, all on Train 94, which the Superintendent blamed on fast running.

At first the C&S planned to keep the Tunnel line open and even ordered another rotary snowplow in 1899 to be sure of it. That rotary, the #99201 now at the Colorado Railroad Museum, arrived in February, 1900, but proved too heavy for the route and was assigned to standard gauge lines. It seemed every winter the C&S had a battle to keep the line open, with closures from a few days to four months. But weather alone was not the deciding factor in the fate of the line. The crash of 1893 had dealt a blow from which the mining industry never seemed to recover. About one-third of the freight to the mines was coal, so any decline in metal mining forced a decline in coal mining, the principal freight item from the Gunnison district. Then in 1907 came another financial "crash" and some historians believe this one was even harder on the mining industry than the 1893 panic. By the time the 1907 hard times exerted their full effect, the South Park was left with few operating mines and mills on its lines, and fewer customers for Baldwin coal. Some of the coal was hauled all the way to the Denver market, where it had to compete with abundant and not too inferior coal from fields much nearer to Denver.

It was standard practice for the C&S to keep one crew at Gunnison, so that they could handle local work during periods when the Tunnel was closed. Usually they left two engines at Gunnison, generally two of the older Consolidations. During the February, 1901, tie-up of the Tunnel, due to no engine being usable at Gunnison, they rented Class 56 D&RG 2-8-0 No. 70, obtaining the engine late in the afternoon of February 19th, to work the Baldwin Branch. That first day it was tied up on return at 1:30 A.M. The 20th, the same crew worked from 10 A.M. and returned the engine to the D&RG at 10 P.M. Meanwhile C&S Engine No. 38 and caboose departed from Buena Vista at 8 A.M. on the 21st, with a D&RG pilot on board, making the trip to Gunnison via the D&RG. The trip cost the C&S 50 cents per mile, the pilot's wages, 50c per tank of water, and cost of coal taken at D&RG points. A large number of coal cars were normally kept on the Gunnison side of Alpine Tunnel, so that the coal mines could keep working.

On September 21, 1910, C&S President Darius Miller wrote D&RG President Jeffery to suggest a plan for "mutual economy" in the operations of the two railroads, whereby the D&RG would operate the C&S line to Pitkin and the coal mines, permitting the C&S to discontinue running trains west of St. Elmo. The C&S would take over operation of the D&RG's Dillon Branch. Jeffery responded encouragingly, and D&RG Vice-President C. H. Schlacks, who was at the time in New York with Jeffery, left on September 24th for Denver to confer with officials there to see what could be effected.

C&S trains began moving cars out of the Gunnison area and by the time the Tunnel was closed, it was estimated over 200 cars were in the Buena Vista area. On October 15, 1910 the Rocky Mountain Fuel Co., then principal mine operator at Baldwin, made a contract with the C&S stating that it agreed to "so far as it effects the operations of its mines in Gunnison County, . . . to the abandonment and closing of said line of railroad from Garos to Pitkin" and waived any claims, etc. that may occur "by reason of the abandonment and closing . . ."

No public announcement of cessation of train operation seems to have been made — quite the contrary. What it amounted to was that one day in October Train 93 was annulled beyond Hancock and just never scheduled again. No. 94 apparently operated on October 20th for the last time through from Gunnison. There were no news stories or any mention of it being a last run, for the simple reason that it was not then known to be the last run. If there had been an outcry of patrons there would have been the possibility of resuming runs, but patrons were so few, their traffic so meager, that the line stayed closed. While there were reports accepted since of a small cave-in as the reason for cessation of operations, nothing in the operating records examined indicates this. In fact it is quite clear that, but for excessive ice in the Tunnel, Superintendent Bacon was planning to move equipment and material from Gunnison via the Tunnel as soon as the ice melted in the summer of 1911.

On July 5, 1911, Bacon reported to General Superintendent J. D. Welsh that: "The haul from Gunnison over our line would be very expensive. On Thursday, June the 28th I inspected the Alpine Tunnel and found the ice for a distance of 600 feet to be 8 and 9 feet in depth. I do not believe this will melt away this year. I understand there are a number of rock slides between Alpine Tunnel and Quartz which would cost considerable to remove. I believe it would be cheaper to let the D&RG move our cars and scrap from Gunnison to Leadville."

The November 1, 1910, timetable showed no train service between Hancock and Quartz. There was no indication why, or that this was temporary or permanent. And so matters rested for years, the C&S quite willing to pay the Gunnison county taxes, the line just laying almost forgotten with management hoping they would never have to operate it again.

In the late summer of 1910, as word got around that closure of the Tunnel was near, morale of the employees suffered. In his report on one fireman quitting without notice at Gunnison, Trainmaster and Traveling Engineer Gray reported: "At this time we were having considerable trouble with the lack of spirit or interest shown by the men account of the road closing down and several had quit on short notice and others appeared to be trying to make it as disagreeable as possible for the company." When on October 19, day before the last run east through the tunnel, a fireman quit at Gunnison, they had to take the fireman off the Baldwin train to take his place, and the engine foreman at Gunnison fired the Baldwin train that day.

After closing, two engines were left at Gunnison, with one crew. Three times a week they made a run to Baldwin, alternating with three runs to Pitkin. There was little business, mostly coal sent out over the D&RG. On November 1st the Kubler mine closed for the winter. An item in the Denver Post reported that 350 C&S cars had been leased to the D&RG and a number of engines had been offered as well, but apparently the latter were not taken by the D&RG. At Como the Master Mechanic's office was busy through November issuing discharges to enginemen as the town's population, mostly railroaders, dwindled to a handful.

At the time formal abandonments were not required by the I.C.C. and the C&S did not make such announcements. Track was left intact and even when the Roadmaster took some of the good steel rail east of the tunnel to put in other track, he was careful to relay it with old 35 pound rail, so that track was still intact. Except for one train that came up from Gunnison late in 1910, apparently to haul out material, the trackage remained idle until taken up years later. The track inside the tunnel never was taken up, and is still there. The large cave-in on the east end occurred sometime in the 1930s, as visitors reported walking through the tunnel in the early thirties. One visitor peering up at the roof inside the east portal discovered the pair of red and white lanterns (used for the doors) still hanging on their hooks nearly 40 years after operations ceased.

When on February 14, 1911, the C&S closed its stations at Pitkin and Ohio City, another abandonment other than railroad occurred but was overlooked — the telegraph line. The Stark Brothers at St. Elmo were both experienced telegraph operators and for years continued the operation of the telegraph line on a commission basis for the Western Union Telegraph Co. They did

just enough maintenance between Nathrop and Pitkin to keep the line operable. By the fall of 1920 the line as far as St. Elmo was in poor condition; 60 poles needed resetting, some arms had come loose and 28 insulators needed replacing. Two linemen were assigned this work, so the line could last through the coming winter. The Western Union people, with railroad agreement, turned the line over to the Starks, as neither felt they would ever need to re-establish telegraph service between Nathrop and Pitkin, and it would cost several hundreds of dollars to repair it, a sum more than the net salvage value of the line. So the Starks, for one dollar and some paragraphs of legalistics, became operators of the line. Though no hands were there to manipulate the dusty Alpine Tunnel key, apparently the facility continued to exist for years, awaiting calls that never came for "UN". The Starks and their sister became legends at St. Elmo. When all other population had left, they maintained the weatherbeaten store and offered phone service at least in their final years of residence in the 1950s.

Tunnel Disaster

"Disaster" is what the DL&G officials termed the happening that occurred when reopening the Tunnel in the spring of 1895, resulting in the deaths of four men. There had been no train service through the Tunnel since 1889, even though the famous snow plow "trials" had been held with much publicity early in 1890, and track reopened. The Union Pacific, becoming increasingly troubled financially, had simply saved money by discontinuing the costly operations on the route. Now under the new receivership of the combined Gulf and DL&G lines, and bright prospects for the coal traffic, a force of men was gathered and sent to reopen the line. Andrew Lejune, Gunnison area mining man, brought a group of men to the east end of the tunnel and set up camp at Atlantic, the siding just outside the portal. The single locomotive used in maintaining the modest operations on the Pitkin-Baldwin line, DL&G 62, and its crew, came up from Gunnison to assist.

There was a large cave-in near the east portal of the Tunnel, inside the Tunnel, but not completely filling the hole to the roof level. Water had backed against this mass, and was three feet deep for a distance, despite the 4% slope. The miners at the east end were working at clearing away what they could. Attacking the problem from the west side was another matter, requiring going through the nearly one-third mile of tunnel to reach it. Nothing could be done until the water was removed, so the B&B men made a "pipe" which was placed across the top of the cave-in, with hope of syphoning the water out to the east side.

The day before the disaster, the men had at one time been in the cab of the engine discussing the problem, and the dangers, and all apparently agreed that to run the engine into the tunnel to provide steam to make the syphon work would be dangerous. On June 8th Lejune warned his foreman Mike Flavin as well as the others to be careful, cautioning him to come out of the tunnel at once "if they felt any ill effects from operating the engine in the tunnel." Engineer Nathan Martenis and Fireman Mike Byrne were experienced men, well aware of the problems of smoke and gas in the tunnel when trains were operated. Elmer England was the conductor.

About 4:30 P.M. the engine entered the tunnel, and a steam line was connected to the syphon pipe. But it did not work, so apparently to get up a better head of steam the fireman started the blower and fired up the engine, immediately filling the tunnel with dense smoke and gas. When they began to feel dizzy, the several B&B men and Conductor Elmer England started out, passing the engine tender. Carpenter Harry James and the conductor staggered out of the tunnel, stopping to bathe their heads in water; Edward Swanson worked about 40 minutes on the syphon when he had "to make for the outside" and in climbing over the tender found George Shields overcome and "insensible" and carried him about 200 feet toward the west end, "then had to drop him to save myself as I was nearly overcome and with difficulty reached the end of the tunnel safely."

Conductor England found several men outside the tunnel and ordered them to take a push car and go into the tunnel to get the men overcome by smoke. They found Shields lying by the track but before they could get the push car to him, they heard the engine coming, backing out, so England ordered them to take the push car out or if they could not to let it go and save themselves. Evidently realizing their danger, the men with the engine had cut the hose to the syphon and had started out with it, but as they reached the laborers, someone shouted to the engineer telling him there was a man laying on the track and not to run over him. Martenis then reversed the engine, evidently immediately collapsing and the engine at full speed ran down into the water and stuck in the slide. One laborer said "she went into the dirt at full speed." It was about three hours before rescuers could get back to the engine, making several attempts to do so.

On the east side, smoke and gas boiled out of the hole across the slide, forcing those men and Foreman Lejune to flee. One, Oscar Cammann, left his coat behind and despite warnings went back to get it. He was found later with the coat on, one button buttoned, lying dead across the track. The other men cleared snow away from the doors and opened those, hoping this would help. Most of the men at Atlantic went over the top to the west end to help.

The push car rescuers had some success, loading Shields unconscious onto the car and bringing him to the portal with one of the rescuers also on the car unconscious. Apparently no telegrapher was present, so Conductor England loaded two of the men and himself on a flat car and coasted to Pitkin to notify Superintendent Rainey from that point. It was not quite dark as they left, England becoming unconscious as he was standing holding on to the brake wheel.

About 8 P.M. the rescuers brought the bodies of the other three men out of the tunnel. Foreman Flavin was found lying face down in the coal of the tender, his feet toward the firebox. Engineer Martenis was dead in the cab and they managed to carry him 400 feet before the gas and smoke caused them to leave the body and flee. The throttle was found "wide open" on the 62.

With no other engine available, contractor Lejune went to Pitkin, obtained two teams the next morning and started out to meet his men "who will pack them down Tunnel Gulch" and he expected to be back in Pitkin by 5 P.M. where he had ordered "three rough boxes made here to ship them to Gunnison."

Meanwhile Superintendent Rainey at Platte Canyon urged his superiors to get an engine from the D&RG "so we can send to Pitkin for the bodies." Relatives of two of the victims wired the Denver offices, urging them to obtain an engine from the D&RG to take them to the Tunnel as "there is no other way to get there." Rainey, reaching the tunnel the next day, had the Coroner of Chaffee County investigate, it being determined the accident occurred in that county. The latter briefly declared no inquest necessary, "their deaths resulting from their own carelessness."

Work continued on the tunnel, the B&B foreman reporting the "work catching up slide or cave in Alpine Tunnel is progressing slow. It is a difficult job to catch and hold the ground. Mr. Lejune the man in charge is doing the best he can. We have put in extra timbers at weak places we can get at . . ." Rainey ordered another Mogul sent from Como to Buena Vista and thence by D&RG around to the Gunnison side as "Engine 62 in Tunnel dead and stuck in dirt."

One curious sidelight is the specific reference to engine "62", although previous South Park locomotive rosters have not shown any such number. A search of C&S and Union Pacific records indicate that, in the 1885-1890 period, some of the Brooks moguls were rebuilt with 14x18″ cylinders — one inch smaller than the original 15x18″. One explanation has it that this facilitated reboring in subsequent shoppings. Another, perhaps more logical, explanation has to do with the engines' reputation as bad steamers — "cold water Brooks". Although Brooks moguls of this same pattern were used with success on many narrow gauges, the South Park's were among the largest and apparently the boiler capacity was not adequate for the larger cylinders, and in addition operation at high altitudes would have aggravated the poor steaming qualities. Thus smaller cylinders might well have alleviated the problem and resulted in a better running (even though theoretically less powerful) locomotive.

The first of these rebuilds was UPD&G 151.

After rebuilding, and apparently to differentiate it from 15x18″ Brooks engines, the UP gave it a new number — 59. Over the next several years, four of the identical DL&G Brooks were also so rebuilt, becoming DL&G 60-63. The latter two eventually became C&S 2 and 3, but were soon disposed of. Thus the central figure in the Alpine Tunnel disaster of 1895 was gone within a half-dozen years.

Statements were taken from various participants in the tragedy as a part of the investigation, and provide interesting accounts of the events of the day. Perhaps the best is that of Conductor England, reprinted at right. The DL&G officials showed a sympathy for the widows and children unusual for that time, and personally did whatever they could to help. Cash settlements of $400 to $500 were made to the surviving heirs of the victims. Free passes to points beyond their lines were secured, as well as free passage of household goods. The road had not incurred any liability and at the time was piling up discouraging losses in operations.

The rare view above shows No. 9 coming into the west end of the Pitkin yard with the "Gunnison Flyer" during the brief period of C&S operation of a through Gunnison-Denver passenger train. (Lad Arend Coll.)

Statement of Conductor ELMER ENGLAND
Gunnison, June 18th, 1895

About 4 P.M. on Saturday, June 8th, 1895, M. W. Flavin, Nathan Martenis, Michael Byrnes, myself and four of Flavin's laborers went into west end of Alpine Tunnel, on engine, under instructions of M. W. Flavin, to syphon the water out of the tunnel. We went into tunnel about sixteen hundred feet, when, after reaching the water, which had accumulated to a depth of about 3 feet, we took the syphon off the tank, carried it over the cab and running-board, connected it and started to turn the steam on. The syphon would not work, so we took up the hose and saw that the hose was broken. Harry James, the carpenter, and myself spliced the hose, when we succeeded in getting the syphon to working.

About this time I began to get dizzy. Martenis and Byrnes were on the engine, and Flavin was on a pile of dirt about 30 or 40 feet from the engine, where Flavin was the last I saw of him. When I began to get dizzy, I started along a walk above the water and slipped into the water, caught myself, went back to the engine and climbed on the running-board into the cab. There were 3 or 4 men on the engine; can not give their names, as I was dizzy and excited. I made the remark, "I will have to get out of here." Some one replied, "It is not bad yet," when I said, "I will have to go," and started, accompanied by the carpenter. When I started I was dizzy and staggered.

When I arrived at the mouth of the tunnel and came to my senses, I enquired if the engine had come out, and was informed by some of the men that it had not come out. I then started back into tunnel again. Could not tell how far back I went when I met Ben Anderson coming from towards engine. He told me to bring the push-car; that there was a man lying alongside of the track, apparently dead. I went outside again and returned with the push-car and three or four men. We entered about six or seven hundred feet, when I heard the engine coming. I told the boys to get the car out of tunnel, so the engine could get out. The engine came up the grade until it reached the place where this man was lying by track, (his name is George Shields), when some one hallooed to the men on the engine to stop, — that they had

a dead man there. The engine was reversed and immediately started back and did not stop. There were three or four men standing about the man who was lying alongside of track, who were evidently the laboring men who had been with the engine.

I began to get dizzy again, and started out of tunnel, leaving these men in there with man whom I supposed was dead. I again secured the assistance of some men with hand-car and entered tunnel to where the man was lying. We put him on the hand-car and started towards mouth of tunnel. Another man and myself were about overcome from effects of gas and lay down on car with the man we picked up, while the other men pushed car out. When we reached outside they took these two men (one found along track and the one who was overcome and lay down on hand-car) to a cabin. By this time some additional help arrived and we started into the tunnel to see if we could not rescue men on engine. Two men and myself took the lead, while some more men followed with the push-car. We took push-car with us, as we expected to find them dead. We walked back pretty near to where engine was, when one of two men with me made the remark, "We will have to get out of here," when we turned and retraced our steps towards entrance on west end. When we got out, we found the push-car there. The men did not enter tunnel with car as far as we did on foot. When we left the tunnel the last time, I suggested that Superintendent Rainey be notified from Pitkin. In company with two others I started on flat-car for Pitkin. The last thing I remember before becoming unconscious was that I was standing on flat-car, holding on to brake-wheel, going to Pitkin. Do not think it was quite dark when we left the tunnel for Pitkin.

I do not remember whether the blower was put on engine or not, when we started to syphon water. We had been operating syphon about twenty-five minutes when the smoke became very dense and I left engine for mouth of tunnel. There was nothing said about danger connected with taking engine into tunnel, by Mr. Flavin. I was the Conductor of this crew, but acted under instructions of Mr. Flavin, who it was understood had full charge of the tunnel work on the west side.

(signed) ELMER ENGLAND

Baldwin-Pitkin

The C&S was accustomed to operating the line from Pitkin through Gunnison to Baldwin as an isolated branch, unconnected with the rest of the South Park system, whenever Alpine Tunnel was closed. However, this was always done on the premise that the closing was temporary, and that the tunnel would be reopened as soon as weather and circumstances permitted, so that equipment could be exchanged and traffic again routed through to Denver on the C&S' own line. Finally, when outright abandonment of Alpine seemed imminent, C&S management also concluded that some escape from the burden of operating the low-traffic and uneconomical Pitkin-Baldwin stretch was necessary. They also perceived that the D&RG was saddled with operating their Blue River branch, from Leadville to Dillon, paralleling the C&S in an area where mining traffic had all but disappeared. Accordingly, in September, 1910, C&S President Darius Miller wrote to D&RG President Edward Jeffery suggesting they each cut their losses by trading their two white elephant branches. Jeffery promptly replied approvingly:

New York, Sept. 23, 1910

Dear Mr. Miller,

Your letter of the 21st inst., came this morning, suggesting a plan for mutual economy in the operations of the Denver & Rio Grande and the Colorado and Southern, whereby the former would operate, from Gunnison, the Colorado & Southern line to Pitkin and to the coal mines in the vicinity of Gunnison, permitting that Company to discontinue running trains west of St. Elmo on that line; and the Colorado & Southern would operate between Leadville and Dillon, using Denver & Rio Grande tracks west of the Divide to Dillon, and the Colorado & Southern tracks east of the Divide to Leadville, the Denver & Rio Grande to discontinue its operations between Leadville and Dillon. I note, also, that by this arrangement the Colorado & Southern would discontinue train service between Como and Breckenridge and serve Breckenridge from Leadville via Dillon.

I am very glad to have suggestions of this kind and to some extent this matter has been on my mind for some years, as I have all along felt there were a number of places in Colorado where operations were so difficult that the service might be combined or exchanged, so as to save us all some money.

Mr. Schlacks, who is with me, leaves tomorrow for the West, and will take with

him to Denver a copy of your letter in order that he may talk the matter over with, and elicit the views of our Second Vice President and General Manager, Mr. Horace W. Clarke, and our General Traffic Manager, Mr. A. S. Hughes, and you will hear further, either from Mr. Schlacks or myself at an early date.

With kind regards and hoping that if from time to time any other suggestions occur to you I may hear from you, I am,

Yours sincerely,
(Signed) E. T. JEFFERY

Representatives of the two roads met on February 4, 1911, in the office of D&RG Second Vice President and General Manager H. W. Clarke to discuss "matters in connection with the operation of tracks in the Gunnison District by the Denver & Rio Grande, and between Leadville and Dillon by the Colorado & Southern." A further meeting on February 13 resolved final details, and the proposed agreement became effective two days later.

Each company was to inventory and pay the other for supplies, tools, materials on hand, or the original owner could remove such items. Each company was to pay the other per diem on cars under load or being unloaded or loaded. The C&S was to be permitted without charge by the D&RG to store its locomotives and passenger cars in the Gunnison C&S roundhouse, and empty C&S cars could be stored free in the yard. The D&RG took over trackage from Quartz to Baldwin; the C&S the entire Blue River Branch. The C&S intention was to let the unneeded rolling stock remain near Gunnison until summer, when "it is possible we may attempt to move the engines and cars over Alpine Pass to get them to Denver, or if this is not feasible, we may move them around through Leadville."

On February 15th C&S Superintendent Bacon met with D&RG Superintendent Ten Eyck to make a joint inspection and inventory of the Gunnison and Quartz line, but with snow one to four feet deep on the route, this had to be given up until some later date. Next day they had the same results in their attempt to inventory the Baldwin line: two to four feet of snow, with some drifts six feet deep.

At first they planned to lock up engines 59 and 65 in the roundhouse, but Denver reversed that decision and ordered the train made up for Leadville. With a pilot crew provided by the D&RG, the last C&S train left Gunnison at 7 A.M. Sunday, February 19, under veteran Conductor Markle and Engineers Colligan and Richardson, with consist, in addition to the two 2-8-0s, of combine, caboose, flanger, tool car, cinder car, two empty flats, a refrigerator and a box loaded with material and supplies, and two empty box cars. The two engines worked hard on the tonnage train, using three additional tanks of water and taking on four tons coal each at Sargent before tackling the Marshall Pass 4% grades. On Monday the 20th, they headed out of Salida, stopping at Buena Vista and Granite tanks and arriving at Leadville at 12:20 P.M. noon, supposedly the last narrow gauge train under steam operated between Salida and Leadville.

The D&RG promptly put on scheduled mixed runs, using the same engine, combination car and crew to run to Pitkin tri-weekly, Monday, Wednesday and Friday, and then on Tuesday, Thursday and Saturday to Baldwin. For awhile a schedule to Kubler mine was shown as well. With very little change, except when coal mines would close down temporarily at Baldwin, this operation continued for over 20 years.

Late in May the joint inspection and inventory of the Baldwin-Quartz line was accomplished, the deep snows having vanished. Much scrap or surplus track material was found, including many of the Fisher bridge rail joints, peculiar to South Park tracks. Superintendent Bacon also was asked about the possibility of bringing this material and the idle C&S cars through Alpine Tunnel and to Denver. On May 27 he reported that "parties who have walked over the Range (report) there is a great deal of snow and from about the center to the east end of the tunnel ice is from 2 to 4 feet deep. It seems to me we should be able to move trains through the Pass along in July or August." Meanwhile he found the Gunnison water tank dry and in danger of collapsing and persuaded the D&RG to pump some water in it to correct its dangerous condition.

The final decision not to open Alpine Tunnel was made on August 21, 1911, when General Superintendent J. D. Welsh and Superintendent William Bacon sat down in the former's office, discussing the problems of the car of scrap at Gunnison and eight other cars still on those lines. Bacon, on July 5th, had reported his inspection of the area: "The haul from Gunnison over our line would be very expensive. On Thursday, June 28th, I inspected Alpine Tunnel and found the ice for a distance of 600 feet to be 8 and 9 feet in depth. I do not believe this will melt away this year. I understand there are a number of rock slides between Alpine Tunnel and Quartz which would cost considerable to remove. I believe it would be cheaper to let the D&RG move our cars and scrap from Gunnison to Leadville." In July the cars went east on a D&RG freight, the empties to "go home" via Leadville, the scrap, after transfer to a standard gauge car at Salida, on to the Pueblo mill.

The D&RG had built a connecting track from their line at Parlin to the C&S line, and ceased to use the C&S line between Parlin and Gunnison. They notified the C&S that effective January 1, 1912, this line was being turned back to the C&S. It was to lay disused for the next 11 years. Operation of the "Pitkin Flyer", as local folk dubbed it, was a losing affair for the D&RG, and the losses got worse as the years went on. Generally a C-16 2-8-0 was the motive power, and in winter a second engine was added with flanger coupled between. By mid-'20s it was a weedy, rotten-tied line, whose trains even in good weather suffered delays slipping on weeds. Western State College at Gunnison had an annual picnic on the branch, using a T-12 4-6-0 for power and a C-16 for helper if needed.

The line faced abandonment in 1926 when a mining firm insisted on having cars spotted at Quartz for loading ore. Nothing had run over the three miles beyond Pitkin for years, and despite protests by both the owning C&S and operating D&RGW, the P.U.C. ordered service. A 300 foot spur was built off the main just before it curved over Quartz Creek.

By 1929 the rail on the Baldwin Branch was so worn that even at slowest speeds with the lightest engines on hand, the C-16 class, it was unsafe. The gross revenues did not pay operating expenses, and the loss per year was $24,000 on the combined Baldwin-Pitkin branches. There was some thought of jointly seeking abandonment of the lines, but it then developed that the Baldwin mine was increasing its output, had spent $38,000 on improvements in 1929 and was expecting to ship 60,000 or more tons a year. About 65% of this production was destined to points in Nebraska and South Dakota.

A 1929 inspection trip on the two lines brought this report: "On the trip from Parlins to Pitkin, the train consisted of one small locomotive, one empty box car, two empty coal cars, and one combination coach. On the return trip the train consisted of engine, two cars loaded with mine props, and one combination coach. This is about the average run of traffic on this branch. Running time average ten miles per hour."

The inspector went on to say the rail was worn 1882 40 lb., needing about 300 ties per mile, and about 40 to 50 rails so badly kinked, etc., they should be replaced as "defective".

Inspecting the Baldwin Branch he reported "Traffic much heavier on this branch. On the up trip, train consisted of one small engine, five empty box cars, four empty coal cars and one combination coach." "On the down trip, train consisted of one engine, nine loads of coal and one combination coach. This is about the average traffic for six months of the year when coal is being moved. After coal season, traffic is as light as on the Pitkin Branch." He described the track as "very rough" and described the 35 and 40# rail in the track as "nothing but scrap." Even at the average speed of 8 miles per hour, it was recommended the rail be replaced if operation was to continue.

In June, 1932, the I.C.C. held hearings on abandonment of the Pitkin line. The decision, in the railroad's favor, was rendered on July 31, 1933, effective in 30 days, or on August 31, 1933. But protestants obtained delays and a rehearing was obtained; nevertheless, on May 8, 1934, the line was again authorized to be abandoned effective 30 days from that date. Work commenced in mid-month by C&S forces, using a motor car and some small equipment found useful earlier on the Clear Creek lines. The final carload of rails and scrap was transferred at Salida to standard gauge on July 31, and it might be noted that among the items were 19 harp switch stands and 1100 Fisher joints, destined to the CF&I at Pueblo for scrap.

The C&S and D&RGW came to an agreement in 1937, and filed with the I.C.C. for their approval, for the C&S to give the Baldwin Branch to the D&RGW, the C&S supplying enough 70 lb. rail (from the recently dismantled old main line to Falcon) to relay the Baldwin line. The C&S would receive all the scrap from the line. Approval came from the I.C.C. on August 13, 1937, and this, coupled with abandonments earlier that year, reduced the South Park mileage to just the 29 miles from Denver to South Platte, the Silica Spur, and the Leadville-Climax line.

In the applications to the I.C.C., figures were quoted showing 1447 carloads shipped from the branch in 1936, of which 1282 were from the Rocky Mountain Fuel Co.'s mines, 67 from the old Richardson mine that pre-dated the DSP&P, and 12 from the Ohio Creek Coal Co., also an old name in coal mining. A few cars of anthracite were included. Balance of freight was cattle and hay. Passenger revenue on the mixed run was trivial toward the last of the tri-weekly schedule, dropping to $8.85 in 1932, $1.05 in 1933 and nothing thereafter.

Rebuilt by 1939, the Baldwin line supplied a great deal of freight to the D&RGW over the years. Its light bridges were the reason the road hung on to two C-16 1882 2-8-0 (Nos. 268 and 278) until the final runs in 1952. Though the material to improve the bridge over the Slate River was on hand for years, it was always cut out of budgets. Last vestige of C&S times was the tank in use until the end at Castleton. In the abandonment of all Gunnison trackage by the D&RGW in 1954, the Baldwin Branch was finally dismantled.

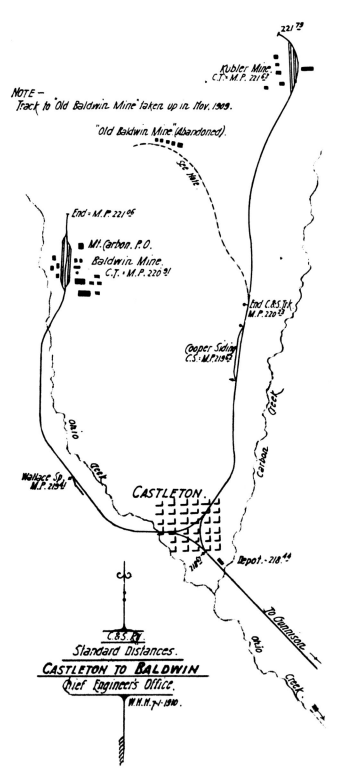

The diagram above shows the trackage at the end of the Baldwin Branch in 1910, shortly after the "Old Baldwin Mine" branch trackage had been abandoned. At right, opposite, DL&G 216 is shown at Old Baldwin about 1890 with a mixed train. Mt. Whetstone is in the distance. This trackage was taken up in November, 1909. (Gary Christopher Collection.)

The Rocky Mountain Fuel Co. had purchased the Baldwin mine in 1907, and up to the time of the 1937 application had shipped over 1,000,000 tons, estimated at over 42,000 carloads. The mine was nearing depletion that year and the owners were preparing to re-open at the closed Kubler Mine site, and had already loaded a few cars by trucks at Cooper Siding, the extent of operable track extending up Carbon Creek from Castleton. Long disused track on to Kubler still lay in place. The mine at Baldwin, called the Alpine mine, was 2½ miles north of Castleton up Ohio Creek, about half of the grade being what remained of the unfinished Ohio Creek Extension of the 1880s.

Confusingly, the name "Baldwin" has been applied to three different railroad points within a few miles of each other. When the DSP&P issued its first passenger timetables reaching to the unfinished Alpine Tunnel, its map of proposed lines north of Gunnison showed only "Richardson" before the dotted line reached Irwin. Sylvester Richardson, founder of Gunnison, had opened a coal mine at Mount Carbon and a townsite was platted. When the DSP&P reached the point known later at "Castleton", M.P. 216.5, at the junc-

tion of Carbon and Ohio Creeks, they gave it the name "Baldwin". Then when track was extended soon to the new large mine up Carbon Creek, 2.8 miles further, that place was named "Baldwin", and Castleton became the depot name at M.P. 216.5. The former Richardson Mine became known as the Alpine Mine with new owners in 1895, and was designated as the terminus of the "Mt. Carbon Branch" which extended 2.5 miles to "Mt. Carbon" (ex-Richardson, ex-Alpine). About half way up this distance, sharp eyes can still find the slight traces of the site of the switch with the never-finished main line toward Ohio Pass.

The Old Baldwin mine having closed down, track to it was removed on the Carbon Creek line in 1909, and in 1910 the timetable designated the main line "Como to Mt. Carbon". That was in January. By June, a further name change had been accomplished and it was now "Como and Baldwin", Mt. Carbon having been renamed Baldwin! In another year, the Kubler Branch was added to the timetable, that mine having become a shipper. Kubler was 3.2 miles beyond Castleton, a mile and a half past the first ("Old") Baldwin mine.

Buena Vista-St. Elmo

Scattered mine traffic originated on the Alpine Tunnel line from Hancock and St. Elmo and the Chalk Creek Canyon District, and this traffic had to be handled out through Buena Vista with a stub run during periods when through service was suspended.

One example of the manner of this operation when the tunnel was closed temporarily, which was rather frequently in winter months, is seen by the report of one run on March 16, 1901. With engines 65 and 71 on the head end, a flanger, 8 empty coal cars, a merchandise car and combine, they left Buena Vista for a round trip to Romley, having come from Como that morning and due to return that day. They ate at Schwanders about 1 P.M. and the crew members discussed possible ice problems, remembering their troubles with 8 to 16 inches of ice at two places east of Fisher, and another bad spot above St. Elmo. The conductor, described as in a bad mood, suffering from a bad cold, ended the discussion by telling the brakeman to "shut up" and the brakie did, saying later at an investigation "I thought he was crazy." At Mt. Princeton they wyed the 71 and it backed up behind the coach. 65 had gone ahead light to Mt. Princeton, 71 bringing the train. The conductor at one point argued with the helper engineer, saying he was not doing his part and might as well cut him off, as the conductor had gone on top of the train watching couplings and felt the helper was really only pushing the rear car and two freight cars ahead.

At St. Elmo the conductor got on the lead engine and examined the sand dome, arguing with that engineer about not using sand when he should. Engineer Stancliff ordered him off the engine and made as if to throw him off; then, the argument getting hotter, he threw a coal pick at the conductor, missing him, at which point the conductor drew a revolver and fired from the ground at the engineer standing in gangway, who fell back in the tender. It turned out he was not hit, had just fallen out of the way. The conductor went back to the combine, the rest of the crew did the work, but on the way back, the lead engineer at Schwanders got off his engine and went back to take the gun away, beating up the conductor in the attempt. The helper engineer pulled him off, went back to the combine and finally got the gun, by promising to return it on arrival at Como. The trip was completed without any more difficulty among the crew, and the gun was handed over at Como.

By 1910 the C&S had changed the through runs from Como to Gunnison to make Buena Vista an intermediate terminal, trains operating between Buena Vista and Como, and Buena Vista and Gunnison. After the tunnel was closed in October, 1910, a tri-weekly train was scheduled to make runs from Buena Vista up the Chalk Creek valley to St. Elmo, Romley and Hancock, as there was still considerable traffic from the mines of that region. Westward they still bore the old designation Train No. 94, eastward Train No. 93. This became an isolated operation, not connected with the balance of the C&S system, as further washouts in Trout Creek Canyon ended train service between Macune and Garos.

One crew worked out of Buena Vista making a round trip on Monday, Wednesday and Saturday. On alternate days they worked on their equipment, in the case of the engine crew drawing regular pay for this. As the D&RG had a third rail in their main line Salida to Leadville, cars reached smelters and the balance of the C&S via mixed gauge runs on the D&RG, the bulk of traffic being to the Leadville smelter. When in need of another engine or cars, the Leadville connection made it easy for the branch to obtain what was needed.

Records show the tri-weekly train handling one to three loads of freight outbound, usually box cars of concentrates, less frequently gondolas of ore which generally came from St. Elmo. A small amount of l.c.l. was handled in the combination baggage-coach. Occasionally a refrigerator car came in loaded, which may have been necessary for perishables transferred from the D&RG local freight, or even that popular carload traffic to the mountain communities: beer. Coal was the most important inbound freight. The single engine would handle the train as far as it could, then would double the rest of the way to St. Elmo and Romley. Hancock was useful only for its wye and tank, and the single engine had to fight snow to get there.

The branch was not a profitable operation. Mileage was reduced in 1915 by ending runs at Romley, saving the 2½ miles to Hancock with its snow and other maintenance problems. The turntable at Gunnison was taken up in July and hauled around via D&RG, then installed at Romley and was ready for use on August 18. The cheapest installation was settled upon, installed at the edge of the grade, rather than try to dig into the rocky slopes. This almost guaranteed the sort of accident that occurred on February 21, 1920.

The crew had spotted engine 67 on the turntable

152

After both Alpine and Trout Creek were vacated, the Buena Vista-St. Elmo line became an isolated, impoverished, down-at-the-heels branch line almost devoid of traffic or population to serve. The photo at left shows the St. Elmo mixed creeping along the rickety track in the upper Chalk Creek Canyon, a solitary box car and combine trailing along after 2-8-0 No. 62 (Frank J. Duca Collection). Below, St. Elmo in the thirties was a nostalgic example of a barely inhabited Colorado ghost town, so "off the beaten track" that it was rarely visited by outsiders (Lad G. Arend photo).

and had it about one-quarter turned when the turntable stuck, as the engine had tilted to the rear. The engineer, to obtain better balance, moved the engine forward slightly and when the turntable tipped forward quickly, he reversed the engine and applied emergency air brakes, but it continued forward, knocking out timbers in the turntable wall and headed down the mountainside about 30 feet below the turntable and turned over on the left side in about 7 feet of snow. The tender went 30 feet further. There was considerable damage to the engine, but the engineer escaped unharmed.

With the engine now about 125 feet from the main track and the tank about 160 feet, Superintendent E. B. Mitchell figured it would take a 300 foot shoofly temporary track cut into the mountainside to reach the engine and tender and pick them up and re-rail. As it would "be difficult and expensive" to recover the engine at that time account the deep snow, he recommended deferring the chore until spring when the snow would be gone. So No. 67 waited for spring.

Cloudbursts were a problem along this branch. On September 9, 1919, the 67 ran into a washout three feet deep and 30 feet long about three-quarters of a mile east of Nathrop. The engine had "three pair drivers off track and tank entirely derailed and partly turned over . . ." The engine was rerailed the 12th with an engine from Leadville but other washouts kept the line out of operation another week. There was a 600 foot washin at Schwanders 2 to 4 feet deep (a continuing problem from Trout Creek), another washin 800 feet long near Nathrop, and a slide from the Chalk Cliffs covered 750 feet of track with material up to 7 feet deep.

In 1914 C&S revised its system maps on employee timetables eliminating the line between Garos and Macune and all road beyond Hancock. In January, 1916, the map further eliminated Hancock, yet the last South Park timetable (1922) continued to list all this long idle or abandoned mileage.

The 29.19 mile Buena Vista-Romley line was no money maker. The mining districts continued their decline, especially after 1916. In that year 16,420 tons of freight were hauled, of which 6,680 tons were coal and 7,914 tons were ore. By 1923, in the post World War I mining slump, this had dropped to 1,186 tons of which 46 tons were coal and 918 tons of ore, for a gross revenue of $2033.40. Fifty-five carloads had been hauled in the entire year, ranging from but two to eight cars per month! The road filed to abandon the line in 1924, citing revenues in the first six months of only $877.24.

Passenger revenue for 1916 was for 3711 "local"

passengers grossing $4009.18. There were no interchanged passengers. This dropped to 430 passengers in 1923 and 124 for the first half of 1924. In the last several years most trains had but one or two passengers, and often none at all. Six times in as many years were there as many as 10 passengers. The trains of August 8 had record loads, some unexplained special movement, 13 on the outbound trip, 23 on return trip. Only once does there seem to have been a need for something other than a combine, a coach being sent from Leadville for some brief use in 1915. In May 1917, combine 21, which had served all these years, was traded off for No. 22, which lasted through the final run.

On October 3, 1924, the operation of the branch was discontinued, and abandoned as of October 11th. Track was not taken up until 1926, the work being completed on November 15. Engine 62 and cars were moved to Leadville. Included were two outfit cars, flanger 016 and combine 22. These along with 98 old gondolas on the C&S lines were sold to the A. T. Herr Supply Co., a dealer in machinery, who did some business with logging lines. Herr sold gondola 4089 at Leadville and a load of trucks from other scrapped gondolas to the New Mexico Lumber Mfg. Co. at Dolores on the Rio Grande Southern R.R. There was some urgency early in 1925 to ship this car before the D&RG started taking up the third rail between Leadville and Salida, the car departing February 10 as the final interchange of C&S narrow gauge with the D&RGW. Unable to find a buyer for the combine, flanger and outfits, Herr had these burned in July, 1928, for their scrap.

Snow Fighting

On January 4, 1890, the Gunnison *Review-Press* reported enthusiastically "the new rotary snow plow of the DL&G is said to be an annihilator of snow banks, is working like a charm and keeping Alpine Pass open." Not two weeks later under date of February 1 the same paper reported "Alpine Pass is closed. Six engines are stalled and dead near Alpine Tunnel." On February 2 the report was made that "8 engines came to Gunnison and were sent out over the Rio Grande on Sunday, February 2." That same month the General Superintendent of the Colorado Division (UP) had reported to his Omaha superiors that when he freed the six engines snowbound near the Tunnel, the line would be closed for the winter. The same paper on April 19 reported the coming snow trials from Hancock as: "Two rotary snow annihilators have been sent up to Alpine Tunnel to reopen the South Park. Approaches are hidden by snow, tunnel is full of ice."

It cost $368.70 freight to bring the first rotary from the builder at Paterson, N. J. to the UP at Omaha. It cost over $1100 freight charges to the Museum to bring the last rotary from Leadville via the D&RGW to Pueblo. The DSP&P paid $15,000 for "Rotary Steam Snow Shovel #064" built by the "Rotary Steam Snow Shovel Co." (better known as Leslie Bros. Mfg. Co. of Paterson, N. J.) The machine was built for them by the Cooke Locomotive & Machine Co. of that city. The plow was acquired in March, 1889, and lettered for DSP&P RR. The snow plow trials on the east approach to Alpine Tunnel from Hancock in April, 1890, received national publicity as they were a test of the Leslie type rotary and the Jull Centrifugal Snow Excavator. The Tunnel line had been closed since early in the year when (with some difficulty) six stalled engines were extricated. The Jull machine was somewhat like a giant auger, and demonstrated a tendency to derail. In fairness, it was a standard gauge machine, there were bad ice conditions, and operators of the rotary 064 had much experience on the South Park. Nevertheless, the Jull was purchased (DL&G 066), but was sent to Trinidad where it was used to fight the bad drifting problems on the lines south to Texas. It survived until the late 1920s. Only 11 of the Jull plows were built, of which this one was his second. None were built after 1892.

The single rotary was generally based at Como, from which point it could attack the worst snow problems, principally over Boreas Pass and on to Leadville. Occasional trips to open badly drifted lines in the open South Park itself were necessary. And Alpine Tunnel required annual attention apparently, but often that line was just left closed for weeks or months. At first the C&S gave it number 01, then in the 1907 renumbering it became 011, and again in the 1912 renumbering it gained its final number 99200. It was stored in the wooden portion of the Como roundhouse in 1935 when a fire destroyed that part of the roundhouse. Rebuilt, it was standard gauged in 1943 when the Climax Branch was changed, and ended its career in 1951 when the main shaft broke while in use. When the machine was backed up at a slide area, the huge wheel stayed in place on the track, a wrecking task that tied up the line a while.

The "new" rotary snow plow of the DL&G was to become the "old" snow plow before long, as on October 21, 1899, a new one was ordered, hopefully to be delivered by "middle of December." On August 15 that year General Superintendent T. F. Dunaway had written C&S President Frank Trumbull:

I would respectfully recommend the purchase of another Rotary Snow Plow, at an estimated cost of $17,500, for use on the South Park line.

Our equipment on this line at present, consists of one Rotary Snow plow which, during the season from November 25th to May 1st, is in use almost daily between Como and Leadville — leaving the line between Como and Gunnison unprotected, and it is impossible to keep it open without a Rotary Snow Plow.

If it is decided to purchase an additional Rotary, the order should be placed at an early date, as the Locomotive Works where these are built, are crowded with orders.

The accepted order called for a machine with wheels set to standard gauge, with "wheel fit extra long to allow of wheels being set to 3′0″ gauge." Price $16,500 F.O.B. Paterson, N. J. John S. Cooke, Vice-President of The Rotary Snow Plow Co. handled the contract. President Trumbull wrote Dunaway to "get earlier delivery if possible, bearing in mind size of Alpine Tunnel, two hundred feet east end." Dunaway was in New York City at the time. It was decided the Plow could be 4 inches wider across the center of the hood than the earlier machine. By late November an argument via mail and telegrams ensued. Winter was becoming worse, Colorado railroads were having great difficulty operating, and Mr. Cooke was pleading delays in obtaining material and was "hoping" to get it shipped the first week of January, but was uncertain. Dunaway wired on November 29 "the storms are commencing in the mountains, which reminds us we will need this machine as soon as we can get it." By December 11th Dunaway was becoming very anxious and wrote Cooke asking if he could depend on shipment between 1st and 10th of January. Cooke reassured him on the 16th, that it would be first machine shipped from their shop after first of year and "have offered our foreman special inducements to get the work out on time."

On the 19th Dunaway wrote again, using a little extra pressure by stating "we will be in the market for a large number of engines in the near future and expect, of course, to ask you to bid on them." Dunaway also instructed on the lettering and number "No. 3". Meantime President Trumbull had become very concerned as Dunaway had written him in New York on December 10:

Considerable snow on Gunnison District this A.M. but has stopped snowing, now cold clear, and windy. N.G. engines have been doing *poorly* for past 10 days. All seemed to let down at once. We have been unable to account for it. Forster is at Como giving personal attention and we have turned the force all to N.G. work until get them straightened out. Got out 5 engines last night and all seem to be doing better this A.M. Hope to get cleaned up today and tomorrow. BG engines doing well.

Again on December 15, Dunaway wired Trumbull: "South Park engines doing better but heavy snow over entire line. Weather clearing up this afternoon." Things got worse, and on the 28th Trumbull wired the manufacturers: "We need the rotary every minute." Their answer: "Our understanding was that if possible would ship rotary first week in January. Are straining every nerve to hasten completion but cannot consent to modify written agreement." That same day Trumbull gave the ultimatum: "If rotary is not shipped by January tenth you may cancel order. We consider your word as good as your bond and expect you to carry out your promises whether written or verbal." John Cooke replied in two pages citing they had promised to deliver the machine in January. The rotary was shipped from Paterson on January 26, rolling on its own wheels. C&S officials kept after the routing as it was feared it might take 20 days to reach Colorado and it came via Erie R.R. to Chicago, then by CRI&P. With boiler full of water, it weighed 143,650 lbs., without tender.

It was used only a few days on the narrow gauge, then brought back to Denver and standard gauged. In October, 1901, after laying idle ever since its brief South Park use, it was offered for sale, but no sale was consummated. Considered too heavy for the South Park line, at least in earlier years, it was generally stationed at Cheyenne for use on the northern standard gauge lines. The 59th Rotary built, it was at first numbered 3, then 03, becoming 0270 in 1907 and, finally, 99201 in 1912. It was used in the 1930s on the South Park when snow troubles were severe; by that time all the old iron rails had been replaced and management felt more confident about letting it venture out onto the narrow gauge.

The C&S' second rotary seems to have been traded back and forth as to gauge, as needed, but being a larger machine spent most of its life stationed at Cheyenne, to tackle the occasional conditions up on that end of the C&S where engine plows were unable to open lines. It was used on the Boreas Pass line in 1936, and then went back to standard gauge. Extensively rebuilt with a boiler from a scrapped standard gauge engine in 1949, it was sent to Leadville and used on the last remnant of the South Park main occasionally, sometimes nearly five years between need. In 1972 it was deemed no longer needed. Widening of cuts, efficient use of bulldozers and the effectiveness of diesels equipped with pilot plows made it not

worth the cost to maintain. Donated to the Colorado Railroad Museum, at the instance of President John W. Terrill of the C&S, it was hauled on the rear of a D&RGW ballast train out of Leadville, and behind a C&S freight out of Pueblo. For the first time since 1889 there were no rotaries on standard gauge railroads in Colorado. Two narrow gauge rotaries remain on the states-owned Cumbres & Toltec Scenic Ry. at Antonito, Colo. and Chama, N. M.

The South Park during a couple of its worst tie-ups in the Alpine Tunnel area borrowed D&RG machines to help out. Prior to the rotaries they protected the worst places on the line with extensive snowsheds, a practice with all the Colorado roads. The sheds, however, were very vulnerable to fires, and many of them were destroyed. The sheds were expensive to maintain, and when the rotary came on the scene in 1889, sheds had to be torn down or rebuilt in some places for clearance. Sheds also sometimes formed snow blockades, when freakish winds would fill them with drifts, and nothing except hand shoveling would open them. The long snowshed of the Alpine Tunnel area, extending from the tunnel almost continuously to alongside the stone engine house, vanished after the rotary arrived.

In March, 1887, the DSP&P received two new flanger cars, one with 26″ wheels, the other with 30″ wheels, costing $856.90 and $893.02 each. With rebuildings such cars lasted until the end of the narrow gauge. For all the mileage involved, a meager three or four flangers sufficed.

After the closure of Alpine and during the two year closing of operations over Boreas, November, 1910-January, 1913, the narrow gauge rotary was stored; then in August, 1913, it was changed — at least on the records — to standard gauge. From then on and through the year 1916 the total of snowplows stands at "three standard gauge", none for narrow gauge. Apparently when the rotary was needed in that period on the South Park, it was temporarily put on narrow gauge trucks.

Generally for opening the lines, the engines were equipped with the Priest Flanger, a patented device whose rights were sold on a royalty basis by Quincy, Manchester, Sargent Co. The royalty was $50 per standard gauge engine and $25 for a narrow gauge engine. In 1909, for instance, two passenger engines and 7 freight engines were so equipped, and rotary 011. Three standard gauge engines were also equipped, the total of 13 costing C&S $400. The licensing firm had to check now and then on this, as due to shoppings, flangers were changed from one engine to another and generally it was confused in the records. Worse, from the Master Mechanic's viewpoint, one would be removed and left laying around, not in use.

In the winter of 1908 the Kubler mine on the Baldwin Branch was going to stay open, so needing a flanger for the engine usually on that branch, No. 59, they removed the flanger from the rotary and put it on No. 59. Next winter they decided to have 2 flangers back on the rotary, reversing the plans of a year ago, the winter of 1908-1909 having demonstrated a Priest flanger was a good idea on the rotary. It might be noted that for the winter of 1909-1910, 2-8-0s No. 38 and No. 52, normally assigned as road engines on Trains 81-82 Como-Leadville, were Priest equipped. Best laid plans for record keeping went astray on railroads and sure enough in January, 1910, the Division Master Mechanic, J. C. Lord, found to his embarrassment he had 11 flangers on engines and rotary. Moguls 4 and 6 were so equipped; 38 and 52 for Leadville District, while Gunnison District had 59, 63, 64, 67, 71 and 73. The Superintendent of Motive Power asked "I do not see how it could be applied to 011 and at same time to engine 59 . . ." Mr. Lord admitted making another, and the patent holders got another $25 late payment! Moreover they pressed him into making proper requisition for the cost and finally he came through with a requisition on March 21, 1910, for a conversion done in September, 1909. It took: One second-hand flanger cylinder 8″ x 12″, 2 flanger saddles, steel, new 180 lbs.; 1 tumbling shaft 7′ x 2″ x 2″ wrought iron 95 lbs.; 2 steel guides, new 40 lbs.; 1 flanger crossbar and knives, wrought iron, 240 lbs.; 2 shaft brackets wrought iron ½″ x 3″ 30 lbs. Cost of applying, $35. Total cost was $96.03, labor and material, after figuring in some pipe fittings, and pipe overlooked earlier.

The use of the Priest flanger was gradually increased. Prior to December, 1902, the C&S had only two, both on narrow gauge engines. That month they put one on a broad gauge engine, then in March, 1903, on four more narrow gauge. Gradually it was increased to ten narrow gauge in all.

In the view below, C&S mogul No. 10 has paused with a passenger train at Halfway, on Boreas Pass, in 1901. The snow and ice-encrusted locomotive and cars and the bleak, wintry landscape give visual evidence of the rigors of narrow gauge railroading in that time (Museum Collection).

The winter of 1899 was one of the severest on record, and the South Park's rotary was kept busy in the early months of the year trying to keep Boreas and Fremont Passes open. Above and below, five engines push the rotary along as it chews its way through the accumulated drifts. As was usual practice, the last engine faces backwards to facilitate dragging the whole outfit back out whenever the rotary got stuck, as the track sometimes partially filled in with snow after the rotary had passed over it. Page opposite, the rotary slowly works its way through a rocky cut, descending the west side of Boreas Pass. (Views this page, Mrs. C. J. Pharnes from R. B. Jackson; opposite, R. H. Kindig Coll.)

The Colorado & Southern had developed snow fighting to a fine art by the 1930's, when Tommy St. John and Pat Colligan posed before leaving Leadville one winter morning with the Denver passenger. No. 9 fitted with pilot plow leads the consist, followed by a flanger, No. 537, and the train — a typical make-up for dealing with "routine" snow. At times the snow was something more than "routine" — as at left along the Tenmile in early February, 1936, and below near Robinson in 1915 — when the train had to be dug out. (Upper two, Lad Arend Coll.; lower, Public Service Photos from John Maxwell.)

The winter of 1936 witnessed continuing and heavy snowfalls, requiring repeated use of the rotary to keep the line open. On this page, three C&S 2-8-0s help the rotary open the line between Leadville, Climax and Dickey on April 9, 1936. The view above is near French Gulch Tank, some 9 miles from Leadville, while below the outfit is just west of Robinson. (Both, Museum Coll.)

Passengers on the
Leadville train in
1936 were treated
to some spectacu-
lar sights. On
February 26, four
engines and the
rotary combined
to lift the east-
bound train up
Boreas; above,
they are pulling
over the top of
Boreas, while be-
low they are
climbing near
Baker Tank.
(Both, Lad Arend
Coll.)

Four engines and the rotary fill the sky with smoke, steam and snow in the 1936 view above. The rear engine is D&RGW No. 345, as it was also on the train opposite. Below, five engines and a combine follow the rotary up the Blue River through Breckenridge on March 29, 1936. (Both, Lad Arend Coll.)

The upper view is typical of many South Park "wrecks" — the Leadville switcher got in trouble around 1900, and is in the process of being jacked up while an assemblage of school boys watches (A. M. Payne Coll.). Below is the aftermath of a South Park wreck — No. 72 was running light on Boreas in 1905, hit a rock at Peabody, and suffered considerable damage (W. V. Murdock photo, G.E.L. Coll.).

Wrecks

No treatment of the South Park line's history would be complete without some coverage of wrecks on the line, replete with breath-catching photos. And there are certainly a great proliferation of photographs available. This is probably largely due to the fact that a wreck provided excitement and diversion from the hum-drum, and thus was a popular subject for picture-taking, rather than a testimony to the South Park's accident rate. For the passenger, in fact, the South Park was a remarkably safe line to ride; passenger fatalities (or even serious injuries) during its sixty-odd years of operation were few. There were no instances of speeding passenger expresses roaring into each other head-on, with hundreds of deaths resulting — South Park trains moved too slowly, and generally moved station to station unopposed by any other passenger trains of opposite direction. Nor did any heavily-laden South Park passenger trains plunge through bridges burnt-out, flood-destroyed or weakened by rot — the South Park took care of its bridges and trestles.

There were, of course, wrecks, and they fell into various categories — the most harrowing being runaways on the long, steep 4% grades. Freight trains were generally controllable on grades if carefully handled, but if allowed to get rolling a few miles an hour too fast they were then often difficult to slow down again. In winter, ice and snow would add another hazard, freezing in the tracks and causing derailments. The South Park's track was not always in the best repair anyway, and not infrequently trains would derail as they were plodding along level track. Sometimes a locomotive, tender or car would end up askew on the grade as the train quickly lurched to a halt; sometimes a ragged pile of several locomotives and cars would result if the train's speed was too great. Usually, when one of these disasters would materialize, the crew would unload as quickly as possible, but sometimes a good engineman or brakeman would not be able to "step off" in time and would then become another South Park fatality.

Crews, despite rules, sometimes picked up bad habits. On July 11, 1905, Engine 45, the rear helper of a westbound, extra stopped and was cut off at Park Siding to unload some freight from the caboose behind it. The head end of the train went on, as the engineer thought, to Buffalo. Soon the 45 started for Buffalo too, but when he came around a curve he found the head end stopped at the tank, a half mile closer! The rear gondola was caved in and one pair of trucks knocked out from under it in the ensuing crash, but the 45 hit so hard that the smoke box of the engine was also caved in, pilot and pilot beam broken off, and headlight knocked off and smashed. Rules required crews to couple up and proceed, not to break a train up like this. Everyone got 10 to 40 days suspension for this affair.

The Leavick branch had a tri-weekly scheduled run in the early years, shown as a timetable train only from Hilltop Jct. on the Alma Branch. There was a wye at the junction and another at Mudsill, at foot of the steepest portion of the branch and less than a mile from the end. The top of this grade was marked by a large tree stump, which served unofficially as a mark to crews struggling up to Leavick that they had topped the steepest part. On June 8, 1913, this grade of 6% was too much for Extra 70, which ran away out of control. They had doubled into Leavick, on the first trip the 70 pushing up four empty gondolas. They then wyed the engine at Mudsill, and backed up, a car of powder ahead, caboose 1007 next to the engine. Leaving the powder car on the main they then coupled eight loaded ore behind the caboose and just before they got to the famous stump, on a grade of about 5½%, they stopped to adjust some brake trouble on a car. Apparently all being well, they started down with all hand brakes set, just as it began to rain. The conductor was tending the caboose and also brakes on the first two gondolas, while the brakeman had the next two which had brake staffs together. The engineer kept making applications of air but it seemed to do no good, so with engine in reverse as they approached a sharp curve just before Mudsill both enginemen got out on the running boards ahead of the cab. When asked why they did this, the fireman replied "So I could jump clear if we turned over." Hitting the curve the engineer was thrown off and one brakeman just before jumping off himself said as he passed him he saw him "on ground when I went by him, blood all over his face." The conductor got off as they passed the east switch. Meanwhile the fireman was the only person on the train and when asked "Why did you return to the cab?" replied, "after we passed that one bad spot, I was not scared." He got the engine under control on a "kind of a level place," then went back to help the engineer who was not badly hurt. The investigation found no one at fault, but decided the engine crew could stand some further instruction on steep grades, principally perhaps to take it a little slower in starting such a train.

One of the South Park's Baldwin 2-8-0's came to grief in a curving cut somewhere on the line (probably on Boreas Pass) back about 1890. The way in which the locomotive is jammed sideways in the cut, above, indicates it must have been a high-speed runaway. Below, all of the other debris has been cleared away and now engines 208 (foreground) and 196 (rear) combine with cables and pulleys and a "dead man" to right the derelict. (Both, Denver Public Library, Western Hist. Collection.)

One day in 1895 DL&G 115 (later C&S 10) was pulling the eastbound mixed on the Leavick Branch when the whole outfit derailed and turned over onto the side of the embankment, just below Mudsill. Above, a relief train has come up from Hilltop Junction, while below the wrecking crew has brought out its jacks and paraphernalia preparatory to putting the 115 back on its feet. (Both, Lad Arend Coll.)

A double header was dropping down the west side of Boreas Pass one February morning in 1901 when they hit a patch of ice over the tracks at Washington Spur, about 4 miles from Breckenridge. No. 70 and the flanger went one way (above), the 60 (below) went the other. (Both, A. M. Payne Collection.)

One of the last wrecks on the South Park occurred on July 25, 1936, when rented D&RGW 2-8-0 No. 346 ran away on Kenosha Pass. The engine left the rails about one mile below the top of the pass, burying itself in the turf and carrying engineer McGowan to his death. (Right, J. W. McCoy Coll.) Immediately brought in to the C&S shops at Denver, it was loaded onto a standard gauge flat by the 30th (below, Museum Coll.) and ferried over to the Burlington shops for rebuilding. "Before and after" photos appear subsequently in the locomotive roster section later in this book. The locomotive's present appearance at the Colorado Railroad Museum still shows evidences of the Burlington's handiwork.

No. 35, shown in the builder's photo above (Lad Arend Coll.), was typical of the large number of "cold water Brooks" 2-6-0's purchased. Poor steamers and light, they were disposed of early. A few 2-8-6T's were obtained (below, Museum Coll.) before the Mason Bogie concept was abandoned. Ultimately successful power was typified by DSP&P 112, one of the 1884 Cooke moguls, shown here with experimental extended smokebox (Denver public Library Western Hist. Coll.).

Locomotives

The three new Baldwin 2-8-0s ordered by the Gulf Road in 1896 were urgently needed. Superintendent of Motive Power M. F. Egan summed up the situation in October: "The Colorado Central had but six engines, all Moguls, four of them Brooks, two were Cooke." The Cooke engines were used on the Denver — Silver Plume passenger and considered "good" engines. The Brooks Moguls were too light for economical passenger or freight service, "have such small fireboxes they cannot make steam readily enough for use, and their cost for repairs, supplies and wages of crew is almost the same as for engines that are able to haul twice their tonnage." They were then renting and using daily five DL&G engines, two Moguls and three Consolidations, using only one of their own Brooks Moguls (on the Central City Branch). He urged management to purchase two Moguls for passenger service weighing not less than 64,000 lbs. each and four Consolidations of not less than 77,000 lbs. each. He also recommended early retirement of the Brooks engines.

The order for three consolidations was placed with Baldwin on November 10, 1896, for delivery in December, and the engines arrived at Jersey (the shops leased from the UP) on January 10, 1897. The extreme dimensions were the maximum for clearance on the line: 8 feet for the cab, 6'10" at the cylinders, from rail to top of stack 13'11". The photograph of this class of locomotive supplied by Baldwin was of Interoceanic Railroad No. 48, the Mexican narrow gauge. These engines were fitted with three pocket drawhead for coupling to both broad and narrow gauge.

And though for the next 35 years operating and mechanical people were to frequently raise hopes for more new narrow gauge engines, these were the last to be obtained for the lines. Meanwhile they did the best they could. Commencing in the summer of 1900, the shops turned out rebuilt Moguls and by July, 1902, seven of them, Nos. 4 through 10, had received new boilers of 54" replacing the 50", and the boiler pressure raised from 150 to 190 lbs. They also received new cylinders, with slightly different dimensions of 15x18. The drivers were now evenly spaced, 5' on centers, where before the space betwen first two was 5' and the last two 4'6". In the rebuilding the engines' weight on drivers was raised from 54,000 lbs. to 64,000. Where tractive effort before had been 11,200 pounds, it now was over 16,000 lbs. This meant that though these Moguls had been rated

previously at 80 tons up Kenosha they now could handle 125 tons, which made them very good passenger engines and accounts for their good performance until the end.

Engines 37 to 56, the 1884 Cooke 2-8-0 series, became the freight workhorses, although they actually had somewhat less tractive effort than the Moguls, at 13,600 lbs. With their 145 lb. boiler pressure unchanged, they rated only 110 tons west up Kenosha. It can be seen why, after a serious decline in operations commencing in 1910, they gradually vanished from the roster, all gone by 1921. And until 1921 the remaining three classes of 2-8-0 were the most powerful of the roster: 57-62, 63-70, 71-73.

Gradually new I.C.C. regulations forced the C&S to rebuild some engines. When the new methods of figuring the factor of safety were computed, it was discovered some of the not yet rebuilt engines would have to be reduced to but 125 pounds pressure. The Master Mechanic said that if this was enforced, the engines would be useless, virtually unable to propel anything but themselves at that low pressure.

Automatic couplers came in the 1903-04 period, along with automatic air brakes. In 1905 hearings were held on requiring driver brakes on engines. It seems that on both the D&RG and South Park these had been removed, even though engines had them when they came from the builders.

It was also C&S practice to have flanges on all drivers, though on many roads such as the D&RG it was customary for a large portion of engines, especially the 2-8-0 types, to have two blind drivers.

In preparation for formation of the C&S, a general renumbering of engines was planned. Narrow gauge were to be given the lowest numbers. The numbering would start with the smallest engine and work up to the heaviest, combining the roster of the UPD&G and DL&G. For those who study rosters, this meant the fourth time many of the engines were numbered, for in addition to their original numbers, many of the engines had been renumbered in an 1885 UP system renumbering, then both the DL&G and the UPD&G had done renumbering, the latter only two years before the C&S was formed.

At the same time they were preparing for the new company in 1898, business went on as usual, disposing by sale or dismantling of unwanted or worn out rolling stock. One of the last financial acts of the DL&G, on its final day of existence, January 11, 1899, was to voucher to the C&S $4,750 for three locomotives sold just before the C&S took over. No. 193 had gone to Alabama, 61 to the Little Book Cliff R.R., while No. 60 went to the

Burns-Biggs Lumber Company at Chama, N. M., and became New Mexico Lumber Co. No. 1 when received in September, 1898. The Brooks engines were not popular, and continued to be disposed of by the C&S, except for the two rebuilt in the 1890s by the DL&G, Nos. 21 and 22.

In the older rolling stock was another Brooks Mogul, UPD&G No. 4, which had been built for the Colorado Central in 1881 as No. 12, becoming No. 154 in the 1885 renumbering. Nos. 154 and 153 had been smashed in a staged head-on collision on September 30, 1896, anticipating that the directors of the UPD&G were going to authorize purchase of some more engines. They didn't; so both were fixed up and put back into service. The 154, now renumbered 4, might have become a C&S engine, but in the closing weeks of the UPD&G's existence was sold to Chicago equipment dealer F. M. Hicks for the Amos Kent Lumber & Brick Co. of Kent's Mills, La. Relettered "Amos Kent No. 2" the engine and tender were loaded onto two standard gauge cars, delivered to the B&M transfer track on December 10, 1898, just nine days before the C&S was formed. Hicks paid $1600 for the engine, which was a fairly substantial price for such an engine at that time, indicating that it must have been very thoroughly rebuilt after its planned wreck. No conclusive evidence has turned up concerning its career in Louisiana and no photos taken after the staged wreck. Even less is known about the 153 (UPD&G 2); it simply disappeared before 1899.

Though the C&S prepared to renumber and use all the engines on hand when it came into being, there is some question if some of the engines ever were put in use by the C&S. Sometimes in describing engines as "scrapped" they meant set aside in some place and designated as scrap, though the physical hulk remained for years. In October, 1900, F. M. Hicks, the Chicago dealer, purchased C&S Mogul #18 and Consolidation #33, two engines that according to the General Superintendent had been in the scrap category since 1892! Hicks paid $600 for the #18, $1350 for the 2-8-0. He also agreed to take engine #35 at the same price. For this price the C&S agreed to supply all missing parts but to do no work on the engines, just load them. Apparently engine #35 had never been re-lettered to C&S for it still bore the number 196, its DL&G number, and in the Bill of Lading, etc., is referred to by that number, confirming that the C&S had never renumbered it as planned.

They tried to sell the derelict #17 for $600 too, but the buyer who seemed interested, an Omaha manufacturer's agent, apparently never closed the deal and the engine was eventually scrapped. All of these were original South Park engines.

The records of the engines during the first years of the C&S are not complete. Due to a fire destroying the Mechanical Engineer's office in 1905, original drawings, blueprints and other records were lost. Then in 1921, after the release from U.S.R.A. control, management found that in the Denver yard area there were over 30 box car bodies used by the various departments to store old records and files. More space was needed: more box cars! The auditor authorized the destruction of the bulk of "useless" old records and called on the department heads to see which could get rid of the most pounds to the paper shredding mill. The mechanical department didn't win the contest, but they did turn in over 13,000 lbs. of old records, and certainly among that 6½ tons of dusty, sooty paper were the bulk of the historical record items — and trivia — on C&S and predecessor roads' engines and cars.

After the third rail was added between Denver and Boulder in 1905, so that through train service to the "Switzerland Trail" could be operated, there was a great deal of narrow gauge summer excursion business. The C&S would rent engines for $8.00 per day, this including the portion of the trip over C&S trackage; but if engines were running light an additional 5 cents per mile was charged. Crew's wages were additional. No doubt the largest movement was for the Grocers' Picnic on Thursday, August 20, 1908. 12 C&S engines were rented. Two of them, Nos. 51 and 66, ran light to and from Boulder; ten other engines ran as doubleheaders, departing from Denver with five specials for Glacier Lake between 6:25 A.M. and 9 A.M. The engines used were Nos. 48 and 70, 37 and 71, 40 and 72, 54 and 45, 39 and 42. The trains required from one hour and 36 minutes to 2 hours each for the one way trip to Boulder, 29.5 miles. Superintendent S. S. Morris of the Northern Division protested when his people were criticized for the delays and slow time made: "It is a mistake on our part to handle a crowd like this with narrow gauge power from here to Boulder. Had we put broad gauge power on these trains we could have run them over there in about an hour with safety."

In addition to such special service, there was a narrow gauge passenger train operated in summer between Boulder and Denver both directions.

The C&S in its first report to the Board of Equalization listed its 66 narrow gauge engines as follows:

3 First Class Valued at $1539 each
14 Second   "   "   " $1099 "
39 Third   "   "   " $720   "
10 Fourth   "   "   " $225   "

They corrected this listing as of December 31, 1899, to:

11 First Class
4 Second Class
39 Third Class
10 "Very old"
2 "scrap"

15 engines were sold, none scrapped, between 1899 and 1902, and 10 of those engines were built in 1880, the others in 1881-1882, wiping out all pre-1883 power with one exception, No. 30.

So by the end of 1902 the C&S had disposed of engines 1-2, 14 through 20, 31 through 36. By June, 1900, 12 of these engines were gone, leaving 54 on the roster. Three more followed within a year, and the final sale was apparently of No. 31 in 1902, which is the relic surviving to this day at the Colorado Railroad Museum.

Evidently 50 engines were more than adequate as some were laid up long periods. Soon after closure of Alpine Tunnel in 1910, 14 engines were in storage in white lead in the Como roundhouse, some of them never to run again on the C&S, and most of them to spend nearly a decade in forgotten storage, being stripped of parts to keep operating engines in repair.

In 1914 No. 41, demolished in a wreck on Boreas Pass five years earlier, was scrapped. In 1916 No. 38 left Como for a similar fate. Hallack & Howard Lumber Co. purchased four of the Como-stored engines, 39 in 1917, 45 in 1918 and Nos. 48 and 54 in 1920. H&H had a large logging operation at La Madera, N. M., and though this was a long way from the C&S and connected with the D&RG, the latter company had nothing much in the way of locomotives to offer. Engines 52 and 53 were scrapped in 1918, and 55 was sold to the CMStP&P for their Bellevue & Cascade narrow gauge in Iowa.

A most unusual transaction took place in January, 1921, when on the 20th an agreement was signed between Morse Bros. Machinery & Supply Co. of Denver and the C&S. It called for the exchange to the C&S of three locomotives from the Denver, Boulder & Western (which Morse Bros. had dismantled). In settlement for the price of $27,000 for the three engines, Morse was to receive five old C&S engines then in storage, priced at $1,600 each, plus 760 tons of old 50 pound rail, priced at $25 a ton. The C&S engines had been stored for years at Como, had a scrap value of only $625 each, minus about $125 in cost of scrapping. Each would have cost over $3,000 to make serviceable, but were considered too light to warrant this expense. The $1,600 price was based on sales of similar engines in better condition to various buyers. The rail was old, definitely second grade and not suitable for relaying on the narrow gauge lines.

The three DB&W engines were Brooks 2-8-0 built in 1898, with tractive effort of 21,172 lbs., which made them desirable as the three largest C&S engines then in use had a tractive effort of 19,869 lbs. It was planned to retire several lighter engines which would soon be in need of $3,000 or more repairs each. So DB&W numbers 30, 31, 32 became C&S 74, 75, 76. As the third rail was gone from the Boulder track, engine 30 had to come via standard gauge car from there, arriving on February 2. The other two came in standard gauge cars from Morse Bros. yard, located on the UP in Denver. C&S loaded 42, 43, 47, 49 and 50 similarly for shipment to Morse Bros. Originally it was planned to trade 30, 40, 42, 43 and 49. 30 and 40 on inspection were judged fit only for scrap. The movement of engines was completed by February 26, and nothing much has been learned as to what became of the engines after they were received by Morse.

DB&W 30 and 31 were quickly readied for use on the C&S, but No. 32 had to be reflued. One of the trio showed evidence of being fired up with low water and had to have a crown sheet patch. But as the C&S had for years done various repairs for the DB&W, working on these engines was nothing new for the Denver force.

General Manager J. T. Blair of the Colorado & Northwestern Ry. (original name of the DB&W), when considering ordering three new engines in March, 1898, had considered ordering three Baldwins like the newly arrived UPD&G 9, 10 and 11. But after studying the specifications, he returned them with his thanks, and advised he was ordering ". . . from the Brooks Locomotive Works; 16x20 cylinders, weight on drivers 85,000 lbs., on trucks 11,000, total weight 96,000. I think engines of this weight ought to handle our business." The Gulf's new engines had a total weight of about 80,000 lbs.

Last of the engines stored in 1910 was No. 30, which was brought to Denver in 1921 with No. 40, another engine stored at Como, to be scrapped. As both these engines had been stripped of many parts, including driver springs, it was necessary to get springs and other parts from another engine, send these to Como, install them on No. 30, haul it to Denver, then send the springs again to Como, to make No. 40 able to manage the trip.

As each of the engines came up for disposition, their condition and cost of rehabilitation were estimated, as well as their usefulness if rebuilt. To bring some of them up to latest ICC requirements would require very extensive boiler work. Some like No. 30 would only handle 90 tons on 4% at best. There was always the hope that management would eventually buy some new power, as it would

In an early example of motive power standardization, the South Park was equipped, in 1878-1880, with 19 new Mason Bogie 2-6-6T's. Before the last of them had arrived, however, the road had acquired the first of its Baldwin 2-8-0's, followed by other heavier power, and the Masons were soon obsolete. Most were gone within a decade or so. The 40 (above) and 55 (below), originally the 3 "Oro City" (first of the group) and 22 "Crested Butte", lasted long enough to be included in the 1889 DL&G numbering scheme. (Both, State Hist. Society of Colorado.)

be a better investment than overhauling the old power, often described as "worn out."

The serious traffic decline of the post-World War I period was in large part due to further serious drops in mining traffic. The number of engines had declined by 1930 to just 18. That year the Burlington's 537, an outside-frame 2-8-0 from the idle Black Hills line, arrived as reinforcement, to stay until the 1937 main line abandonment. It was rented for $1.20 per day. Despite the depression, this was not enough help and inquiry was made of the D&RGW.

The D&RGW was hard hit by the depression and had lines of dead engines, among them some of the heaviest power. The newest K-36 and K-37 Mikados could handle the main line trains; so they talked of Class K-27 2-8-2 "Mudhens". The D&RGW of course had many idle 2-8-0, but most of these were not as good in tonnage or factor of adhesion as the C&S power. However, a C&S official concluded that the mudhens were "altogether too heavy for our railroad."

In a July 24, 1931, discussion of the situation H. W. Ridgway, C&S Superintendent of Motive Power, said "The next best engine they have, C-19 Consolidation type, develops 18,947 lbs. tractive power and has a total weight of 64,000 lbs. on the drivers. This engine develops somewhat more tractive power than our 68 and 69 but has less adhesion on the drivers and I question very much if any of them would give us as good service as our 68 and 69, because from the figures, they only have a factor of adhesion of 3.37 and which I think is altogether too light for our railroad, when you consider the curves and worn rail conditions, which would make these engines very slippery and I do not believe they would handle the tonnage successfully."

By March 1928 it was agreed that no more engines could be retired. The only possible avenue for improvement in performance and reducing cost increases, it was pointed out, would be to acquire three new engines of a suggested 30,000 lbs. tractive power each. This would allow six of the oldest and smallest engines to be retired and reduce the "excessive engine miles in proportion to train miles" (due to the mileage of helper engines running light). It was estimated that the three proposed engines would have saved 32,629 engine miles in the year 1927, almost 30% of total engine mileage that year.

After the ICC turned down the 1928 application to abandon, in June, 1930, Mr. Ridgway went to investigate the Uintah Railway's power, especially the mallets. It was found, however, to try to adopt such engines to the C&S was not a practical matter, not only because of their cost but the "im-

mense expense of fitting up the Platte Canyon line to carry the same." In 1927 it had been suggested perhaps the "Santa Fe type" (2-10-2) would be a solution. Baldwin Locomotive Works quoted prices of $32,500 for 2-10-2s and $29,000 and $48,000 for Mikados and 2-6-6-2 mallets. But after all the thought, study and recommendations, in the summer of 1931 repair of several engines, held waiting decisions, was resumed.

In September, 1931, a study was made of converting the engines on the South Park from coal to oil. The difference in cost of the two fuels, f.o.b. Denver, indicated a saving if oil were used of $10,040 just on fuel cost alone. But as there were no facilities for handling oil, other than at Denver, the cost of tank cars to move it, as well as estimates on facilities needed at various points, killed this idea. As a test, engine 70 was put in service on the Clear Creek line that fall as an oil burner. Since it could make the round trip (if crews were careful) without refueling, there was no need for additional installations on that line. Incidentally, 3½ barrels of oil were considered equivalent to one ton of coal. Oil then was 60c a barrel, coal was $2.70 a ton at the mines.

To convert to oil was estimated to cost $33,770 — which was for storage tanks at three points, $15,000; converting 16 engines to oil burners, $12,800; building ten tanks and placing them on former coal cars whose sides would be removed and equipping them with valves, $5,970. 16,735 tons of coal were used on the South Park Division in 1930.

The Great Depression was on. Economy was a must on all railroads and there just was no money to spend on branch lines that kept losing money and which offered no hope of improvement in traffic and revenues. But then, a slight improvement in traffic began to take place. Gold mining in South Park required a number of box cars being repaired and assigned to that service on the Alma Branch. Molybdenum production kept climbing at Climax, providing shipments of machinery and supplies inbound, concentrates outbound all the way to Denver, there to be transferred for shipment to Pennsylvania.

Early in 1935 the motive power situation became acute; there just was not enough power available for trains. In 1930 Baldwin Locomotive Works had quoted a tentative price of $48,000 for a 2-6-6-2 articulated "simple" engine much like the Uintah, though with a tender. When contacted in early 1935, the price had risen to $56,500. The specifications were for a simple articulated engine with four 15x22 cylinders, 42 inch drivers, 210 pounds pressure, weight in working order of engine of 197,000 pounds, tender loaded with 8 tons coal and

5,000 gallons of water, 100,000 pounds. The rigid wheel base was only 7'8". Tractive power 42,100 and ratio of adhesion 4.0.

But all the discussion of a mallet ended as it became clear management was preparing to again file application to abandon the South Park between Waterton and Climax. By September, 1935, the application was being readied.

So as a temporary solution pending the outcome of the abandonment application (which could become a drawn out affair) they again went to the D&RGW and rented three of the Class C-19 2-8-0, Nos. 343, 345 and 346, which arrived from Alamosa early in 1936. They were equipped with the distinctive cinder catcher of the C&S, but retained their D&RGW numbers and lettering.

Roundhouse records show them ready to roll in February. They were used only on the Denver-Leadville run, almost entirely on freight, and only in an emergency on the passenger train. The custom at this time was to run a couple of four-engine freights a week west out of Denver. Many freights had one or two of these engines on the Denver-Como portion of the run. In winter, they would be employed as helpers for the tri-weekly passenger train. A C19 would often be coupled with a flanger car ahead of the road engine and its two passenger cars.

The C-19s were not liked by the South Park men as well as their own engines. They had a tendency to derail when working hard in the Platte Canyon. The delays generally were slight as they were quickly re-railed, with generally no damage to track or engine. They were classed as the CB&Q 537 in this regard and brought on an investigation. The decision was that there was little danger in using them, as they only derailed when working hard, which was always at low speed of 12 miles an hour or less. They did not derail when running light, which often was at greater speeds. The derailing was blamed on the blind center drivers and the very worn condition of much of the rail in the Platte Canyon.

Of the trio, No. 346 suffered the only major wreck while on the South Park. On July 25th it was one of the helpers on an eastbound freight from Como to summit of Kenosha. Then it was cut loose, to run light ahead. It did not go far — about one mile from the summit, running too fast, it jumped the rails and turned over on the first sharp curve. The fireman jumped or was thrown off before reaching the curve, but Engineer Eugene K. McGowan was entangled in pipes, and badly scalded before being rescued from the cab. He died July 26.

When the engine was brought into Denver and loaded on a standard gauge flat car to go to the Joint Shop it appeared badly battered. Most of the damage was superficial and minor, as the derailment site was soft, marshy ground. The engine was out of the shop and back to the C&S by early September, with some changes that were to last. In place of the standard wooden cab, it now had a steel one. The shopmen, unable to replace the upper broken steam dome ring or moulding, didn't bother. They managed to patch the bottom one. The tender, badly dented, was straightened and repaired. And, they turned a small flange ("half flange") on the two pair of intermediate drivers, this being done as had been done earlier to the Q's 537 with the idea that this might prevent some of the derailments. To this day the engine bears these changes made by the Joint Shop long ago. And on the steel plate to the right of the smoke box, a patch can still be seen indicating where the cinder catcher had been.

On April 7 346 handled the last South Park stock train. In the system report for the 24-hour period, among the stock trains listed, is "346 stock extra, 15 cars Denver to Jefferson." The roundhouse register shows that morning an 8 A.M. call for the crews of 346 and helpers 345, 58 and 65. The three helpers made it into Como 14 hours and 40 minutes later, while 346 made it in just 5 minutes under the 16 hour limit at 11:50 P.M. with two cars of coal and caboose 1006. The four engines started off for the return trip to Denver the next day around noon. The two C-19 engines headed back for Denver at 11:05 and 11:10 A.M. the next morning, running light, their final trip from Como. They stayed in the Denver roundhouse, were prepared for joint inspection, and on April 18 and 19 the two roads' mechanical people completed the joint inspection and the C-19s vanished from C&S records, heading back on flatcars to Alamosa. No wonder the ex-fireman of that July 25 wreck stared in amazement in 1958, when he saw 346 once more in the C&S yard, after 21 years, again on a flat car. The Kenosha wreck had decided him on taking up a career of switchman, and he never expected to see THAT engine again, he said!

Big Power *comes to the South Park: Utah & Northern 261 (above, opp.; Rex G. Beistle Coll.), shown here with a South Park freight at Wheeler, on the Tenmile, was one of six 1886 Rhode Island 2-8-0's transferred to the DL&G in 1890, still lettered "Utah & Northern" on the cab. On the C&S it became No. 58; of the group (57-62), No. 60 is preserved at Idaho Springs. At the same time, the DL&G obtained eight new Baldwin 2-8-0's of similar size, Nos. 266-273, which became C&S 63-70. The 270 has apparently just been relettered and renumbered C&S 67 in the lower view (Denver Public Library Coll.).*

The 28 engines obtained from Cooke in 1883-84 were fine engines by the standards of the day, and saw many years' use on the South Park. 8 were moguls (with two more on the Colorado Central) like DL&G 115 (ex-DSP&P 73), which became C&S 10. By the first decade of the century, the group generally looked like No. 8 (center). The other 20 Cookes were 2-8-0's like No. 47, shown below at Pitkin about 1905. Never rebuilt or modernized, the 2-8-0's were largely idled by the closing of Alpine and were all sold or scrapped by 1921. (Denver Public Library Western Hist. Coll.)

First engines to follow the Masons were 8 Baldwin 2-8-0's in 1880. By late 1890's they were obsolete and all but one were sold off, largely through sales to lumber roads. Above, DSP&P 51-DL&G 191-C&S 31 was sold to lumberman Ed Hines, and was No. 7 on his Washburn & Northwestern in Wisconsin when this photo was made in 1903 (Howard Peddle Coll.). Later it went to the Thunder Lake Lumber Co., and after rusting away at Rhinelander for forty years was recently brought back to the Colorado Railroad Museum.

C&S 34 had been DSP&P 55 and DL&G 195. Shortly after this photo was made at London Jct. in 1899, it was sold to R. G. Peters' Manistee & Luther RR in Michigan, where it became No. 4 (Fred Jukes Coll.).

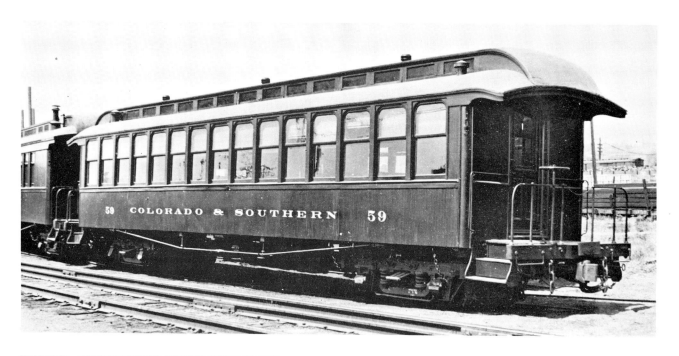

Photographed in 1929, these two coaches show the wide diversity of design in South Park equipment. Above is coach No. 59, while the two lower interior and exterior views are of coach No. 58. Different still were the coaches usually seen on the Leadville train in the final years. (Three photos, Richard B. Jackson.)

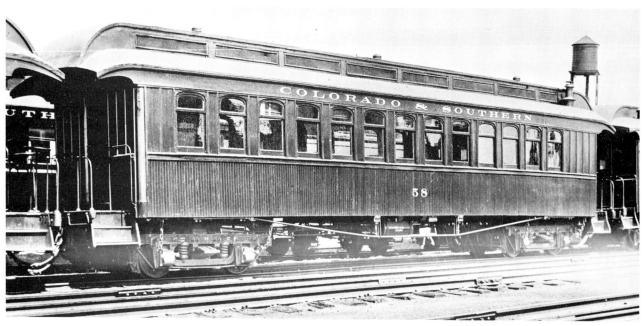

Rolling Stock

Under date of January 1, 1899, Master Car Builder W. E. Fowler issued instructions to each Car Foreman as follows: "Before leaving Repair Tracks all UPD&G and DL&G Cars must have the markings changed to "COLORADO & SOUTHERN" and the new numbers applied . . ." They were to check their blueprints and see that length and marked capacity corresponded with the blue print record, and make daily reports of all changes. A total of 4334 freight and non-revenue cars were listed at the time, a number of which were new cars, some not yet on hand. A report to the I.C.C. on July 1, 1899, listed 4171 cars of both gauges of which 1362 were narrow gauge. This included non-revenue cars.

Included were 566 box cars, 70 flat, 14 stock, 637 coal, 33 refrigerators, 4 tool, 5 wrecking, 11 outfits, and one each Rotary, Jull plow and pile driver. There were also 4 flangers and 15 cabooses. Only the cabooses, flangers and 3 outfit cars did not have air brakes. 608 units still had link and pin or other semi-automatic couplers. Orders for new narrow gauge cars placed in the late 1890s had specified air brakes and automatic couplers.

To the new merged company the DL&G contributed 25 passenger cars and two "Official" cars (which were counted as additional passenger cars). Combination car 709 didn't quite make it to the C&S by a few hours, turning over at Alpine Tunnel on December 27, 1898, in one of the wintry troubles at that place and destroyed in the ensuing fire. The Gulf Route's contribution to the combined roster was 34 cars, including Officer's Car No. 1, 1 baggage, 3 mail, baggage and express, 2 combines, 18 coaches and two chair cars. There were 7 of the open observation cars.

In 1896, as the receivership obviously was nearing an end, officials discovered that subsidiaries of the Union Pacific had surplus narrow passenger cars and tried to obtain them. At first, in early 1896, it was arranged to trade two standard gauge Gulf Route mail and express cars for four narrow gauge coaches at Salt Lake City owned by the Oregon Short Line. After delays, due to obtaining approval of various Receivers, then court approval, a trade of UPD&G 1162 mail car for coaches 131 and 140 was finally carried out. The mail car went to Omaha, and the two coaches were placed on broad gauge trucks and delivered at Denver, where their narrow gauge trucks, coming via a coal car, were again put under them. They became Gulf cars 189 and 192. Hopes of getting other cars were

ended, however, when the UP decided to place its Kansas Central narrow gauge passenger cars on broad gauge trucks and use them on that widened line. The OSL officials held on to their other cars for use on the Garfield line which had been delayed in standard gauging. So the Gulf Route ordered four new coaches later that year for the increasing needs of the narrow gauge lines.

Gulf Route combination car 735 must have been the first narrow gauge passenger car to be lettered for C&S. On December 15, 1898, it was changed to No. 120 and initialed for "C&S". As the new company was not incorporated until four days later, it makes a researcher wonder if the relettering of this car might have been some kind of commemorative observance of the day the new company was started on its way? Passenger cars were rushed through the shops and changed quickly to the new road name and numbers, but it took several years for the freight cars to be changed over. The passenger cars were assigned numbers above 100, between 101 and 199, while the standard gauge C&S cars were numbered under 100. This did not work out too well when more cars were received and in 1906 everything was renumbered, just the reverse, with narrow gauge cars receiving numbers under 100, starting with baggage car No. 1, except that the excursion cars were given numbers 120 through 148. The standard gauge cars received new numbers, all above 200. But for a while it must have been very confusing in the Denver yard and shops and especially in switching trains at the Union Station, as car numbers could no longer be counted upon to indicate the gauge of car. The duplication of numbers for a while was bound to cause problems.

Gulf Route was busy in the 1890s converting its freight and passenger cars to automatic couplers, so that by time of the C&S virtually all of the "broad gauge" were converted. On the narrow gauge the passenger cars were nearly all Miller Hook, the semi-automatic coupler then a favorite on most roads, which was an interim coupler between link and pin and the automatic. Some cars had the Miller coupler on one end, link and pin on the other for a while. This occurred on R.P.O.-Baggage cars and some combination cars, apparently because these cars would be coupled most of the time to a link and pin tender coupler.

As long as freight cars did not cross state lines, those in Colorado could remain link and pin coupler-equipped for a few years into the early 1900s, but the C&S rapidly converted the narrow gauge cars once they had caught up a little with their standard gauge problems. It was a good investment on a mountain narrow gauge and the much larger D&RG system was completing its work of this nature in 1903-04. Interchange because of couplers was no problem on the C&S.

With only one Railway Post Office route, the DL&G only had three cars with RPO compartments. Also but three baggage cars. They had 12 coaches, and a gradually declining group of combination cars totalling seven by end of 1898. This mirrored the slim passenger traffic on most of the South Park, with the combination cars generally on all Gunnison District trains, and used as well on the night mixed or "fast freight" between Denver and Leadville. The Gulf had only three RPO compartment cars, as it too had but one such route. With only the Central City Branch, it had but two combination cars, only one baggage car, but the large amount of its passenger revenue is reflected by the 20 coaches and chair cars in 1898, plus seven open observation cars.

The freight cars reflected the type of traffic very well, with one exception. At turn of the century, railroads supplied few if any specialized types of cars, unlike now. The large traffic in coal and ore was handled by the fleet of 637 gondolas of which nearly 200 were new in 1896-1898. Peculiar is the small number of stock cars, hardly enough to make one "stock extra", just 14 cars. No explanation of this has been encountered. No payments for rented or leased stock cars has been noted, though there were a number of companies engaged in such rentals. It's unlikely the South Park could have borrowed any from the D&RG, as that road seemed to be absolutely strapped for enough such cars every spring and fall, often having to delay movements for weeks. While the C&S-UPD&G had surplus at times of standard gauge stock cars, as is evident from the use of "lined stock cars" as box cars, it's not clear if any were temporarily placed on narrow gauge trucks for South Park use. The movements of restless cattle in oversize cars would make such usage dangerous and derailment prone. The flat car fleet was augmented from time to time, down to the end of the South Park by removing sides from gondolas. The refrigerator fleet was important, many freights using one of the cars to handle l.c.l. perishables, and of course the beer requirements alone of the mountain towns would keep a number of such cars busy.

Through the decade of the 1890s the DL&G totals varied slightly for freight cars, from 1117 in 1890 to 1086 in 1897. Cabooses led a hard life, as one-fourth of the 16 they had in 1890 vanished by 1898. All four-wheelers, they were easily derailed (though often just as easily re-railed, being so light), but simply could not stand hard handling such as pushing.

Under the C&S the total of freight cars, with the new cars purchased in 1898-1900, rose to nearly 1400 cars; but even with an addition of many new box and stock cars built at the C&S shops 1907-1910, the total went down as older cars were scrapped or sold to used equipment dealers.

In the spring of 1900 the C&S ordered 50 stock cars at the same time it ordered nearly 300 standard gauge coal cars. With only 14 stock cars on hand the need was urgent. The new cars arrived in Denver between May 30th and June 15th. They were loaded into the empty broad gauge coal cars built at same time at the St. Charles, Mo., plant of the American Car & Foundry Co. Numbered 7015-7064, the last one of the series had a lengthy career, eventually going to the Rio Grande Southern R.R. in 1938 and is now preserved at this Museum, the sole survivor. When built the cars cost $550.00.

C&S cars were interchanged with the D&RG of course, but not in large numbers. A few rarely showed up on the far away Rio Grande Southern. And of course there was interchange with the "Switzerland Trail" line at Boulder after third rail was laid to there in 1905. No doubt the most distant point reached by a C&S narrow gauge car was one box car, shown on the Coahuila & Zacatecas in Mexico in 1917. The circumstances are obscure, but apparently it was returned to the C&S. As the box cars used on the C&Z in later years appeared very much like the C&S cars, one might almost wonder if it was a sample or pattern?

The officials of the Gulf-South Park receivership were placing orders for new cars even before a name was certain for the new combined road. Passenger cars, when ordered, seemed generally to be for the Gulf Road, while freight cars were on behalf of the DL&G. One exception was six refrigerator cars ordered on August 20, 1898, cost $700 each. The cars, numbered 550-555 and lettered for the C&S, were received in Denver on November 10th. Management had specified they be canary yellow, have the same lettering as box cars except for the word "refrigerator" on "right side, both sides." The manufacturer was pressed to send them as soon as possible as the lines were very short of cars of this type.

Also in 1898 they ordered 160 50,000 lb. capacity coal cars and 40 box cars of the same capacity. The specifications for painting the coal cars were:

> Entire outside of car to receive three coats of Sherwin and Williams paint, U.P.D.&G. standard color, not more than one coat to be applied in 24 hours. Side sills of cars to be stencilled with pure white lead in linseed oil, with 10″ Roman letters also with number in same size and style. All outside iron work to have one coat of asphaltum black. Ends of cars to be also stencilled in 5″ letters and figures

with same markings; the same to be also stencilled on coal sides between the two center stakes, with 5″ letters and figures. The length and capacity of cars to be also stencilled on side sills, as nearly as possible over body transom over left end of car, in 3″ letters and figures, and the words "Air Brake", in 3″ letters, at left end of car. Each car to be weighed separately, and the weight, and name of place, and date weighed, to be stencilled in 2″ letters at right end of car as nearly as possible over body transom. Car also to be stencilled at each end with the words "Selden Automatic Coupler".

and for the box cars:

Entire outside of car to receive three coats of Sherwin and Williams paint, U.P.D.&G. Standard color, not more than one coat to be applied in 24 hours; all outside iron work to have one coat of asphaltum black.

Cars to be stencilled with pure white lead in oil, with 10″ Roman letter "U. P. D. & G." The number in same size and style on the right side of cars, the initials being on left.

Side doors and end doors to be also stencilled in 5″ letters and figures, same as on sides of car.

Inside dimensions of car, capacity, and the words "Air Brake" to be also stencilled in 3″ letters on lower part of body of car over body transom at left side of side doors. Each car to be weighed, and weight to be stencilled in 3″ figures over body transom at opposite end.

Cars to be stencilled at each end with the words "Selden Automatic Coupler". (This was a link and pin coupler with draft gear and a pin lifter.)

Before the cars were shipped, they had at first ordered them lettered "Colorado & Seaboard Ry. Co.", but four days later, on October 26th, this was changed to "Colorado & Southern Ry. Co." The manufacturer, however, found the name much too long to fit on the coal cars, and shortened it to the initials, which drew criticism from the C&S people, who ignored the fact that the side stakes would have made the spelled out name fit oddly on the cars. The gondolas cost $315 each, the box cars $415 each. This was the series of gondolas numbered 4086 to 4245 and box cars numbered 8026 to 8065. It might be noted that in 1925 the bulk of these gondolas were out of service needing major repairs and not deemed worth it, so 93 of them were sold at prices of $78 to $105 each to a materials firm then supplying logging railroads, the A. T. Herr Supply Co. A further batch of these cars were sold to the same firm in 1929, the Denver car force mistakenly repairing them, installing new center sills on some and new flooring on others bringing a rather sad comment from the Superintendent that "it seems a shame that we went to all this expense on cars which did not belong to us . . . and then turn them over at practically a scrap price."

An important change in brakes on the narrow gauge cars, commenced in 1909, brought on an important increase in safety of operations on the heavy grades, and reduced the numerous wrecks. Between July 27 and August 11, tests were conducted on the Gunnison District of cars re-equipped by the Westinghouse Air Brake Co. with their Type K-1 Triple Valve and Duplex or double weight retaining valves. The tests were made to demonstrate that freight trains could be successfully handled on long continuous 4% grades by air brakes alone, unassisted by hand brakes. The cost per car to convert from the "H-1" type triple valve to the K-1 was $5.25 and the change in retaining valves from the single weight type then in use to the new Duplex 10 and 20 lb. was $2.25 each, actually costing somewhat less as the older valves were usable on standard gauge cars. The total cost was estimated at $6.75 per car for material plus 25 cents for labor. The Superintendent of Motive Power felt the change would "give us a decided margin of safety."

So the sight of the crew out on top of the train, in all kinds of weather, setting brakes to aid the air brake system controlled by the engineer gradually vanished. Prior to the K-1's advent, crews were required to "be out on top" on all the principal grades. Thus the change for the employees too was of great importance, lessening greatly the dangerous character of their work. Runaway trains were noticeably fewer after 1910.

Under the U.S.R.A. nothing of importance occurred in car changes. At time of return to the railroad company, there were still 80 passenger cars, 402 box cars (of which one, No. 8242, reflected the change of the times, being an "automobile" car), coal cars had dropped from the January 1, 1918 total of 607 to 490, but flat cars had increased from 20 to 33 (a mere shift of status of coal cars), 26 refrigerator cars, 115 stock, 54 non-revenue dropped to 49, for a total decline during USRA from 1,152 freight and non-revenue cars to 1,124.

In summarizing non-revenue equipment in early 1920 it is interesting to note that both rotary snow plows were classed as standard gauge equipment. Also the C&S managed with but three flangers on the narrow gauge in contrast to the large number of such cars on the D&RG. The lengthy standard gauge lines of the C&S, with many snow problem areas, had only two flangers.

On March 1, 1920, the C&S sold 15 gondolas in the 4400 series to its parent CB&Q for use on the Q's Black Hills narrow gauge line. Over the years other sales would occur, such as four flat cars in 1928 to Hallack & Howard. This was an emergency matter, as Hallack & Howard were facing a shut down of their mill at La Madera, N. M. for lack of log cars, and the cars were quickly loaded two per standard gauge car. Sale price was $300 each. The CB&Q had earlier, in 1911, obtained 50 of the coal cars. 17 others went to Morse Bros. Machinery Co. in 1922.

The sale of 98 coal cars to the A. T. Herr Supply Co. in September, 1925, included mostly cars whose bodies were in poor condition. Herr only wanted the trucks and other metal, for sales to logging lines, especially in Idaho.

As non-revenue cars needed any major expenditure, they were generally scrapped. Such was the fate of the wooden wrecking derrick 099 and idler car 99010. The steel underframe idler car was scrapped in August, 1927; the derrick itself in November, 1934, long since retired and in need of major rebuilding.

The increase in heavy and lengthy machinery traffic, such as to Climax, caused the rebuilding in the fall of 1929 of 15 gondolas from solid fixed ends to drop ends. They were renumbered to 4600-4614.

The narrow gauge passenger cars the C&S started with in 1898 were mostly received from builders between 1873 and 1886. Wooden passenger cars had a relatively short life, before needing rebuilding or replacement. Repainting and considerable work was a must at least every three years, while shop and rip track crews were constantly making minor repairs while the cars "laid over" at terminals. When wood was cheap and labor also, this was not too great a cost matter, but lumber costs kept rising, and labor costs followed along. In the early 1900s a repair bill on a car might include but 25 cents or so as the labor cost. Often a repair bill was only a dollar or two, much of the time such things as broken windows, etc., costing much less than $5. These kinds of costs were fine in the era of wooden cars, whose platforms insisted on sagging, whose lines would sag or hump with use or mis-use of cars. With steel underframe cars coming in, the stresses on all wooden cars increased, and the dangers in their use. Fortunately (?) when all-steel cars began to be adopted on broad gauge lines in the early 1900s, this practice did not spread to the narrow gauge lines, or else wooden cars would have vanished long before the lines themselves vanished. The head of the car department was titled "Master Car Builder", a title frequently found throughout the railroad industry in the era of wooden cars, and a title self-descriptive of his task. Contributing to the decline and abandonment of the narrow gauge lines were the increasingly higher costs of maintaining in serviceable condition the wooden cars, both freight and passenger. The visitor to the Colorado Railroad Museum and other display points need only examine surviving wooden cars to see how the cars, whether in use or not, require continual maintenance, far in excess of steel or other metal cars.

As Colorado slowly emerged from the devastating Crash of '93, business picked up in the latter 1890s, though was never again to reach the pre-1893 levels in the mining regions. On June 11, 1896, the UPD&G contracted with the St. Charles Car Co. of St. Charles, Mo. for four first-class passenger cars at $3,000 each. They were to be 40 feet over sills, and 8 feet wide. Master Car Builder Fowler sent the St. Charles company blueprints showing the position of passenger cars when on a 30 degree curve, for their guidance in fitting the underframes of cars. They were to seat 44 persons, to be lettered with the road name spelled out and numbered 194 through 197. The cars weighed 17 tons.

It was to be a standard gauge coach that was first to receive the new name "Colorado & Southern". It and a large number of freight cars ordered at the same time for the DL&G were nearly lettered "Colorado & Seaboard". That was the name the general office force thought had been adopted on October 22, 1898, for the new company. On the 25th General Superintendent Dunaway wired them not to letter any cars then being completed, until further word. On October 26th he wrote them that the name to be lettered on the cars would be "Colorado & Southern" for the coach, and "Colorado & Southern Ry. Co." on the narrow gauge freight cars.

The next new coaches were three more first class ones, again to be built at the St. Charles plant, which meantime had become a part of the American Car & Foundry Co. About the only change in specifications for those was to have them fitted with the builder's "medium high-back seats" instead of the more famous Scarrett Seats, at the time a much advertised feature of passenger cars. Price to be $3,166.00 each. The order was nearly cancelled in late May of 1900 when delays in delivery seemed likely. However on August 6th they left St. Louis via the Frisco and Santa Fe for Pueblo and arrived in Denver on the 9th. The speed of the trip indicates they probably made the trip on broad gauge trucks, as was frequently done. These were coaches 172, 173, 174.

In 1890 it was proposed that the idle narrow gauge Pullman cars be used on the night freight to Leadville — though how much sleep anyone would have been able to achieve on the end of a freight train equipped with link and pin couplers is doubtful. Maybe that is why the idea was shelved. The cars had occasional use on specials, and on the Alpine excursions which involved overnight travel for two nights. Their use became more limited as time passed, and General Superintendent Dunaway told Receiver Trumbull "if we cannot exchange the sleepers for coaches or cars of some kind, we will take the berths out and use them as day coaches." In 1904 the last two still equipped for sleeper service were placed in storage, one being stripped of its furnishings which were placed in the other car, and it in turn stored in the Golden roundhouse.

In April 1896 the Gulf people had offered to trade the three narrow gauge 10-section sleepers to Pullman for four of the idle Tourist Sleepers. On May 22 Dunaway asked the Master Car Builder, W. E. Fowler, to go to the Rio Grande yards and examine car 466 and see if it could be used on "our" narrow gauge lines, keeping in mind the car was 8'2" wide at the eaves. Fowler reported the car no wider over sills "than our widest coaches" and would be "O.K." So on May 25th Dunaway told the Pullman people they would take car 466 at the agreed price of $1250 and directed them to have the D&RG switch it out and set over in transfer track. The price was exclusive of equipment, as it became Gulf coach No. 193. In June, 1898, the Gulf shops at Denver took on a conversion job for the new Colorado & Northwestern Ry. at Boulder. They had purchased from the Pullman Palace Car Co. narrow gauge Pullman Tourist Sleepers Nos. 465, 467, 468 and 469, which were held surplus at the D&RG in Denver since that road standard gauged its main line. The cars were changed to coaches Nos. 6 through 9.

In early 1906 it was decided that the Railway Post Office could be more efficiently handled in a combination R.P.O.-coach, and on May 3rd the remaining three ex-Pullmans, numbers 146-147-148, were delivered to the Pullman shop at Denver, where they were rebuilt. All three were returned to the C&S on July 14th as R.P.O.-coaches numbers 41-42-43. Cost per car ranged from $2,285 to $2,402. A fourth car was ordered from Pullman and built new at a cost of $2,789; it was received on August 25th, as number 40.

There was little change in the total number of passenger cars until the 1920s. With the big drop in excursion business, especially on the Georgetown Loop line, the older open excursion cars were sold off in 1923. The balance of the excursion cars were dismantled in the fall of 1928. The regular passenger trains on the Loop had been discontinued in April, 1927, and excursion usage on the South Park was insufficient to warrant expense of rebuilding the cars for continued use. Regular coaches handled excursion business up through the final summer of 1936.

Meantime as various older non-revenue cars were judged in need of heavy repairs, it became the custom to substitute some passenger car not needed. Coach 28 was converted to a scale test car as of September 30, 1922, and used on either gauge trucks over the system. Little 26-foot Business Car 912 was changed to 089 Water Service under date of April 23, 1926. This car was a relic of the DSP&P. Combination car No. 21 was sold to the Denver Tramway Corp. on July 28, 1930, for $20. It became a caboose, on 3½' gauge freight car trucks, used on the Denver-Leyden coal trains of that company. As of December 13, 1929, coaches 59-60, 80, and 82-83 were dismantled. And from that time on through the end of South Park passenger service there was a steady decline in passenger cars. Also in March, 1929, Business Car 910 had been dismantled, formerly Gulf Route No. 1. The Business Car 911 was almost scrapped in 1938, at which time it was estimated that it would cost $30 to cut up, or a mere $20 to burn it and then cut up the remaining scrap. Fortunately it was reprieved.

Little 4-wheel caboose No. 1003 pays a visit to Idaho Springs in July, 1940, during the twilight of the Clear Creek line. Two similar cabooses have been preserved; one at Silver Plume, and one at the Colorado Railroad Museum. (Photo, Richard B. Jackson.)

Handsome business car No. 911 (above; Richard B. Jackson photo) escaped destruction because of the low price of scrap; the view here is at Black Hawk in 1940. Below, Express car No. 1 looks clean and well maintained in the Denver yards; there is barely enough room on the letterboard for the full road name (Lad Arend photo).

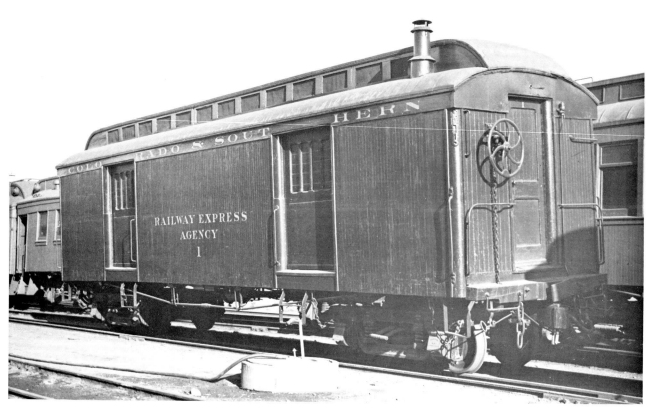

Rotary No. 99200 served the South Park narrow gauge for over half a century before being converted to standard gauge along with the Climax Branch in 1943. It is shown here (above) shortly after having been rebuilt following the disastrous Como roundhouse fire of 1935. Below, flanger plows like the 015 (shown here at Leadville in 1937) were used extensively to keep the line open in winter. (Both, R. B. Jackson.)

The C&S had many freight cars for the South Park system, and while most of them were post-1900, low maintenance levels made them look older. At top, one of many gondolas, this side-emptying car was used for maintenance of way work and still showed traces of the original "C&S" block lettering. Of the two stock cars shown, the lower is a present-day view of the last survivor, now at the Colorado Railroad Museum. (Two upper photos, Lad Arend; lower, Museum Coll.)

Bad-order box 8167 at right also revealed the block lettering from the origins of the C&S, while 8114 below appears well maintained and displays a latter-day lettering style. Bottom, one of the Conoco tank cars. (All, Lad Arend photos.)

First major "abandonment" of the South Park was the never-completed Ohio Pass line, constructed from Gunnison nearly to Irwin, and destined for coal lands beyond and ultimately Utah. In the steep climb from Ohio Creek up over Ohio Pass a great deal of rock work was involved, including some great stone retaining walls similar to those at the Palisades. Seen from the valley today, the great uncompleted walls look like scars across the face of the mountainside (above); up close, the massive nature of the work can be appreciated by the intrepid explorer (left). (Both photos, R. W. Richardson.)

Abandonment

The main line of the South Park was never completed. It was like most Colorado roads — projected ambitiously, perhaps too enthusiastically. The mining industry needed a great deal of coal, every mine had its own blacksmith, and everyone burned coal for office or home or factory. The railroads themselves needed tremendous quantities. The South Park mines at King were poor and never could produce enough coal even for the needs at Como. It was difficult to get miners for them, and the Superintendent complained of this to the Denver office. So they gradually ceased to function and the track was torn up in 1898. The Union Pacific owned vast coal lands in the Gunnison country and the South Park was extended toward that area. Surveys were run in 1881 and grading progressed through the summer. The earliest passenger timetables showed but one station, "Richardson", between Gunnison and the metal mining camp of Irwin. Irwin was booming, so it looked like a very profitable extension to that point, with so much mining potential. By January, 1882, the grade was reported completed except the last three miles to Irwin. A rather mild winter enabled the work to continue, but in the spring of 1882 the workmen were called off the job, to return later; but as it developed they never returned, and tracklaying stopped in the vicinity of Baldwin in 1883. In 1892 the Union Pacific resumed its long deferred intention to reach its coal lands and survey crews were sent out, but this work too stopped in March, 1893. Under the C&S a map has been noted showing a proposed extension about 1904 in that general direction, but apparently nothing serious was done. Meanwhile, under the DL&G in the late 1890s, "Ohio Creek Branch 3.09 miles taken up" during 1897 evidently covers the track so hopefully laid a few years earlier.

The ending of operations through Alpine Tunnel late in 1910 was at first merely a suspension of operations, but coupled with washouts in Trout Creek Canyon late that year it brought on the first big abandonment of South Park trackage. Nothing much was done for about five years, the tracks and structures just left there, occasional grass fires destroying something, slides and washouts taking their toll. Insurance was cancelled. The telegraph department on November 29, 1915, reported completion of changing the wires from the South Park line between Bath and Buena Vista to the Colorado Midland's poles. The water tank at Newett was "abandoned" in July, 1915.

In August, 1912, needing some 56 lb. steel rail, about half a mile of this was taken up just beyond Hancock and replaced with old 35 lb. iron rail, so the track was still intact.

That October the Garos depot was moved to Fairplay, a $210 expense item. In the summer of 1913, with debris now many feet deep over tracks at the mouth of Trout Creek, the coal platform, chute and coaling tracks were taken down and removed, some material being used to erect a 16 x 64-foot coaling platform at Buena Vista.

1915 was the year in which it became clear trains would not again run through to Gunnison. Water tanks were removed at Gunnison and Parlins and Newett. The turntable at Gunnison was moved to Romley. Buildings at McGees, Schwanders and Parlin were sold and removed by the end of 1916. In September, 1915, the old bridge timbers remaining from the flood destroyed structures in Trout Canyon were sold to two bidders for a total of $53. One of them bought the tool house and coal house at Bath for another $5, and the section house for $50. The Schwanders tank, once a *must* for all trains, stood until 1920, when a local man paid $25 for it. The Castleton depot was destroyed by fire on December 13 of that year.

The first recorded rail removal was that reported as "completed" in November, 1918, of "Taking up track and abandoning Tunnel M.P. 162 to M.P. 163." $734 was spent on this project, but since the track still lays inside the Tunnel to this day, it can be assumed the clerk, in entering a ledger item and having but meager space for the entry, entered only a portion of the intended work. Whether at that late date they removed the turntable, or other items, is uncertain from the record. On September 17, 1923, the rail of the line between Quartz and Hancock was sold, with mileage given as 160.55 to 173.81, except 162.71-163.42 (the tunnel.) However, the purchaser left behind much of the yard rail and almost a mile of main line. About the time of World War II the yard was largely salvaged, but still a good portion of main remained untouched. Also on September 17, 1923, the rails of the long idle Parlins-Gunnison line were sold. This trackage had not been used since 1911, as the D&RG in its operation of the Pitkin line had employed its own line between Parlins and Gunnison.

The Garos-Schwanders line was dismantled in the summer of 1922, the work being completed in October. On the part through South Park a saddle-tank locomotive was used by the contractor, the only portion of the abandonments where this sort of motive power was employed. Four years later on November 15, 1926, work of taking up the Buena Vista-Romley line was completed.

The D&RGW had continued to operate the Pitkin line, but revenues were small for the tri-weekly operation from Gunnison. Abandonment was authorized and the line torn up in the summer of 1934. All that now remained of the Gunnison line was the Baldwin Branch, which the D&RGW operated until they abandoned their own lines into Gunnison in 1954, at which time all were torn up. The stone South Park depot, long used by D&RGW section men as a residence, was demolished when U.S. highway 50 was relocated. Until then too, the stone foundations of the round-house could be seen and the red yard shanty still stood. The last structure, the distinctive C&S water tank at Castleton, lasted until the end. It should be noted that the Baldwin Branch became D&RGW property finally on September 19, 1937, when it was retired from C&S accounts.

On September 22, 1928, the C&S filed an application with the I.C.C. to abandon their entire South Park line beyond Waterton, 185.05 miles of main line and branches. The deficits per year ranged from $514,314 in 1923 to $426,505 in 1927. The City of Denver wanted the initial mileage beyond Waterton to Buffalo abandoned for water purposes (a dam), and the C&S pointed out that the line's major revenues were through Denver-Leadville traffic, which would be lost by such a partial abandonment as the City required. The exhibits showed a dreary picture of heavy deficits from 1910 onward, in only two years being under $100,000. At times the percentage of this deficit to total operating income of the C&S was around 20%, with a few years much higher, in 1923 being 61%! The railroad made a good case that the continuance of the line would indeed be a "heavy burden on interstate commerce." The moly mine at Climax, soon to become the largest traffic source, was at the time diverting considerable incoming freight via the Leadville route of the D&RGW because the rate was better.

The railroad disputed major claims of its detractors and then countercharged with the following offer:

> Protestants asserted that a great saving could be made by the railway company in operating the line in question by securing new and heavier motive power. The opinion was expressed that three of the engines now used on the line are only 65 to 70 per cent efficient and the others only 20 to 25 per cent. It was thought that eight new locomotives would be sufficient for the line and that they would cost about $50,000 each. Materially heavier engines, however, would require the rebuilding of the road with heavier rails, all of which would involve greatly increased expenses. The railway company does not consider these expenses advisable in view of the

industrial conditions shown by the record.

> If the abandonment sought is permitted, the Colorado & Southern offers to donate the line to be abandoned, or any part or parts thereof, to such local interests or communities as may desire to continue operation. It also offers to donate for that purpose such of the locomotives and other rolling stock used on the line as may be necessary for its continued operation. It further states in its brief that assurance has been given by the trustee of the refunding and extension mortgage that arrangements will be made for a release of the line from this mortgage in case we authorize the abandonment and the company's offer to other interests is accepted. It is stated that the only other mortgage on the line is now being paid off.

On June 2, 1930, the I.C.C. handed down its decision that "present and future public necessity and convenience are not shown to permit the abandonment . . ." At the same time they denied the application of the city and county of Denver seeking authorization to abandon the Waterton-Buffalo portion. They left the door open to renewal of the case in 36 months if the "situation has not materially improved." They suggested possible economies might be effected by reducing passenger service, changing freight schedules and "perhaps improvement of equipment." A reduction of taxes was suggested. It also counseled the public to "appreciate the necessity of providing it (the railroad) with sufficient traffic to enable it to live."

The I.C.C. called on all, the carrier, the State and the territory served to use this "probationary period" to make a "united effort to save these lines of railroad." The railroad was urged to study the Uintah to see what that road had accomplished with steep grades and sparsely settled territory.

The offer to give away the line attracted one serious bidder in Victor A. Miller, then Receiver of the Rio Grande Southern R.R. He sent his Superintendent Forest White and his "Motor Mechanic" Jack Odenbaugh to Denver to take a sort of incognito trip over the South Park. Paying fares like any other passengers they rode the two car passenger run, closely observing the condition of the line, what freight and other traffic was in evidence, all with the end view of a report on whether use of motor cars similar to the Rio Grande Southern's famous "Galloping Goose" would be practical instead of the steam powered passenger. White had been a conductor on the RGS for many years before becoming Superintendent when Miller became Receiver. Odenbaugh was the genius who built the successful motor cars and kept them running on the bare bones budget of a railroad sometimes unable to make its meager payroll, and with no dollars to waste on anything. Their report to Miller was enthusiastic, assuring him that the South Park main line could be changed successfully to Goose type operations. Moreover they saw a chance to obtain engines and freight cars for the RGS, ending dependence on the D&RGW and the high cost of rental of engines.

On July 14, 1932, Miller and the C&S negotiated a contract and the headlines in the papers read "Railroad Gives Leadville Line to Youthful Denver Lawyer." It looked like the South Park was saved. So the I.C.C. set a hearing for November 21. Miller organized his company as the Denver, Leadville & Alma R.R.

The publicity inspired a rival bidder, a Mr. W. C. Johnstone, who organized the Denver, Intermountain & Summit Ry. His company prepared elaborate evidence of traffic possibilities for the South Park and what they could do with the line. However, the I.C.C. turned both applications down, stating "we think that neither applicant has made satisfactory proof of its ability to keep the lines in operation under present conditions, and both applications must be denied." That was on November 29. Johnstone made strong representations, alleging heavy costs in presenting his case, of over $160,000. There had been objections too by shippers and other interested parties that sale should not be permitted as the C&S had not been authorized yet to abandon the line. Files of the Rio Grande Southern indicate a very serious effort would have been made with the South Park and one is left to muse on what might have been.

The winter of 1935-1936 demonstrated the need of train service to the small mountain communities, otherwise dependent on gravel roads often closed for periods by winter weather. The exploring visitor today, traveling all weather paved roads, has no conception of the travel problems of that time, nor the inadequate forces of Colorado's Highway Department then.

On February 19, 1936, train No. 70 left Denver on time with Engine 8 and two cars. It departed Como only 20 minutes late, after coupling D&RGW 343 and flanger ahead. They lost one hour 27 minutes over Boreas "account snow conditions" although the weather report was "calm and clear and light snow conditions in afternoon." The train lost another hour and 38 minutes Breckenridge to Leadville, arriving three hours and 25 minutes late. The return trip to Denver the next day saw them leave Leadville 35 minutes late account loading mail and express. The 343 and flanger were cut off at Como. But working across South Park and over Kenosha added delay time and the train was two hours 15 minutes late on arrival at Grant.

Next trip things got worse. Again it left Denver on time but was twenty-four hours and 40 minutes late into Como! The balance of run to Leadville was annulled. Late on the 22nd, the two-car train left Como four hours 20 minutes late as train No. 71 and arrived Denver seven hours late. It lost two hours 40 minutes following the rotary across South Park as far as Kenosha. Downhill No. 8 was able to plow its own way on to Denver.

Strong winds set in, which was really the worst feature of South Park weather. The winds take a small amount of snow and drift it so badly that even in these days of paved roads and modern plows the highway can be snowed in while they are working on it. Train 70 made it to Como on February 24th, and stayed there. No passenger trains operated the next three days. When the winds quieted, the rotary went out and the line was soon open.

March was no improvement, with occasional annulments of part of the passenger runs. The four-engine freights had a rough time of it. Sometimes to aid a desperate shipper or consignee, a car of freight would be in the passenger consist, as in March when refrigerator car 1111 was handled Denver to Dillon, slowing the train down an hour and 25 minutes. Snowslides just beyond Frisco forced the train to go back to Como, from which point the next day it ran on schedule to Denver. Engines 68, 69 and 345 served as helpers out of Como that month, with flanger coupled between the two engines of the passenger. On the 16th westbound 345 and 8 followed the rotary toward Leadville. On the 17th No. 71 was late eastward because of the rotary ahead, taking the siding at Climax for the rotary. Then east of Como the valve yoke broke and engine 345 came to the rescue, finding the train stalled near Michigan.

Summer saw the final excursionists, extra coaches on a few trains for Crystal Lake including parochial school outings. But the only excitement was derailment and turning over of D&RGW 346 on Kenosha Pass, tying up the line while, in the manner of decades of wrecking experience, they used other engines, "deadman" and block and tackle to get it back on the rails, a mud splattered battered spectacle.

The winter of 1936-1937 was kinder to the line. Even the flanger was little used, although the last run of No. 70 west from Como had it behind the engine. There was a four-engine freight nearly every day into Como from one direction or the other. Nos. 8 and 9 were the last Moguls to be run on the passenger, while on the freights were various combinations of engines 58, 60, 65, 68, 69, 71 through 76, 537 and the three D&RGW. However, the lack of troubles permitted setting aside the three D&RGW engines in November, not to show again until March when the roundhouse foreman got them ready for possible use, since they were going to have to be steamed up before return to the D&RGW anyway. The 343 evidently was not used again, but 345 and 346 made one final trip on April 7-8 on a stock extra west, then returning light. The 537 was used also on some final freight runs, after the final passenger. Cabooses 1006, 1008, 1009 were used that final winter and spring, 1009 surviving to this day at the Museum.

In August, 1935, the C&S made the final and successful application to abandon, the only important change being that the line from Climax to Leadville was not included. The testimony showed continued high deficits, diversion of traffic to highways, etc. Moreover the road had looked into heavier motive power without success, as in order to use heavier engines much of the line would need extensive and expensive rebuilding, heavier rails, strengthened bridges and culverts, and important changes in terminal facilities. Among all the charts and statistics was one showing operating revenues of the Denver-Leadville line, 1879 through 1934. 1879 showed $1,826,924; 1934 $254,357. The last million dollar year had been 1892; in only two years after that time did they exceed $700,000 and most years were far under $500,000. Too much of the time the railroad was paying out $3 in operating expense for every $2 they took in, before taxes. Passenger revenue was $6,748 that year, and figured out to average 16 per day. 106 passengers rode the entire Denver-Leadville trip in either direction; the largest numbers were summer excursionists to Platte Canyon places such as Glenisle, Cassells, Buffalo and South Platte, from 146 to 702 each, and Dome Rock had 1168 passengers from Denver. Approximately 4141 cars of freight were handled.

This time the I.C.C. found in favor of the C&S. With the expectation of the train coming off on or about December 10, 1936, the first date set for abandonment of Waterton to Climax, the Post Office Dept. took off the R.P.O. So on December 11, 1936, the postmark "Denver & Leadville R.P.O." was used for the last time. However, the combination baggage-R.P.O. cars continued in the two-car consist.

Engines 8 and 9 generally handled the two-car train in the final months, but for the final run from Denver Engine 60 handled the train into Como. There No. 9 was put on and, with flanger car added, took off at 3 P.M. for Leadville for the last time. The return trip of the 10th saw No. 9 handling the train all the way through to Denver. Strangely it was not considered the final scheduled run, but an "extra", and ran as that with white flags.

The final freight train was when engine 68 made a round trip Denver to Como on Friday and Saturday, April 25 and 26. The final mixed run on the South Park was the Como-Alma and return trip made by engines 8 and 69 on April 11, with caboose 1008 serving as the "combine." Classified as an "extra" and carrying white flags, the train got into Como at 8:45 P.M. with five loads and four empties.

Dismantling contract was let to Platt Rogers Inc. in May, 1938, and their man advised that they would be ready for engines in about two weeks from May 23. The contractor's people selected the cars they needed, including several passenger cars, and two engines, Nos. 58 and 73. The railroad set about converting cars to flats for dismantling use. The scrap was to be brought in to tracks at Dome Rock or such storage tracks as the contractor might build between there and South Platte. Contractor's trains were not permitted to come within 1,000 ft. of South Platte's westerly switch.

Engines 58, 65, 69, 71 and 73 were employed by the contractor, engine 65 replacing 68 on August 9. In passenger cars RPO-baggage car No. 12 and coaches 62, 73, 74, 75, 77 were stripped down and equipped as bunk and living cars. Only four flat cars were given the contractor, plus another 54 flat cars made from gondolas and stock cars, many of them selected because of their steel underframes. The work was completed in October, 1938. Left behind, specifically exempted in the contract, were the Como structures to remain landmarks of the South Park to this day — the engine house, station and hotel. Depots and other structures were generally sold, often in place with the land.

Though the I.C.C. had authorized abandonment all the way from Climax to Waterton, and notices went out for this becoming effective at 12:01 A.M. April 12, 1937, the trackage from South Platte (M.P. 29.4) to Waterton was left in and freight service continued on this nine miles to serve feldspar loadings at that point. After April 12, occasional trains would go that far, taking as many as 15 box cars for loading. In addition trains ran as needed on the 3.8 miles of the Silica Branch from Waterton, and what was called the Lakeland Spur, which was 3 miles of the former Morrison Branch main track from Sheridan Junction. By April, 1939, third rail for standard gauge had been extended to Chatfield (M.P. 14.1), further reducing the need for narrow gauge operations. Sometimes the narrow gauge trains heading beyond Chatfield had orders to do some standard gauge work, but generally their orders were for narrow gauge operations only. A standard gauge flat car equipped with offset dual gauge couplers was kept in event of need.

Coming and Going: *Scrapping was getting under way on July 14, 1938, when a small group of railfan photographers tracked the 73 westbound through Webster with a scrap train. Seconds before Hank Griffiths snapped the train smoking past the old coke ovens there, young Jim Jackson, following his Dad around with a 35mm. camera, caught the outfit going away in the backlighted view below. (Upper, Henry R. Griffiths, Jr.; lower, James R. Jackson.)*

There was little life left in the remaining narrow gauge on the Denver end of what had been the main line. Sugar beets and feldspar moved in narrow gauge cars, but the traffic was dwindling and the track was getting poor. Derailments of loaded cars on the Silica Branch were becoming too common. The Lakeland Spur was removed by September 30, 1938, having been authorized earlier that summer. The Silica Branch was next to go, dismantling being completed on November 27, 1941. Scrappers went to work on the remaining line west of Chatfield in the fall of 1942, with completion reported on December 5. Meanwhile section crews were busy removing 11 miles of narrow gauge third rail in the Denver yard, skipping the rails in street crossings and other paved areas. Frogs and crossings sometimes were left in, some to remain many years. The crossing of the D&RGW a mile beyond Sheridan Jct. had the dual gauge crossing complete for another dozen or 15 years. Another near the Union Station lasted similarly. Today all that remains of the South Park around Denver are such small items as the battered, almost indecipherable sign at South Park Jct., and trackage extending south serving industry in Denver for several miles. There may be a buried piece of three rail track several places. Where the stalls of the C&S roundhouse were, a few rails still are tightly held in concrete.

Dismantling of the South Park from South Platte to Climax got under way in 1938, resulting in a last spurt of activity on the line. Above, Jim Jackson panned No. 69 rushing along near Jefferson on July 15 with a consist of ties and other liberated track material. Left, Hank Griffiths had caught the 73 climbing Kenosha westbound the day previous; the highway (as yet unpaved) was already encroaching on the rail line. And at right, Dick Kindig found mogul No. 9 smoking along near Chatfield on July 29 with 21 flats for the scrapper; assisting at the rear was No. 70. (H. R. Griffiths, Jr.; James R. Jackson; R. H. Kindig.)

Dick Kindig found the scrap train, powered by C&S 58, creeping down the Tenmile near Solitude early in August (top, opposite), leaving behind a lengthening trail of abandoned right-of-way. Later than month he found the train powered by both the 58 and 69, inching over the Gold Pan trestle above Breckenridge at about 3 miles per hour (bottom, opp.) (Both, R. H. Kindig). That July Bruce Triplett journeyed out from Ohio to witness the South Park's final days, and hitched a ride on a freight hauling rail and other salvage before the line was cut east of Climax. No. 74 provided the sometimes smoky motive power on the trip. (Both views this page, Bruce Triplett.)

By September the scrappers had left Como behind and were working their way across South Park. Two men went ahead with a power-operated spike puller (left) removing most of the numerous spikes holding the rails to the old, rotting ties. The scrap train, seen below between Jefferson and the foot of Kenosha Pass, crept along behind them; a winch on the first car was used to pull the rails up a ramp and onto the flat cars. (R. H. Kindig photos.)

No. 71 was slowly climbing towards Kenosha on September 18 as Dick Kindig took this last view of a South Park train silhouetted against its namesake Park (above). The dismantling of the line was completed to South Platte on October 29, and the next day the 71 was sitting dead outside the Denver roundhouse. (R. H. Kindig photos.)

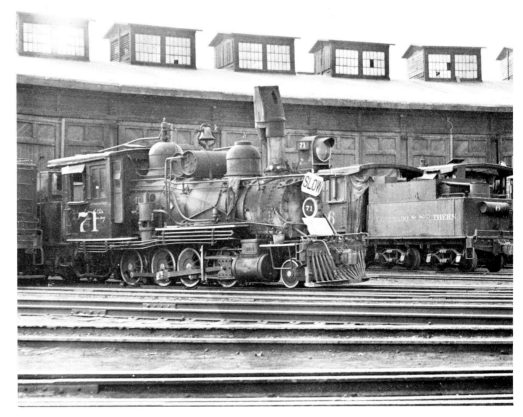

Remnants

After the bulk of the South Park line had been torn up, two segments at either end continued to operate — about 33 miles of track from Denver to South Platte and Silica, and some 14 miles between Leadville and the great molybdenum mine at Climax. It was obvious that both operations were running on borrowed time. The Silica branch was taken up in 1941 and, as a third rail had been laid as far as Chatfield, 14 miles from Denver, to accommodate sugar beet and other local business, the remainder of the Waterton-South Platte line was taken up in 1942. The final South Park narrow gauge operation, however, occurred at the Leadville end. Rather than fade away, business on the isolated Climax branch increased to the point that it was obvious the branch would be around for some time to come. It then became advisable to standard gauge the line for more efficient operation, and to eliminate the costly transfer at Leadville. The last run was made on August 25, 1943, and an ex-Denver, Boulder & Western engine, C&S 76, had the honor of pulling the last narrow gauge train on the South Park.

The Climax run: in 1938 Bruce Triplett obtained this engineer's-eye view of the Leadville yards from the cab of the 74 (left), and made the classic view below of a short freight on the line behind the same No. 74.

Above, Dick Kindig snapped C&S 69 chuffing into Climax with four cars; snow belies the date: June 4, 1938. Below, John Maxwell followed the 75 and 9 cars out of Leadville at 9:30 on May 31, 1941, with the snowcapped peaks of Mt. Elbert and Mt. Massive in the background.

A fair amount of traffic kept the Denver-South Platte section busy as late as 1941, when John Maxwell made these photos. Above, on a warm July morning No. 70 trundled south through a field of daisies near Florida Avenue, trailing 22 assorted cars. Below left, the standard gauge third rail ended in these weeds at Chatfield; right, the Silica branch was taken out in August, and this bridge over a canal salvaged. Above opposite, the 70 and 69 team up to move 24 loads through Chatfield at five o'clock on the ides of March. Bottom, lack of a wye on the stub of line in the canyon made it necessary for the 70 to back up the line with cars for feldspar loading, as shown here passing the old Strontia Springs resort. (All, John W. Maxwell.)

Above, young Dick Jackson in 1890, prophetically posed with a favorite cast-iron locomotive. Below, Dick with his prized live-steamer in his back yard (Richard B. Bagley).

Dick Jackson

South Park Photographer

**a summary of his life
as told to Cornelius Hauck
by his son James R. Jackson
and his good friend
Gerald M. Best**

Richard B. Jackson was born in Denver in 1886, third son (and sixth of eight children) of early settler James W. Jackson. The elder Jackson had come to Denver around 1871, and became the operator of a foundry and manufacturer of machinery — probably accounting for his son Dick's life-long interest in machinery of all kinds, railroad included. Certainly his interest in railroads was apparent at an early age; the photo adjacent showing Dick at four years of age includes a toy locomotive.

In 1906 Dick entered the Colorado School of Mines, and although he did not complete the curriculum there, it did provide him with some early opportunities to ride the C&S narrow gauge. He related riding up to Central City on the train with his Mines class in 1906, and then spending quite a bit of time in Central City in 1907 with a Mines class, staying at the Teller House and frequently riding both the C&S and Gilpin Tram narrow gauge trains. Thus the seeds for his later interest in the narrow gauge lines of Colorado had been sown early.

His career, however, took another direction. Sometime in the 1908-10 period he formed a partnership with a boyhood friend, Oliver E. Wood, and under the name Jackson & Wood retailed and manufactured automobile accessories, with offices at 1634 Broadway. By 1911 the partners were manufacturing headlights ("electric projectors") for automobiles. Offered in three sizes (the smallest also being suitable for use as a sidelight or, with extension cord, as a trouble light), the lights were apparently of sufficient promise to warrant a half-column write-up in a national automotive magazine of the time, *The Horseless Age*. Unfortunately success eluded the venture — perhaps because automobile manufacturers adopted the practice about that time of including electric lights as standard equipment on all new cars. By 1912 Dick's partner, Oliver E. (Ellsworth) Wood, was a partner of the Wood-Wight Manufacturing Company, and Jackson & Wood apparently disappeared.

Subsequently Dick moved to Los Angeles, where he was mustered into the service in 1917. After World War I he worked as a machinist and supervisor in Los Angeles until about 1931, when he was able to retire to his Beverly Hills home and devote his time to his hobbies — railroads, and working with machine tools.

One of the earliest known examples of Dick's combining his railroad interest and his craftsmanship was in 1908, when he built an operating model single-truck electric street car to 1/20" to the foot scale, for operation on 15/64" track. This model was rebuilt in 1920 into the style of a Pacific Electric locomotive, and still operates on its 7" diameter circular track.

Dick was greatly interested in Ward Kimball's Grizzly Flats Railroad project at San Gabriel (after all, how many railfans could have their own full-size narrow gauge back yard railroad in the thirties?). Above right, he is standing on the back platform of the first Grizzly Flats R.R. invitational run in 1939, and left, standing behind Ward Kimball and Tom Taber seated on a push-car. Below, Dick works on a part for Kimball's "Emma Nevada" Baldwin mogul in his immaculate shop. (All, G. M. Best photos.)

During the twenties plans to revive the 1/20″ scale project were shelved when Dick's interests became focused on the possibility of building a live steam passenger-carrying railroad. This idea took shape as the one-inch scale "Colorado Central" railroad about 1927 or 1928. Dick spent several years building a handsome 4-4-0 locomotive, No. 900, designed along the lines of the Denver & Rio Grande Western's 760-class 4-6-0s. Meanwhile an elaborate track layout was under construction back in Colorado, at half-brother Stanley Jackson's summer cottage twenty miles west of Denver, not far from Golden and the Clear Creek Canyon. Beginning at a terminal with a turntable, siding and engine-house, the line curved along the mountainside for some 300 feet, and then around a loop of 220 feet. The track was laid through pine trees and over several bridges and culverts, through a 60-foot cut and over a high fill, and featured several short grades of from 2% to 4%. Over this line the little engine could haul three cars, carrying eight people, with ease. Operation began in 1930, and each summer Dick would bring the locomotive up from Los Angeles in a specially constructed box.

Stanley Jackson died in 1938 and the Colorado trackage was then dismantled, and a new 300-foot layout built in Beverly Hills. This trackage was relaid in 1972-73, after Dick's death, and is still being operated by son Jim on selected Sundays during California's long annual non-rainy season. In addition, an alternative layout near Tehachapi, California, is now in the early stages of planning.

Dick's interest in railroad history and photography emerged in 1921 and 1922, when he made visits to Hawaii and extensively photographed the little railroads operating there. Many of these photos were reproduced in *Sugar Trains* by Conde and Best (Glenwood Publishers, Felton CA, 1973), and there were scattered appearances in other earlier works. Among the little engines filmed in their natural habitat at the time were those now owned by Ward Kimball and Gerald Best, housed and operated on Kimball's famed Grizzly Flats Railroad, at his home in San Gabriel, California. Another was Godchaux Sugar Co. No. 1, an 1894 Baldwin 0-4-4T that was rebuilt in 1958 as a 2-4-4T for Disney, becoming Santa Fe & Disneyland No. 3.

During the late twenties Dick started snapping photos of Colorado narrow gauges on occasional visits back to his home state, and his production became more prolific during the thirties. He took many static equipment photos, as did most railfan photographers then, but he also spent a great deal of time following the little trains out on the line to get action views. Most of his work was done with a Graflex of postcard size, with which he was able to capture the narrow gauge trains at speed; a 3-A Kodak was tried when the Graflex proved too heavy and cumbersome. He continued taking pictures of the Colorado lines through 1946, covering the C&S South Park and Clear Creek lines, the Rio Grande Southern, the Gunnison and Durango lines of the D&RGW, as well as Ouray, Santa Fe and other Rio Grande branches. In the process he compiled a remarkable photographic record of the operations of these lines during that period, and his work is notable not only for its technical photographic competence but for its composition and artistic excellence as well.

As the railfan and modelling hobbies began to grow in the early thirties, Dick began making a host of new friends. One of these was Gerald Best, who met Dick in 1934, after searching through a new Railway & Locomotive Historical Society membership list for the names of members living in his area. Finding Dick's name listed, Gerry relates that "I called him on the phone, we exchanged visits, and soon became very good friends. I was in the midst of building an "0" gauge model railroad, and since Dick had a complete machine shop in a room at the back of his home, he began helping me with difficult and very small parts I had to make. I soon realized that Dick was an absolute perfectionist in working with machine tools, and my admiration for his skill grew through the years."

Dick's model-making abilities and his generosity in helping others earned for him the friendships of many other enthusiasts over the years, and literally thousands of casual visitors — grownups and children alike — enjoyed riding on his backyard live steam railroad. He was active in the Los Angeles Live Steamers and, as Gerald Best put it, the group's monthly meet in Los Angeles' Griffith Park "would not be complete if Dick was not there." A friend brought Walt Disney over to see Dick's live steam operation in 1946, and Walt became so enthusiastic that he built his own locomotive and backyard railroad. Dick and Walt remained good friends through the years, and Walt made Dick and a few others, who had helped him with his live steam locomotive, honorary Vice Presidents of the Santa Fe & Disneyland Railroad, permitting them to ride on the engine whenever they visited Disneyland. In later years one of Dick's greatest pleasures was making a weekly visit to Disneyland to ride the railroad, taking along a visiting fireman if one turned up. When Otto Perry visited him a few years ago, Dick expressed mild exasperation because Otto visited Disneyland *first* (paying taxi fare to do it) instead of letting Dick take him free on a properly escorted tour.

Although his favorite railroads were the Colorado lines he memorialized on film, Dick was also interested in the little narrow gauge lines of California and Nevada. Gerry Best relates how the two of them journeyed to such legendary outfits as the Pacific Coast Railway, the Nevada County Narrow Gauge, the Eureka-Nevada, the Nevada Central, and the Southern Pacific's Carson & Colorado line. "Dick and I took the West Coast Limited from Los Angeles to Sacramento overnight, and rode the first fan trip staged by the Pacific Coast Chapter of the R&LHS, of which Dick and I were charter members. This was to the Nevada County Narrow Gauge, and was quickly followed by a trip to San Luis Obispo and a ride on a special train on the Pacific Coast Railway. We went to Modesto on one trip; imposed on Al Rose to drive us over to Oakdale so we could ride the Sierra Railway on its early fan trips; and in 1938, accompanied by Phil Middlebrook of San Diego, we drove to Stockton where we joined the group going by special train to Reno to ride on the Virginia & Truckee, and had the experience of a lifetime."

When Ward Kimball purchased Nevada Central No. 2, an 1881 Baldwin mogul, in 1938 and had it shipped to his backyard in San Gabriel, Dick became an "official" of Ward's "Grizzly Flats Railroad" and over the next five years repaired or supplied new parts for the engine as it was being restored. Such things as acorn nuts, flagstaff holders for the pilot, patterns for making various castings, and all manner of fine detail for the engine came from Dick's machine shop — and all contributed free to help his friend's project. It was a great day for Dick as well as everyone else when the engine, now named the *Emma Nevada*, first ran under steam in 1943. Later in 1950, when the *Emma Nevada* was again retired, this time in favor of two little Baldwin 0-4-2T engines brought over from Hawaii by Kimball and Gerry Best, Dick pitched in once more to help in the restoration. The little engines lacked number plates, so Dick designed a pattern accurately scaled from Baldwin drawings, with removable numbers so the pattern could be used for any engine.

Collecting locomotive builder's plates became another of his hobbies, after he saw Gerry Best's extensive collection. He began, characteristically enough, by acquiring damaged plates and carefully rebuilding and restoring them, patching holes or broken pieces, replacing missing letters, and buffing and refinishing the plates until they looked as good as new. Eventually his collection decorated all the walls of his shop.

In a sense, Dick retired from his first retirement at about age 67, in the early 1950's. He had accumulated a fund of historical information and material relating to the local railroads of Southern California as well as Colorado narrow gauge lines, which he freely shared with other rail history enthusiasts. His memory of how the trains operated and how they appeared to him in his early youth, around the turn of the century, was remarkable, and he saw Colorado narrow gauge railroading over a period of 75 years. He was much involved in the growth of Walt Disney's interest in railroads, and provided a great deal of free technical advice, plus producing some of the decorative hardware, for the original Disneyland equipment. Among the live steam model building fraternity in Southern California he became known as the "Dean of Live Steamers".

In discussing Dick Jackson's life, one aspect of his personality always seems to come to the forefront — an honest and open spirit of friendliness for everyone. His friends among railroad enthusiasts were many, but he also seemed to be well received by others with whom he came in contact, such as railroad employees. He once remarked that the "only ill-natured conductor" he had ever run into was a short, testy fellow on the C&S' Clear Creek line, and that all others were "pleasant and seemed pleased to see a person who was interested in their railroad." This happy state of affairs may well have been attributable in large part to the influence of Dick's own agreeable personality.

Eventually, age caught up with Dick. He complained early in 1971, after having suffered a mild strain, that "am very short on energy now, you recover slowly at my age", but then went on to say with characteristic optimism that he expected to be "in good operating condition soon". Optimism couldn't counteract a massive heart attack that summer, however, and he died suddenly on August 5, 1971, in his 85th year.

A tangible memento that Dick left for us is his collection of superlative railroad photographs, providing a record of railroading in an era that is fast fading into dim history. Of special interest is his series of photos of the Colorado & Southern South Park line during its final years in the early 1930's. With the help of his son Jim Jackson, who used to go along with his Dad on these trips taking 35 mm. color while his Dad took the black and white views, we have had virtually all of these negatives carefully printed for reproduction on the pages following. They provide a remarkable picture of the old South Park as Dick Jackson saw it forty years ago.

The South Park

as seen by

Richard B. Jackson

The view at right may be Dick Jackson's earliest action photo of a South Park train — No. 4 with the "Fish Train", No. 72, leaving Denver at 2:00 PM on a Saturday early in the summer of 1929, and taking fishermen up the canyon as far as Grant.

In August, 1929, Dick visited Colorado on vacation and rode the South Park to Leadville and back. At left, mogul No. 10 stands waiting at Denver for the departure, a baggage-express, combine and coach coupled on behind. A small clutch of passengers and seers-off is gathered around the rear platform. At right, the train follows the rushing South Platte up the canyon, and below, the station stop is made at Jefferson to unload some head-end business, much to the interest of a few local youngsters.

JEFFERSON

Right, the train, reduced to two cars when the combine was dropped at Como, crests Boreas Pass and is about to plunge into the snowsheds. Below, No. 10 steams gently as the station stop is made at Dillon, and express is unloaded under the watchful eye of the conductor. On the page opposite, the return trip is made the following day. The platform at Leadville (top) seems almost deserted, but there is quite a bit of bustle at Climax (center). At bottom, the 10 takes on some water at Bakers tank, near the top of Boreas.

Sometime on the same 1929 vacation — perhaps on the same trip — Dick made this portrait shot of No. 6 and the west-bound train standing at Como for the station stop and lunch stop; the express messenger watches idly while engineer "Curly" Colligan oils around. In Colorado again in 1931, Dick made the photo at top, opposite, of C&S 74 working a long string of box cars up the Platte Canyon. There is no explanation for the presence of the fireman on the pilot beam. Bottom opposite, the year is 1932 and the scene is Baileys; the 537 has 7 cars in tow, and the likely explanation for this flood of traffic is some sort of excursion.

On August 28, 1935, Dick was up in South Park when C&S 8 came swooping down from Kenosha with a three-car passenger — the regular mail and express car and coach consist of No. 70, plus a business car transporting some unidentified railroad official. Near Jefferson he tried making a "pan" shot of the little mogul at speed from the highway at a recorded 40 miles an hour — not bad for narrow gauge passenger travel in the waning days of the South Park. Opposite, young Jim Jackson and his Uncle Stanley watch No. 8 crest Kenosha on another day, with a different three car consist, and sending up a towering plume of coal smoke.

April, 1937, found Dick Jackson back in Denver for the last days of the South Park. On the morning of April 8 he followed a 4-engine freight departing for Como and Leadville, and made the photographs shown here. Top left, the 75 and 8 are waiting with the train in the Denver yards while the 76 and 537 do last minute switching. Bottom left, all 4 engines are coupled in and the train starts moving out of the yards. Above, the two pushers, cut in 4 cars ahead of the caboose, make smoke as the outfit reaches open country and, below, passes by the camera near Overland park.

The last passenger runs were recorded, too — above, No. 9 leaving Denver on a dreary, drizzly April 5, and below, No. 58 with eastbound train 71 near Sheridan Junction on April 8, were leading up to the finale.

The final round trip came on April 9 and 10. Dick Jackson was there for the trip, unlimbering his camera as No. 60 gently steamed at the head of the train, and an assortment of railroad officials, passengers and curious onlookers milled about the platform. Even though it was the last trip ever, the single coach was only half-filled.

As the train worked its way west, Dick took photos whenever the opportunities arose. Opposite, top, he jumped off the rear platform and made shots as the train made brief stops at Sheridan Junction (left) and the tank at Waterton (right). He stood in the snow and made the lower photo just as the train was starting up at Strontia Springs, with Otto Perry leaning out of the car window. Above, everyone stretched their legs in the welcome sunshine as the engine took on coal at Pine Grove, but when the train went through Buffalo (below) the scene was almost bereft of human activity.

During the Como station stop, the box car was dropped and No. 60 was exchanged for mogul No. 9. A few passengers, railroaders, and bystanders stood in the lee of the depot, away from the biting wind blowing off the melting snow, and watched the 73 switching the yards. Away from the tracks everything was slush and ankle-deep mud; the lone motorist's Auburn 8-98 cabriolet was wearing tire chains.

At Leadville the next morning (April 10, 1937) everyone prepared for their final ride on a C&S passenger train over the South Park line. Conductor Tom St. John and engineer "Curley" Colligan compared notes by the sturdy Cooke mogul No. 9, while the scattered few passengers milled about and waited for the "all aboard". A little weak spring sunshine broke through the morning haze, to give just a slight lift to the participants' spirits, but there were no brass bands, no mayor's reception, no dignitaries proposing toasts.

Dick Jackson made a series of photos that morning as the train made its uneventful way along the Tenmile and Blue River valleys for the last time. The rugged beauty of the Rockies in snow is pictured from the rear platform of the coach at top, left, as the train climbed towards Fremont Pass. At the top, at Climax, a few passengers ventured onto the ground as the train made the traditional station stop, below left. Above, stops were also made at Kokomo tank (left) and Dillon (right). The first evidence of life and activity around the depot came at Breckenridge (below), before the ascent of Boreas Pass.

Part way up Boreas, the train stopped for an informal "photo stop", at left. When the top of the Pass was reached, everyone could get out and walk around the summit for a few moments, view the ruins of the old stone engine house, and savor the historic significance of the event before resuming the trip. It was the last descent from the top of Boreas. In little more than a half hour, the train had pulled up before the old depot at Como for the traditional brief lunch stop (above). The warming sun, gently steaming locomotive, and timeless vistas of South Park lent a spirit of tranquillity to the scene. Any semblance of permanence, however, was to prove illusory.

As the train moved down the Platte Canyon, it stopped momentarily at Long Meadow siding (MP 61.80, east of Grant) for a meet with a freight headed by No. 65, above. Below, everyone on the back platform seems cheerful as they watch photographer Jackson at work. He has just taken the photograph at right.

Fittingly, the last train on the legendary South Park had an official portrait made — Dick Jackson made it, and this is it: No. 9, train and most of the crew, carefully posed on the famed Second Bridge just above Strontia Springs (Deansbury), near MP 27 in the Platte Canyon. There was no second section, no trip out tomorrow: this was the end.

Even though operations had ceased on most of the South Park, the line between Leadville and Climax continued operating. In July the 60 and 76 were at the roundhouse when the 74 left town with 9 cars and caboose; a few days later the 76 and 75 departed with a long train. Top right, on August 6, 1937, Dick photographed the 74 and 75 nearing Climax, high on the side of the mountain.

Back in Colorado the following summer, Dick found Nos. 71, 8 (dead) and 69 moving east from storage at Dillon. Left, crossing the Blue and picking through a graded-over crossing; above, pulling into Breckenridge depot (almost gone), and below, on Gold Pan trestle; July 6, 1938.

A week later, C&S 73 took a train of coal and cars for the scrapper up the South Platte and over Kenosha Pass, and despite grey skies and occasional rain the action was once again masterfully recorded by the Jackson camera. Top left, the train has paused with the caboose spotted by the little depot at Baileys, while below, a light rain has settled in as the outfit slowly chomps through Shawnee, past the unusual rustic log depot. Above, the 73 picks up speed and throws up a huge plume of coal smoke going through Cassells, while below it is nearly lost in foliage as it picks its way along the stream near Webster.

Following the train up Kenosha, Dick made the photo at left above as the 73 worked its way up the sharp curves of the east side, flanges squealing. Lower left, the train, still climbing, has emerged into the broad, open approach to the top of the Pass. Above, this handsome panorama captures the train drifting down the west side of Kenosha, with the cozy buildings of a ranch nestled at the edge of South Park.

Como — heart of the South Park! Dick Jackson was there the next day, July 15, 1938, while C&S 69 and 73 readied a train for Denver. The air was clear and sharp, and a few fleecy summer clouds were scudding across the sky. At left, the crew is going about its switching chores with the 69 (foreground) and 73 (back by the stone enginehouse); the 71 at far left is not under steam.

While waiting for the departure, Dick went out onto the rise east of town, across Park Gulch, and took the panoramic view at right. Enginehouse and ruins of the old mechanical department buildings are at left, depot and hotel at right. The 69 is about to cross the road crossing, with the 73 partly obscured behind it.

The train finally left Como that afternoon, and included a car of salvaged ties, a long string of flats loaded with rails from west of Boreas Pass, and a small crane loaded on a flat. The heavy rails proved too much for the two engines, and they had to "double" Kenosha, as shown at top left — first the 69 with three cars, then both engines with the remainder of the train. At the summit, the two engines had to reassemble the train for the run down the South Platte to Denver. The operation is mirrored in the pond (below) at the top of Kenosha.

the end

Dick Jackson returned to Colorado the following July (1940), and found one last opportunity to photograph South Park trains in action — this time C&S engines 70 and 69 coming north out of Chatfield with a long string of boxcars, on the Waterton remnant — just a faint vestige of old-time South Park action.

At the turn of the century, a locomotive was highly esteemed as a background for taking photos of railroad friends. Above, C&S 69, a Baldwin-built 2-8-0, is joined by two railroaders and a friend at Dickey, while another pair pose with Cooke-built No. 49 at Pitkin, below. (Upper, Lad Arend Coll.; lower, Museum Coll.)

Less than Carload Lots

Locomotive Roster

A railroad's personality is reflected in its locomotives, and an experienced ferroequinologist can identify a South Park engine at a glance, without benefit of reading markings or insignia. In its early DSP&P-DL&G era, the South Park acquired some 90 locomotives, and the Colorado & Southern added ten more from the CC-UPD&G and other sources. The greatest part of these came in two large lots — the 23 Mason bogies purchased between 1878 and 1880, which provided the bulk of the early motive power for the road during construction, and the 28 Cooke moguls and consolidations (plus two more moguls for the Colorado Central) purchased in 1883-1884. Third largest order was for 10 Brooks moguls in 1882. Most of the early locomotives were gone long before the South Park suspended operations, however, and in later years the line's roster was populated with several smaller groups of Baldwin, Rhode Island and Brooks 2-8-0s, plus the rebuilt Cooke moguls. While most locomotives were purchased new, the South Park was not above acquiring good used machines. Even in earliest days, four of the five Dawson & Baily-National locomotives were second hand, and one of the Mason bogies had been built for the Kansas Central Railroad. The Rhode Island 2-8-0s spent four years on the Utah & Northern before coming to the DL&G, and a U&N Brooks mogul also spent some years on the South Park (and some of the South Park Masons ended up on the U&N as well). The C&S purchased three used Brooks 2-8-0s from the Denver, Boulder & Western, and leased one Baldwin 2-8-0 from the Burlington's Black Hills line and three from the Rio Grande.

Rosters of the South Park's motive power have been under construction and reconstruction for many years, and the data listed below is the result of the input of many researchers. Most recently, added data and details have been unearthed by

Bob Richardson during his examinations of old Colorado & Southern records that have been given to the Colorado Railroad Museum by the C&S in recent years. In presenting the material, we have listed the locomotives in semi-chronological order, starting with the early odd engines, Masons and moguls, and then following with the 2-8-0s. This has resulted in a numerical listing compromise in which the earlier power is more or less in DSP&P numbering order, and the later power generally in C&S numbering order. Numbering and historical records are listed first, with specifications for the various groups listed thereafter. Dispositions are shown where known, but the loss of all early C&S locomotive records has obscured the dispositions and sales records of many of the locomotives disposed of during the "house cleaning" of the first few years — for during the UPD&G and DL&G receiverships the receiver apparently was reluctant to dispose of old junk locomotives or unneeded relics made surplus by declining traffic and newer power, unless handsome sale prices were negotiated, which was not too often. Several South Park locomotives escaped ultimate destruction and exist today: C&S 60 and 71 were put on display at Idaho Springs and Central City by the railroad; C&S 74 (ex-C&N 30, DB&W 30) went to the Rio Grande Southern and subsequently was put on display at Boulder; DSP&P 51-DL&G 191 is undergoing restoration at the Colorado Railroad Museum; and famed Cooke mogul No. 9 is in South Dakota. Sister engine 6 almost made the select circle; C&S records show that the railroad's officials tried repeatedly throughout 1939 to find someone or someplace to preserve the engine, as a free gift, but found no takers and finally cut the engine up in November of that year. The ultimate preservation, that of a Mason bogie, was accomplished for a time at Iowa State College, as detailed later in this chapter.

Two of the Brooks moguls (UPD&G 153 and 154) were virtually destroyed in a staged locomotive wreck at Denver in 1896 (top, Museum Coll.), yet the 154 was rebuilt and sold two years later to the Amos Kent Lumber firm in Louisiana as their No. 2. Kent's No. 3 (center, Leon Ford III Coll.) was also a South Park Brooks, probably C&S 18. At bottom, C&S 34 with a train of logs — in Michigan, on the Manistee & Luther. The Baldwin 2-8-0 was soon renumbered M&L 4 by painting out the "3". (C. T. Stoner Coll.)

Orig. DSP&P No.	1885 DSP&P No.	1889 DL&G No.	1890 UPD&G No.	1885-90 UP Reno.	1896 UPD&G No.	1899 C&S No.	Type, key	
1	4	—	—	—	—	—	2-6-0 (A)	*Fairplay*, Dawson & Baily 3/1874. Condemned by 9/1887, scr. 1888?
2	283	283	—	—	—	—	4-4-0 (B)	*Platte Canyon*, Dawson & Baily /1874. Acquired 11/1874 from Kansas Central. Good cond. 9/1887. Scr. ca. 1890?
3	40	40	—	—	—	—	2-6-6T (C)	*Oro City*, Mason 591 5/1878. Scr. 1890.
4	41	—	—	—	—	—	2-6-6T (C)	*San Juan*, Mason 597 11/1878. Scr. 1889.
5	291	291	—	—	—	—	2-6-6T (D)	*Leadville*, Mason 589 1/1878. Blt. as Kansas Central *L. T. Smith*, returned and resold to DSP 2/4/1879. Scr. 1889.
6	42	42	—	—	—	—	2-6-6T (C)	*Tenmile*, Mason 599 4/1879. Scr. 1890.
7	43	43	—	—	—	—	2-6-6T (C)	*Gunnison,* Mason 600 4/1879. Scr. 1890.
8	44	44	—	—	—	—	2-6-6T (C)	*Lake City*, Mason 601 5/1879. Scr. 1889.
9	50	—	—	—	—	—	2-6-6T (C)	*Kenosha*, Mason 602 5/1879. Scr. 1886 on U&N and replaced by U&N 101, ex-UN 45, Brooks 2-6-0 (see below).
10	45	45	—	—	—	—	2-6-6T (C)	*Granite*, Mason 607 8/1879. Scr. 1890.
11	46	46	—	—	—	—	2-6-6T (C)	*Ouray*, Mason 608 8/1879. Scr. 1890.
12	47	47	—	—	—	—	2-6-6T (C)	*Como*, Mason 609 9/1879. Scr. 1890.
13	48	48	—	—	—	—	2-6-6T (C)	*Ruby*, Mason 610 9/1879. Scr. 1890.
14	58	58	—	—	—	—	2-6-6T (E)	*Twin Lakes*, Mason 611 10/1879. Gone by 1894.
15	51	51	—	—	—	—	2-6-6T (E)	*Breckenridge*, Mason 612 10/1879. On U&N 1887, gone by 1894.
16	52	52	—	—	—	—	2-6-6T (E)	*Eureka*, Mason 613 11/1879. On U&N 1887, gone by 1894.
17	140	—	—	—	—	—	2-6-0 (F)	*Wm. H. Baily*, National Locomotive Works 2/1875. Ex-Cairo & St. Louis nos. 19-24, purch. ca. 11/1879. Scr. 1889.
18	141	—	—	—	—	—	2-6-0 (F)	*Wm. H. Baily*, National Locomotive Works 2/1875. Ex-Cairo & St. Louis nos. 19-24, purch. ca. 11/1879. Scr. 1889.
19	142	—	—	—	—	—	2-6-0 (F)	*Wm. H. Baily*, National Locomotive Works 2/1875. Ex-Cairo & St. Louis nos. 19-24, purch. ca. 11/1879. Reblt. 5/1884. Scr. 1889.
20	53	53	—	—	—	—	2-6-6T (E)	*Silverton*, Mason 614 11/1879. Gone by 1894.
21	54	54	—	—	—	—	2-6-6T (E)	*Pitkin City*, Mason 615 12/1879. Used on U&N, gone by 1894.
22	55	55	—	—	—	—	2-6-6T (E)	*Crested Butte*, Mason 616 12/1879. Used on U&N, gone by 1894.
23	56	56	—	—	—	—	2-6-6T (E)	*Grant*, Mason 617 2/1880. Gone by 1894.
24	57	57	—	—	—	1	2-6-6T (E)	*Buena Vista*, Mason 618 2/1880. Sold, see following account.
25	240	240	—	—	—	—	2-8-6T (G)	*Alpine*, Mason 623 6/1880. Gone by 1894.
26	241	241	—	—	—	—	2-8-6T (G)	*Rico*, Mason 624 6/1880. Gone by 1894.
27	242	242	—	—	—	—	2-8-6T (G)	*Roaring Fork*, Mason 628 8/1880. Gone by 1894.
28	243	243	—	—	—	—	2-8-6T (G)	*Denver*, Mason 632 10/1880. Gone by 1894.
—	—	—	150	—	5	15	2-6-0 (H)	Brooks 403 3/1880. Ex-CC 8, 150. In use on DL&G 1893. Sold by 1902.
—	—	—	—	59	—	—	2-6-0 (H)	Brooks 404 3/1880. Ex-CC 9, 151, 59. Reblt. and reno. 12/1885, used on DSP&P-DL&G. Sold to Little Book Cliff RR 1898. Scr.?
—	—	—	152	—	6	16	2-6-0 (H)	Brooks 464 10/1880. Ex-CC 10, 152. In use on DL&G 1893. Sold by 1902.
—	—	—	153	—	2	—	2-6-0 (H)	Brooks 465 10/1880. Ex-CC 11, 153. Wrecked 1896 in staged locomotive collision. Sold or scr. by 12/31/98.
—	—	—	154	—	4	—	2-6-0 (H)	Brooks 547 6/1881. Ex-CC 12, 154. Wrecked 1896 in staged locomotive collision. Reblt. and sold 12/1898 for $1600 to F. M. Hicks Co. for Amos Kent Lumber & Brick Co. as *Amos Kent No. 2.* (Later Kentwood, Greensburg & Southwestern RR Co.)
—	—	—	155	—	3	14	2-6-0 (H)	Brooks 548 6/1881. Sold by 1902. Ex-CC 13, 155.

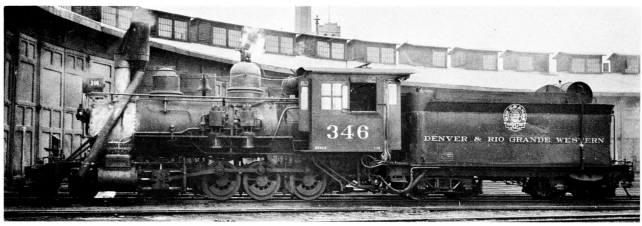

D&RGW 346 looked like this (left, G. M. Best) before going to the C&S, and after its wreck as below (R. B. Jackson), with new cab and mismatched dome covers.

When CB&Q 537 arrived on the C&S, it appeared as at right, with old cab and a mix of dome covers. (Gary Morgan Coll.) Despite the shiny paint, the C&S apparently quickly rebuilt it with new steel cab, air pumps and tanks, steam and sand domes, smokebox and stack, and perhaps other improvements not visible, as in the lower view (Lad Arend).

Orig. DSP&P No.	1885 DSP&P No.	1889 DL&G No.	1890 UPD&G No.	1885-90 UP Reno.	1896 UPD&G No.	1899 C&S No.			
—	101	101	—	—	—	—	2-6-0	(I)	Brooks 801 10/1882. Ex-UN 45, U&N 101. Replaced DSP 50, see above. Gone by 1894. May have been sold to New York Equipment Co. 1893, to Kaaterskill Ry. #3 7/1893, to Catskill & Tannersville #1 ca. 1898. Retired 1908.
29	156	156	—	—	—	21	2-6-0	(H)	Brooks 713 5/1882. On U&N, 1887. Reblt. and reboilered 12/1892. Scr. 8/1923.
30	157	157	—	61	—	—	2-6-0	(H)	*Morrison*, Brooks 714 5/1882. Reblt. ca. 1890. Sold to Little Book Cliff RR 12/1897 for $1200. Scr.?
31	158	158	—	62	—	2	2-6-0	(H)	*Hill Top*, Brooks 727 6/1882. Reblt. ca. 1890. On U&N, 1887. Sold by 1902.
32	159	159	—	60	—	—	2-6-0	(H)	Brooks 728 6/1882. Reblt. ca. 1886. Sold to Burns-Biggs Lumber Co. 9/98; became New Mexico Lumber #1. Scr.
33	160	160	—	63	—	3	2-6-0	(H)	*Webster*, Brooks 742 7/1882. Reblt. ca. 1890. Sold by 1902.
34	161	161	—	—	—	17	2-6-0	(H)	*Alma*, Brooks 743 7/1882. On U&N, 1887. Derelict and not used by C&S; scr. 1900-01.
35	162	162	—	—	—	22	2-6-0	(H)	*Dillon*, Brooks 755 8/1882. Reblt. and reboilered 7/1894. Scr. 3/1927.
36	163	163	—	—	—	18	2-6-0	(H)	Brooks 756 8/1882. Retired 1892. Sold 10/1900 to F. M. Hicks Co. for $600; may have become Kent Lumber & Brick Co. #3.
37	164	164	—	—	—	19	2-6-0	(H)	Brooks 782 9/1882. Sold to Montrose Lumber Co. ca. 1902.
38	165	165	—	—	—	20	2-6-0	(H)	*Chihuahua*, Brooks 783 9/1882. Sold by 1902.
39	109	109	—	—	—	4	2-6-0	(J)	Cooke 1550 2/1884. Reblt. 6/1900 and 1917. Scr. 7/1934.
40	110	110	—	—	—	5	2-6-0	(J)	Cooke 1551 2/1884. Reblt. 8/1901 and 1917. Scr. 3/1939.
69	111	111	—	—	—	6	2-6-0	(J)	Cooke 1552 2/1884. Reblt. 7/1900 and 1917. Scr. 11/1939.
70	112	112	—	—	—	7	2-6-0	(J)	Cooke 1553 2/1884. Reblt. 7/1902 and 1917. Wrecked 3/1928, scr. 10/1929.
71	113	113	—	—	—	8	2-6-0	(J)	Cooke 1554 2/1884. Reblt. 6/1901 and 1917. Scr. 9/1939.
72	114	114	—	—	—	9	2-6-0	(J)	Cooke 1555 2/1884. Reblt. 4/1901 and 1917. Exhibited New York Worlds Fair 1939-40, Chicago Railroad Fair 1948-49; sent to Hill City S. D. (Black Hills Central RR) for display 1957.
73	115	115	—	—	—	10	2-6-0	(J)	Cooke 1556 2/1884. Reblt. 11/1900 and 1917. Scr. 6/1934.
74	116	116	—	—	—	11	2-6-0	(J)	Cooke 1557 2/1884. Scr. 6/1918.
—	—	—	107	—	7	12	2-6-0	(J)	Cooke 1558 2/1884. Ex-CC 14, 107. Scr. 8/1923.
—	—	—	108	—	8	13	2-6-0	(J)	Cooke 1559 2/1884. Ex-CC 15, 108. Scr. 8/1923.
75	—	—	—	—	—	—	unk.	(-)	Reported as "dinky engine" rebuilt at Omaha Shops for South Park RR early 1883; presumably light used engine utilized briefly as switcher.
50	190	190	—	—	—	30	2-8-0	(K)	Baldwin 4917 1/1880. Scr. 2/1921.
51	191	191	—	—	—	31	2-8-0	(K)	Baldwin 4919 1/1880. Sold 1902 to Ed Hines Lumber Co. for Washburn & Northwestern RR (ex-A. A. Bigelow & Co.) #7, 1905 to Thunder Lake Lumber Co. (Robbins RR) #7, 1932 to Rhinelander Logging Museum, 1973 to Colorado Railroad Museum.
52	192	192	—	—	—	32	2-8-0	(K)	Baldwin 4926 1/1880. Sold 1901 to J. J. White Lbr. Co., McComb Miss., later Deerfield RR #1.
53	193	193	—	—	—	—	2-8-0	(K)	Baldwin 4930 1/1880. Sold ca. 1894-98 to Oak Grove & Georgetown RR, Oak Grove, Ala.
54	194	194	—	—	—	33	2-8-0	(K)	Baldwin 4950 2/1880. Retired 1892, sold 10/1900 to F. M. Hicks Co.
55	195	195	—	—	—	34	2-8-0	(K)	Baldwin 4951 2/1880. Sold 1899 to R. G. Peters for Manistee & Luther RR, Eastlake (Manistee) Mich. #4. Retired ca. 1914?

Orig. DSP&P No.	1885 DSP&P No.	1889 DL&G No.	1890 UPD&G No.	1885-90 UP Reno.	1896 UPD&G No.	1899 C&S No.			
56	196	196	—	—	—	35	2-8-0	(K)	Baldwin 4955 2/1880. Sold 1900 as DL&G 196 to F. M. Hicks Co. for $1350; to Clarkson Sawmill Co., then Deerfield RR #2. Not used by C&S.
57	197	197	—	—	—	36	2-8-0	(K)	Baldwin 4957 2/1880. Sold 1899 to R. G. Peters for Manistee & Luther RR, Eastlake (Manistee) Mich. #3. Retired ca. 1914?
41	198	198	—	—	—	37	2-8-0	(L)	Cooke 1478 6/1883. Scr. 11/1921.
42	199	199	—	—	—	38	2-8-0	(L)	Cooke 1479 6/1883. Scr. 8/1916.
43	200	200	—	—	—	39	2-8-0	(L)	Cooke 1480 6/1883. Sold 6/1917 to Hallack & Howard Lumber Co. #4; scr. 1927.
44	201	201	—	—	—	40	2-8-0	(L)	Cooke 1481 6/1883. Scr. 2/1921.
45	202	202	—	—	—	41	2-8-0	(L)	Cooke 1482 6/1883. Wrecked 3/1909, retired 12/1909, scr. 10/1914.
46	203	203	—	—	—	42	2-8-0	(L)	Cooke 1483 6/1883. Traded to Morse Bros. Denver 2/1921.
47	204	204	—	—	—	43	2-8-0	(L)	Cooke 1484 7/1883. Traded to Morse Bros. Denver 2/1921.
48	205	205	—	—	—	44	2-8-0	(L)	Cooke 1485 7/1883. Scr. 10/1914.
49	206	206	—	—	—	45	2-8-0	(L)	Cooke 1486 7/1883. Sold 9/1918 to Hallack & Howard Lumber Co. #5; scr. 1927.
58	207	207	—	—	—	46	2-8-0	(L)	Cooke 1487 7/1883. Sold 7/1916 to Hallack & Howard Lumber Co. #2; scr. 1927.
59	208	208	—	—	—	47	2-8-0	(L)	Cooke 1494 8/1883. Traded to Morse Bros. Denver 2/1921.
60	209	209	—	—	—	48	2-8-0	(L)	Cooke 1495 8/1883. Sold 8/1920 to Hallack & Howard Lumber Co. #9; scr. 1927.
61	210	210	—	—	—	49	2-8-0	(L)	Cooke 1496 8/1883. Traded to Morse Bros. Denver 2/1921.
62	211	211	—	—	—	50	2-8-0	(L)	Cooke 1497 8/1883. Traded to Morse Bros. Denver 2/1921.
63	212	212	—	—	—	51	2-8-0	(L)	Cooke 1498 8/1883. Scr. 10/1920.
64	213	213	—	—	—	52	2-8-0	(L)	Cooke 1499 8/1883. Scr. 6/1918.
65	214	214	—	—	—	53	2-8-0	(L)	Cooke 1500 9/1883. Scr. 6/1918.
66	215	215	—	—	—	54	2-8-0	(L)	Cooke 1501 9/1883. Sold 5/1920 to Hallack & Howard Lumber Co. #8; scr. 1927.
67	216	216	—	—	—	55	2-8-0	(L)	Cooke 1502 9/1883. Sold 5/1918 to CMStP&P RR for Bellevue & Cascade RR #4; retired 7/1923, scr. 1/1936.
68	217	217	—	—	—	56	2-8-0	(L)	Cooke 1503 9/1883. Scr. 10/1914.
—	—	260	—	—	—	57	2-8-0	(M)	Rhode Island 1592 2/1886. Ex-U&N 260, rec'd 9/1890. Scr. 3/1923.
—	—	261	—	—	—	58	2-8-0	(M)	Rhode Island 1593 2/1886. Ex-U&N 261, rec'd 9/1890. Scr. 4/1939.
—	—	262	—	—	—	59	2-8-0	(M)	Rhode Island 1594 3/1886. Ex-U&N 262, rec'd 9/1890. Scr. 4/1925.
—	—	263	—	—	—	60	2-8-0	(M)	Rhode Island 1595 3/1886. Ex-U&N 263, rec'd 9/1890. To Idaho Springs for preservation, 5/1941.
—	—	264	—	—	—	61	2-8-0	(M)	Rhode Island 1596 4/1886. Ex-U&N 264, rec'd 9/1890. Scr. 1/1930.
—	—	265	—	—	—	62	2-8-0	(M)	Rhode Island 1597 4/1886. Ex-U&N 265, rec'd 9/1890. Scr. 12/1927.
—	—	266	—	—	—	63	2-8-0	(N)	Baldwin 11331 12/1890. Scr. 5/1929.
—	—	267	—	—	—	64	2-8-0	(N)	Baldwin 11332 12/1890. Sold to Sosa & Garcia Co., Mexico City, 9/1921.
—	—	268	—	—	—	65	2-8-0	(N)	Baldwin 11340 12/1890. Scr. 4/1939.
—	—	269	—	—	—	66	2-8-0	(N)	Baldwin 11353 12/1890. Scr. 9/1923.
—	—	270	—	—	—	67	2-8-0	(N)	Baldwin 11333 12/1890. Scr. 2/1927.
—	—	271	—	—	—	68	2-8-0	(N)	Baldwin 11352 12/1890. Scr. 5/1939.

Orig. DSP&P No.	1885 DSP&P No.	1889 DL&G No.	1890 UPD&G No.	1885-90 UP Reno.	1896 UPD&G No.	1899 C&S No.			
—	—	272	—	—	—	69	2-8-0	(N)	Baldwin 11355 12/1890. Sold to U. S. Army 4/1943 as WP&Y 20. Scr. at Seattle, Wash. 1/1946.
—	—	273	—	—	—	70	2-8-0	(N)	Baldwin 11356 12/1890. Oil burner. Sold to U. S. Army 4/1943 as WP&Y 21. Scr. at Seattle, Wash. 1/1946.
—	—	—	—	—	9	71	2-8-0	(O)	Baldwin 15142 12/1896. To Central City for preservation 4/1941.
—	—	—	—	—	10	72	2-8-0	(O)	Baldwin 15143 12/1896. Scr. 10/1940.
—	—	—	—	—	11	73	2-8-0	(O)	Baldwin 15144 12/1896. Scr. 10/1940.
—	—	—	—	—	—	74	2-8-0	(P)	Brooks 2951 4/1898. Ex-C&N 30, DB&W 30; from Morse Bros. Denver 2/1921 in trade. Sold to Morse Bros. 3/1945, to Rio Grande Southern RR 74, 11/1948; to Boulder for preservation 8/1953.
—	—	—	—	—	—	75	2-8-0	(P)	Brooks 2969 6/1898. Ex-C&N 31, DB&W 31; from Morse Bros. Denver 2/1921 in trade. Sold to Morse Bros. 3/1945; to Cerro de Pasco Copper Co., Lima, Peru 1948; scr. ca. 1960-65.
—	—	—	—	—	—	76	2-8-0	(P)	Brooks 2970 6/1898. Ex-C&N 32, DB&W 32; from Morse Bros. Denver 2/1921 in trade. Sold to Morse Bros. 3/1945; to Cerro de Pasco Copper Co., Lima, Peru 1948; scr. ca. 1960-65.
—	—	—	—	—	—	537	2-8-0	(Q)	Baldwin 14792 4/1896. Property of CB&Q; ex-Deadwood Central 5, Burlington & Missouri River 496 in 1901, 537 in 1904; leased to C&S 9/1930 to 2/1939; scr. 8/1939.

Abbreviations: DSP&P = Denver South Park & Pacific; DL&G = Denver Leadville & Gunnison; UPD&G = Union Pacific, Denver & Gulf; C&S = Colorado & Southern; U&N = Utah & Northern; CC = Colorado Central; WP&Y = White Pass & Yukon; C&N = Colorado & Northwestern; DB&W = Denver Boulder & Western; CB&Q = Chicago Burlington & Quincy.

Specifications

Type, key		UP Cl.	C&S Cl.	Cyl.	Dr.	Eng. Wt.	Remarks
2-6-0	(A)	DF-1	—	11x16	34″	40,000	
4-4-0	(B)	Odd	—	13x18	44″	46,000	
2-6-6T	(C)	DH-1	—	13x16	37″	43,850*	*Wt. on drivers
2-6-6T	(D)	Odd	—	12x16	34″	42,000*	*Wt. on drivers
2-6-6T	(E)	DI-1	—	14x16	37″	45,000*	*Wt. on drivers
2-6-0	(F)	DI-3	—	14x22	47″	52,000	No. 18/141 rebuilt in 5/1884
2-8-6T	(G)	EJ-1	—	15x20	36″	55,340*	*Wt. on drivers
2-6-0	(H)	DJ-1	B-3B	15x18	38″	60,000	Ex-CC engines shown as 52,000 wt. UP 59-63 were rebuilt with 14x18 cylinders. DL&G 156 and 162 (C&S 21 and 22) were rebuilt and reboilered 1892-1894, new wt. 63,250. C&S 21 received 41″ dr. and 22 40″ dr. about 1910.
2-6-0	(I)	DI-2	—	14x18	42″	50,000	
2-6-0	(J)	DI-2	B-3A	14½x18	40″	61,300	Ex-CC engines shown as 59,900 wt. C&S 11-13 received new 15x18 cylinders ca. 1903-1906. C&S 4-10 rebuilt 1900-1902 with following new dimensions:
			B-3C	15x18	40″	74,700	
2-8-0	(K)	EJ-1	B-4A	15x18	37″	61,750	
2-8-0	(L)	EJ-1	B-4B	15x18	37″	66,000	
2-8-0	(M)	—	B-4C	16x18	37″	71,000	
2-8-0	(N)	—	B-4D	16x20	37″	76,000	C&S 70 converted to oil burner 10/1931
2-8-0	(O)	—	B-4E	15½x20	37″	80,500	
2-8-0	(P)	—	B-4F	16x20	37″	95,500	C&S 74 has slide valves, 75 and 76 had piston valves
2-8-0	(Q)	—	—	17x20	38″	97,000	Outside frame

255

Probably most famous of all the South Park's locomotives was mogul No. 9. Not only was it frequently used on the Leadville passenger in later years, thus gaining maximum exposure to railfans and railfan photographers, but it was also the last of the moguls to see service and only one to be preserved. Here it is (top left) nearing Denver on a February afternoon in 1937 with the Leadville passenger (Otto Perry photo); freshly painted for exhibit at the New York World's Fair two years later (Ted Wurm photo); and on the last train at Como on April 10, 1937 (R. B. Jackson photo).

Page opposite, three of the South Park's biggest freight hogs. Top, No. 71, at Como, was typical of the three Baldwins acquired by the UPD&G in 1897. No. 74, an 1898 Brooks, was first of the three DB&W machines and only one with the distinctive canted Brooks slide valves. No. 76 (shown bottom) and sister No. 75 were also 1898 Brooks from the DB&W and the only South Park engines with piston valves. Only No. 74 has survived. (All, Gerald M. Best photos.)

A spread of C&S moguls photographed by Gerald M. Best — Nos. 5 and 6, top; 7 and 8, middle; and No. 10, lower left, all identical Cooke engines of 1884; and an Otto Perry view of No. 22, rebuilt by the Union Pacific from old Brooks DSP&P No. 35, the Dillon.

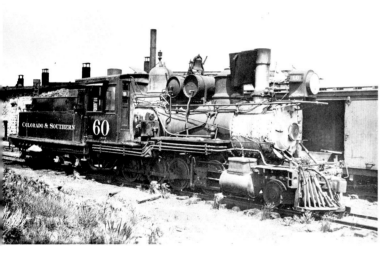

Nos. 58, 59, and 60 (from top left) were typical of the half dozen Rhode Island 2-8-0s acquired from the Utah & Northern, while Nos. 65, 68 and 69 are representative of the Baldwins obtained new in 1890. Only the 60 has survived. (All, Gerald M. Best.)

The photo of DL&G 57 above was taken in Morrison in 1892, and the lower view in the Denver yards in the late 1890's, and they show that the engine was maintained in good condition during that period. (Top, G. E. Lundberg Coll. from Tom St. John; bottom, State Historical Society of Colo.)

the last
Mason bogie

"Engine No. 1 of the South Park Line Sold to a Lumber Camp Outfit." So read the headline on an October 26, 1899 article in the Denver TIMES that was to tickle the curiosity of South Park archeologists for years. The article continued:

> Engine No. 1, the pioneer on the South Park line, was loaded for shipment to the lumber region of Wisconsin yesterday. This is the last of the old lot of locomotives first sent to Denver for use on the famous old mountain line.
>
> The locomotives were of the Mason type, and were said to be the most uncertain propositions ever sent to this country.

Identifying the engine was not difficult; the South Park had, of course, initially used Mason bogie engines almost exclusively, and one of these was still in use in Colorado by 1899 — DSP&P 24, the *Buena Vista*, later DL&G 57, and finally Colorado & Southern 1 —hence the "Engine No. 1 of the South Park Line" designation.

But to whom and where in "Wisconsin"? A canvassing of likely "lumber camp outfits" in that state around 1900 yielded no Mason bogies.

Then a parallel mystery arose in Iowa — the story of an odd old engine preserved (after a fashion) for years on the Iowa State University campus at Ames, Iowa. Unfortunately, the engine had been contributed to the wartime scrap drive in 1942, but old photographs revealed the obvious — it too was a Mason bogie 2-6-6T, remarkably similar in appearance to the South Park machines. However, campus mythology attributed an even more romantic past to the little engine, which had been called the *Iowa*. The accepted story was printed in a lengthy eulogy in the college newspaper when the locomotive was offered to the scrap drive:

> State's famous 87-year-old locomotive is being offered as scrap to the nation's war salvage drive . . . The narrow gauge locomotive earned her right to fame in 1855 when she was ferried across the Mississippi River at Davenport to be second locomotive to enter Iowa . . Her trial run occurred almost one hundred years ago when Rogers, Ketchum and Grosvenor, of Patterson, New Jersey, polished her bronze bell and sent her (on) the way for her illustrious career. There were many adventures in the loco-

motive's life after that first run. She traveled hard and worked hard in her westward pioneering, not admitting defeat until the railroad tracks were widened so that her wheels wouldn't fit. Mystery shrouds the locomotive's pre-Iowa history but when she entered the state she was in the employ of the Mississippi and Missouri Railroad. At this time she acquired the name *Iowa* and continued in the service of the M. & M. Railroad until it was widened from narrow to standard gauge. Following that she found work with the Denver and Rio Grande Railway.

A handsome piece of creative writing, but unfortunately at wide variance from historic fact. Aside from the impossibility of the various exploits attributed to the locomotive, a few hard facts unearthed by perceptive observers before the locomotive's demise pointed in another direction: the words *Denver and South Park* and *Union Pacific Denver & Gulf* were reported to have been cast into several vital parts. It was, unquestionably, a South Park Mason bogie. But which one?

One locomotive historian who accepted the challenge was John Buvinger, who stopped at the Ames campus on trips between Denver and Ohio and read endless strips of newspaper microfilm searching out the story. These efforts, and the input of others as well, have unravelled the story.

The locomotive was found to have arrived on the (then) Iowa State College campus in January, 1905, as a gift from Mrs. Jessie Mallory Thayer, whose father S. H. Mallory had used it in contracting work. Its arrival was heralded by an article in the college newspaper, *The I. S. C. Student*, on February 1, 1905:

> A PIONEER LOCOMOTIVE
> Presented to the Engineering Department By the Mallory Estate. An Interesting Relic.
>
> The Mechanical engineering department has just come into possession of a valuable relic in the shape of one of the first locomotive engines used in the West. It comes through the kindness of Mrs. Jessie Mallory Thayer of Chariton, Iowa, whose father was the last person to own and operate the "Iowa", as it is called.
>
> Early in September President Storms received a letter from Mrs. Thayer offering the engine to the college and from this letter we are permitted to make a few extracts. Said Mrs. Thayer: "We have in the C. B. & Q. shops at West Burlington an old locomotive of peculiar and antiquated design, belonging to my late father's railroad outfit. We intended to have it scrapped, but Master Mechanic Carney insists that the engine is unique and that it is a pity to destroy it for old iron. I am greatly interested in the college at Ames, and before deciding the fate of the engine I wish to know if you have a

The 57 at Ames: as received and, at bottom, as it appeared in the thirties. (Top to bottom, I. S. U. Photo Service, Art Wallace Coll., Frank L. Mott Coll.)

place and would like the engine. Purdue is anxious to have it but we would rather see the old "Iowa" placed in our state if possible." The matter was placed in the hands of Prof. Bissell for report and he entered into correspondence with a view to finding out whether or not the engine would prove of sufficient value to the institution to warrant acceptance by the board. His report was favorable but owing to rush of business, the board did not accept the gift until a month or two later, and it arrived by freight only a week or two ago.

The engine is of a type unlike any in use on the roads of this state today. From Mr. Carney's letter we quote the following brief description: "The engine is a three foot, narrow gauge, Forney type, having outside valve motion and the driving wheels and cylinder on a truck separate from the boiler, which is contrary to more recent methods of construction." It is equipped with the old fashioned funnel stack, small drivers and tender and a headlight seemingly out of all proportion to its weight. It is in a bad state of repair, the wood work being rotted and smashed, and the metal rusted in spots, but a comparatively small expense in repairing and paint which it will receive will not only improve it in appearance but preserve it. For the present or until proper accommodations can be provided for it, it will occupy a shed just west of that occupied by the C. & N. W. engine. . . .

As to the early history of the "Iowa" no large amount of authentic information is to be had. It is doubted that it was ever used in Iowa in the pioneer service. Mr. Carney of the C. B. & Q. writes that it was formerly used by the Denver and Rio Grande and some faint initials on the tender seem to bear out his statement. A large casting on the forward truck intimates that the machine was once the property of the Union Pacific, Denver & Gulf Railway. Other castings including wheels indicated that the Denver and South Park Railroad had a share of the locomotive's service and "Hank" who received his early ideas of railroading in the Rockies, testifies to the fact that the latter road alone used the "sewing machine" type of engine in his day. Mr. S. H. Mallory bought the "Iowa" . . . for use in railroad construction and used it as late as 1902 while putting in double tracks for the "Q" at Red Oak. With his death the engine ended its period of active service and will now soon be at rest. Called "517", "1" and "Iowa" at various times in its history it bids fair to become known to future generations at I. S. C. as "Poor Old Iowa."

Further investigation reveals that the article was remarkably accurate. While Mrs. Thayer received acclamation for making the gift, it seems clear that it was Burlington Master Mechanic Carney's insistence that actually was responsible for the locomotive's preservation. He was, however, misled by the appearance of faint "D&RG" initials on the tender boards; undoubtedly what he saw were the unfamiliar letters "DL&G". The number "517" is also misleading; appearing in faded digits on the sand dome, this resulted from an older "5" and "7" bleeding through on either side of a newer "1" — the new C&S number having been painted on a light coat of paint covering the old number 57 of the DL&G.

The 57 had been in occasional use around Denver during the 1890's. Classified by the DL&G as "too light for use on the South Park", it appears to have been used on the Morrison branch and on similar short, light tonnage runs. Still in operating order when the C&S assumed control, it was numbered "1", but was of so little use that it was sold to the first buyer to appear — Mallory. It is not known where Mallory first used the engine — Wisconsin? He had contracted part of the Missouri Pacific's line to Pueblo a decade earlier, so was an established railroad contractor. During 1901 and 1902 Mallory used the Mason bogie on a major line improvement for the Burlington around Red Oak, Iowa, involving a great deal of grading and the construction of a two-mile fill west of town. Following this work, the engine was left in the weeds for a buyer that never appeared, and later was moved to the CB&Q shops at West Burlington, where Master Mechanic Carney "took pity" on it. Mallory had died and his daughter, Mrs. Thayer, was in charge of his estate. Carney convinced her that the locomotive should be preserved for its historic value. Apparently an offer was received from Purdue, but Mrs. Thayer was interested in I. S. C. and felt the engine should stay in Iowa.

Photographs (and newspaper accounts) reveal that the engine was in terrible shape when it arrived at Ames. The cab was nearly rotted off, and it generally looked like a derelict. It remained in that condition until 1916, when the college appropriated $600 to fix it up and put it out on exhibit near the Engineering Building. There it sat, a popular and beloved if gradually deteriorating monument, until October, 1942.

The wartime mania for collecting scrap metal reached the I. S. C. campus, and the *Iowa* was quickly seized upon by the enthusiastic scrap-gatherers. It was cut up on the spot on November 2 and 3, 1942, and on the 4th the campus paper could piously report that a patriotic contribution had been made of the locomotive, a pile of coat hangers, some old cast iron pipe fittings, a small cement mixer, and some unused refrigerator coils.

Only after the deed had been accomplished were voices raised in objection. But then it was too late, and the last South Park Mason was gone.

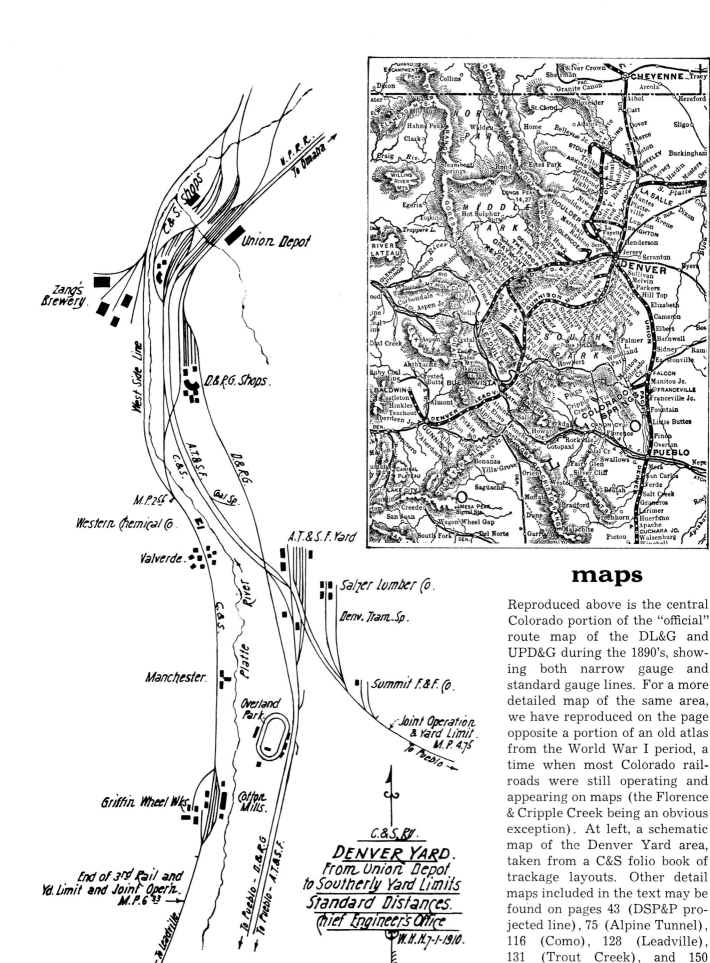

maps

Reproduced above is the central Colorado portion of the "official" route map of the DL&G and UPD&G during the 1890's, showing both narrow gauge and standard gauge lines. For a more detailed map of the same area, we have reproduced on the page opposite a portion of an old atlas from the World War I period, a time when most Colorado railroads were still operating and appearing on maps (the Florence & Cripple Creek being an obvious exception). At left, a schematic map of the Denver Yard area, taken from a C&S folio book of trackage layouts. Other detail maps included in the text may be found on pages 43 (DSP&P projected line), 75 (Alpine Tunnel), 116 (Como), 128 (Leadville), 131 (Trout Creek), and 150 (Baldwin).

a pictorial STATION LIST
Denver to South Park

Water has played an increasingly important role over the years in Colorado's history and politics, and curiously was responsible for a detailed photo study of the South Park line right-of-way during the late winter of 1929. The previous August, Denver's Board of Water Commissioners announced a plan to dam the South Platte at Waterton, creating a lake back as far as Buffalo, to provide added water supplies for Denver. This would have inundated 19.2 miles of South Park main line, and immediately led to the first move by the C&S to abandon the line. As a step in the development of their plans, the Water Board chartered a special C&S train to tour the route. The train consisted of business cars 911 and 910 and one of the moguls. A professional photographer went along and took many photographs en route, some (as shown here) including trains and railroad facilities.

At left, the train is approaching Waterton (MP 20.43); the station is hidden in the grove of trees in the center. The track is delineated by the line of boxcars, and swings off into the canyon beyond. The lower view shows the train deep in the first part of the canyon, at about MP 23. Right above, near Strontia Springs (Deansbury, MP 26.80), the partially finished grade of the D&RG's South Platte extension could be seen across the river; below, the train chuffed through the famed "second bridge" above Strontia Springs (MP 27.52).

Above, at South Platte (MP 29.41) the special pulled ahead on the siding, past the depot and hotel, to the stub switch where the Nighthawk Branch joined (MP 29.52). At Buffalo (MP 39.59) the special again took the siding, to make way for No. 4 with regular passenger train 71.

A brief stop was made at Pine Grove (MP 42.39) for coal (right), and then the train proceeded to Grant (below) (MP 66.14) for a meet with an eastbound freight headed by C&S 73.

Returning, the special (headed by No. 5) is shown above at MP 69.70, near Webster, while a long freight is descending the hillside above from Kenosha, at about MP 71. Left, looking down from MP 71.40, at a point just short of the location of the caboose above; the sidings, water tank and abandoned coke ovens at Webster (MP 69.39) can be seen in the center.

Above, a freight at about MP 78, working its way up Kenosha out of South Park. Below, the east-bound special pauses just beyond Jefferson, at about MP 81. Further data on stations and scheduling can be gained from the pages of Employee Timetable No. 6, of June 10, 1906, reproduced on the pages following.

West-Bound. PLATTE CANON DISTRICT. Denver and

Time Table No. 6.

June 10th, 1906.

Trains running Denver Union Depot to S. P. Junction, will be governed by A., T. & S. F. Time Tables and Rules.

Car Capacity of Sidings, Location of Scales, Water, Fuel, Turn Stations and Wyes.		SECOND CLASS 83 Freight	85 Way Freight	81 Mixed	FIRST CLASS 69 Passenger	79 Passenger	77 Passenger	73 Fish Train	75 Fish Train	71 Denver and Leadville Passenger	Distance from Denver		Miles	STATIONS	
		Leave Daily Exc. Sunday	Leave Daily Exc. Sunday	Leave Daily Exc. Sunday	Leave Daily	Leave Daily	Leave Daily	Leave Saturday Only	Leave Daily Exc. Sunday	Leave Daily					
				6.30 pm	4.05pm	1.00pm	8.05am	2.05pm	5.05pm	8.15 am	.0	DnR		DENVER U. D.	N S
											0 8		0.8	6th Street	
											1.0		0.2	South Park Yard	
		s 8.31	7.15am	6.55	s 4.14	s 1.09	s 8 14	s 2.15	s 5.14	s 8.24	2.0	R	1.0	S. F. Xing and S. P. Junc.	
86		f 8.34	7.20	f 7.00	f 4.19	f 1.14	f 8.17	f 2.17	f 5.18	s 8.28	3.4		1 4	Valverde	
132		f 8.39			f 4.22	f 1.17	f 8.21	f 2.22	f 5.23	f 8.33	4.6		1.2	Denver Mills	
68		f 8.43			f 4.25	f 1.19	f 8.23	f 2.24	f 5.25	f 8.36	5.9		1.3	Overland	
55	O. Y. W	8.48 am	s 7.45	s 7.30	4.30pm	1.25pm	8.30am	s 2.28	s 5.30	s 8.40	7.6	DR	1.7	Sheridan Junction	Sj
			s	s				s	s	s	8.2		0.6	R. G. Xing	
19			s 8.05	f 7.40				f 2.38	f 5.40	f 8.49	11.2		3.0	MacRose	
33			8.35	f 7.55				s 2.50	f 5.51	f 9 01	16.7		5.5	Wheatland	
141	Y. W		s 9.10	s 8.05				s 3.00	s 6.00	s 9.10	20.4		3.7	Platte Canon	
25			9.36	f 8.22				f 3.13	f 6.12	f 9.23	24.6		4.2	Mill Gulch	
			9.50	f 8.33				f 3.21	f 6.20	f 9.31	26.8		2.2	Strontia Springs	
78			10.10	s 8.45				s 3.32	s 6.29	s 9.39	29.4	D	2.6	South Platte	Sp
24	W		10.25	f 8.55				f 3.40	f 6.36	f 9.47	31.7		2.3	Dome Rock	
21			10.38	f 9.08				f 3.51	f 6.46	f 9.57	34.6		2.9	Dawsons	
17			10.53	f 9.15				s 4.00	f 6.51	f 10.02	36.0		1.4	Park Siding	
	W							f 4.07	f 6.58	f 10.14	38.0		2.0	Ferndale	
71			11.16	f 9.31				s 4.11	s 7.02	s 10.18	39.6	D	1.6	Buffalo	Fo
43	Y. C		s 11.35 11.50am	s 9.46				4.18	s 7.10	s 10.28	42.4	DR	2.8	Pine Grove	Ni
43								f	f	f	43.1		0.7	Crystal Lake	
								f 4.27	f 7.19	f 10.39	45.1		2.0	Glenmore Lakes	
26			12.14pm	f 10.05				f 4.29	f 7.22	f 10.42	46.0		0.9	Cliff	
14	W		12.26	s 10.16				f 4.34	f 7.28	s 10.48	47.7		1.7	Crossons	
29			12.57	f 10.36				s 4.45	f 7.40	s 11.05	51.6		3.9	Estabrook	
6								f 4.50	f 7.45	f 11.11	53.2		1.6	Insmont	
31			1.15	f 10.50				s 4.54	s 7.49	s 11.15	54.6	D	1.4	Baileys	Ry
3								f 5.00	f 7.53	s 11.21	56.2		1.6	Glenisle	
								f 5.04	f 7.57	f 11.26	57.5		1.3	Grousemont	
											58.3		0.8	Maddox	
29			1.47	f 11.08				s 5.08	s 8.03	f 11.30	59.1		0.8	Altruria	
2	W		1.56	f 11.12				s 5.10	s 8.05	s 11.33	59.6		0.5	Shawnee	Wa
20			2.14	f 11.22				f 5.18	f 8.12	f 11.42	62.0		2.4	Long Meadow	
11			s 2.30	f 11.29				f 5.23	f 8.17	f 11.47	63.5		1.5	Chase	
								f 5.25	f 8.21	f 11 50	64.4		0.9	Cassells	
95	Y.		3.05	f 11.42				5.35pm	8.30pm	s 11.56am	66.1	DnR	1.7	Grant	Us
43	W		3.38	f 11.59pm						s 12.09pm	69.4		3.3	Webster	
9			4.18	f 12.30am						f 12.30	78.8		4.4	Hoosier	
86	Y.		4.45	s 12.45						s 12.39	76.0		2.2	Kenosha	
76	Y. W.		5.20	f 1.10						s 12.54	81.1	D	5.1	Jefferson	Jn
19			5.35	f 1.23						f 1.02	84.1		3.0	Michigan	
8	Y.			1.40						1.12	87.4		3.3	Coal Branch Junction	
499	O.T.C W.		6.00 pm	1.45 am						1.15 pm	88.2	DnR	0.8	COMO	Mo
		Arrive Daily Exc. Sunday	Arrive Daily Exc. Sunday	Arrive Daily Exc. Monday	Arrive Daily	Arrive Daily	Arrive Daily	Arrive Saturday Only	Arrive Daily Exc. Sunday	Arrive Daily					
Buffalo Water Tank, M. P. 36.8.		(1.20)	(10.55)	(7.15)	(0.55)	(0.55)	(0.55)	(3.30)	(3.25)	(5.00)				(88.2)	

PLATTE CANON DISTRICT.

West-bound trains are superior to trains of same class in opposite direction.

All trains running via D. & R. G. track between 6th Street and Denver Union Depot will be governed by D. & R. G. Time Tables and Rules.

Time Table No. 6. — June 10th, 1906.

Station No.	STATIONS (miles)	FIRST CLASS 72 Denver and Leadville Passenger — Arrive Daily	70 Fish Train — Arrive Daily Exc. Sunday	74 Fish Train — Arrive Monday Only	76 Passenger — Arrive Daily	78 Passenger — Arrive Daily	68 Passenger — Arrive Daily	SECOND CLASS 82 Mixed — Arrive Daily Exc. Sunday	86 Way Freight — Arrive Daily Exc. Sunday	84 Freight — Arrive Daily Exc. Sunday
33	DnR DENVER U. D. (N)	5.55pm	8.40am	10.05am	10.00am	3.40pm	7.55pm	2.30am		
	6th Street (0.8)	f 5.51	f 8.36	f 10.01	9.56	s 3.36	s 7.51	2.24		
	South Park Yard (0.2)	s 5.50	f 8.34	f 10.00	9.55	s 3.35	s 7.50	s 2.20	4.14pm	11.46am
1	R S. F. King and S. P. Junc. (1.0)	s 5.46	s 8.31	s 9.58	s 9.51	s 3.31	s 7.46	s 2.14	s 4.09	s 11.39
53	ValVerde (1.8)	f 5.43	s 8.28	f 9.53	f 9.48	f 3.28	f 7.43	s 2.10	s 4.00	f 11.33
55	Denver Mills (1.2)	f 5.38	f 8.21	f 9.48	f 9.43	f 3.23	f 7.38		3.50	f 11.26
56	Overland (1.3)	f 5.35	8.17	f 9.45	f 9.40	f 3.20	f 7.35		3.45	f 11.22
57	DR SHERIDAN JUNCTION (Sj) (1.7)	s 5.30	8.13	s 9.40	9.35am	3.15pm	7.30pm	s 1.50	s 3.37	11.15am
	D. & R. G. Xing (0.6)									
511	MacRose (3.3)	f 5.20	s 8.05	f 9.31				1.30	3.10	
517	Wheatland (5.5)	f 5.09	f 7.54	f 9.19				f 1.10	2.50	
521	Platte Canon (3.7)	s 4.59	s 7.45	s 9.10				s 12.55	2.15	
525	Mill Gulch (4.2)	f 4.46	f 7.33	f 8.58				f 12.35	1.50	
527	Strontia Springs (2.2)	f 4.36	f 7.25	f 8.50				f 12.20	1.35	
516	D South Platte (Sp) (2.5)	s 4.27	s 7.16	s 8.41				s 12.05am	1.20	
582½	Dome Rock (2.3)	f 4.17	f 7.09	f 8.34				f 11.53pm	1.05	
584	Dawsons (2.6)	f 4.06	f 6.59	f 8.24				f 11.38	12.45	
536	Park Siding (2.9)	s 4.00	s 6.54	s 8.19				f 11.31	12.40	
538½	Ferndale (1.4)	f 3.53	f 6.47	f 8.12						
523	D Buffalo (Fo) (2.0)	s 3.48	s 6.43	f 8.08				f 11.15	12.20pm	
524	DR PINE GROVE (Ni) (2.3)	s 3.40	s 6.35	s 8.00				s 11.00	{12.05pm / 11.35am}	
543	Crystal Lake (1.6)	f	f	f						
545	Glenmore Lakes (2.8)	f 3.32	f 6.25	f 7.50					11.00	
546	Cliff (0.7)	f 3.29	f 6.23	f 7.48				f 10.27		
548	Crossons (2.0)	f 3.23	f 6.17	f 7.42				s 10.16	10.48	
552	Estabrook (0.9)	s 3.10	s 6.04	s 7.29				f 9.58	10.10	
553	Insmont (1.7)	f 3.04	f 5.58	f 7.23						
530	g Baileys (By) (1.7)	s 3.00	s 5.49	f 7.19				f 9.45	9.55	
556	Glenisle (3.9)	f 2.54	f 5.46	f 7.15						
557	Grousemont (1.6)	f 2.50		f 7.11						
558	Maddox (1.4)									
559	Altruria (1.6)	s 2.44	s 5.42	s 7.06				s 9.25	9.36	
532	Shawnee (Wa) (0.8)	s 2.42	s 5.40	s 7.04					9.33	
562	Long Meadow (0.8)	f 2.34	f 5.33	f 6.58				f 9.12	9.20	
564	Chase (0.5)	2.30	f 5.28	f 6.53				f 9.03	9.10	
565	Cassells (2.4)	f 2.28	f 5.26	f 6.51						
538	DnR Grant (Us) (1.5)	s 2.20	5.20am	6.45am				s 8.49	8.55	
569	Webster (0.9)	s 2.10						f 8.32	8.35	
574½	Hoosier (1.7)	f 1.55						f 8.07	8.02	
576	Kenosha (3.3)	f 1.50						s 7.55	7.55	
544	D Jefferson (Jn) (4.4)	s 1.34						s 7.05	7.05	
584	Michigan (2.2)	f 1.26						6.50	6.50	
	Coal Branch Junction (5.1)	1.17								
547	DnR COMO (Mo) (0.8)	s 1.15pm	5.20am					6.30pm	6.35am	
		Leave Daily (4.40)	Leave Daily Exc. Sunday (3.20)	Leave Monday Only (3.20)	Leave Daily (0.55)	Leave Daily (0.55)	Leave Daily (0.55)	Leave Daily Exc. Sunday (8.00)	Leave Daily Exc. Sunday (9.40)	Leave Daily Exc. Sunday (1.25)

LEADVILLE DISTRICT.—Como and Leadville.

WEST-BOUND FIRST CLASS 81 Mixed (Leave Daily Exc. Monday)	WEST-BOUND FIRST CLASS 71 Denver and Lead. Pass. (Leave Daily)	Distances from Denver	Time Table No. 6. June 10th, 1906 STATIONS	Station Numbers	EAST-BOUND FIRST CLASS 72 Denver and Lead. Pass. (Arrive Daily)	EAST-BOUND 82 Mixed (Arrive Daily Exc. Sunday)
2.05am	1.35pm	88.2	COMO .... Mo DnR	547	12.55pm	5.40pm
		90.9	Peabodys	591	f 12.46	5.28
f 2.30	f 1.57	93.9	Half Way	594	f 12.37	5.15
s 3.10	s 2.20	98.7	BOREAS .... Bo DR	599½	s 12.20	s 4.50
s 3.16	f 2.24	99.9	Farnham Spur	5100	f 12.14	f 4.27
f 3.20	f 2.26	100.8	Dwyer Spur	5101	f 12.09pm	f 4.15
		102.0	Bakers Tank	5103		3.55
f 3.32	f 2.35	103.7	Argentine	5104	f 11.54am	f 3.30
		105.3	Pittsburg Spur	5105		f 3.15
		105.9	Washington Spur	5106		2.55
s 3.43	s 2.44	106.5	Mayo Spur	5107	f 11.41	s 2.44
		108.4	Smith Spur	5108		2.00
		108.7	Puzzle	5109		
s 4.00	s 2.55	110.0	Breckenridge .... Hd D	561	s 11.25	s 1.40
		111.1	Bartholomew	561½		f 1.26
f 4.10	f 3.04	113.3	Braddocks	5113	f 11.15	f 1.18
s 4.25	{ 3.18 / 3.33 }	116.4	DICKEY .... Jd DR	563	{ 11.07 / 10.47 }	{ 1.00 / 12.40 }
f 4.35	f 3.44	119.9	Frisco	5120	f 10.39	f 12.22
f 4.45	f 3.50	122.0	Curtin	5122	f 10.33	f 12.10pm
s 5.05	f 4.03	126.1	Wheeler	5126	f 10.22	f 11.55am
s 5.45	s 4.27	132.8	Kokomo .... Ko D	568	s 10.02	s 11.25
f 5.55	s 4.34	134.6	Robinson	5135	f 9.54	f 11.15
		135.9	Buffers Spur	5136		
s 6.10	s 4.48	137.4	CLIMAX .... R	571	s 9.45	s 11.00
		138.0	Wortmans	5138		
f 6.37	f 5.11	144.8	Birds Eye	5145	f 9.20	f 9.50
		149.9	L. M. B. Junction	5150		
		150.4	D. & R. G. Xing			
7.00am	5.30pm	151.1	LEADVILLE .... Vi DR	574	9.00am	9.05am
Arrive Daily Exc. Monday	Arrive Daily				Leave Daily	Leave Daily Exc. Sunday

GUNNISON DISTRICT—Como and Baldwin.

WEST-BOUND SECOND CLASS 93 Mixed (Leave Daily Exc. Monday)	WEST-BOUND SECOND CLASS 91 Mixed (Leave Daily)	Distances from Denver	Time Table No. 6. June 10th, 1906. STATIONS	Station Numbers	EAST-BOUND SECOND CLASS 92 Mixed (Arrive Daily)	EAST-BOUND SECOND CLASS 94 Mixed (Arrive Daily Exc. Sunday)
2.15am		88.2	COMO .... Mo DnR	547	12.40pm	7.30pm
f 2.37		93.6	Red Hill	T 94	f 12.20	f 7.06
f 2.52		97.8	Hay Ranch	T 98	f 12.02pm	6.46
f 3.08		102.5	Arthurs	T103	f 11.45am	6.27
s 3.20		104.6	GAROS .... Gr DR	579	11.35am	6.18
f 3.55		113.5	Platte River	T114		f 5.40
f 4.30		119.9	Bath	T120		s 5.13
f 4.47		123.6	Newett	T124		s 4.45
f 5.05		126.6	McGees	T127		f 4.20
5.40		132.6	SCHWANDERS .... R	T133		{ 3.35 / 2.45 } s
6.50	Arrive Daily				Leave Daily	
		135.8	D. & R. G. R. R. Crossing			
f 7.10		136.8	Nathrop	T187		f 2.22
f 7.40		142.1	Mount Princeton	T142		f 1.58
s 8.15		146.9	Cascade	T147		f 1.28
f 8.25		148.9	Fisher	T149		f 1.20
s 8.56		153.3	St. Elmo .... Rs D	590		s 12.55
s 9.40		155.6	Romley	592		s 12.36
f 10.20		158.1	Hancock	T158		f 12.22
f 10.50		161.0	Atlantic	T161		12.06pm
s 11.00		161.8	Alpine Tunnel .... Un D	T162		s 11.55am
f 11.15		164.2	Sherrod	T165		f 11.35
s 11.25	95 Mixed (Leave Mon. Wed. & Fri.)	164.8	Woodstock	T165½	96 Mixed (Arrive Mon. Wed. & Fri.)	s 11.25
f 11.50am		167.9	Valley Spur	T168		f 10.30
f 12.10pm		171.9	Quartz	T172		f 9.55
s 12.25		174.7	PITKIN .... P DR	599		f { 9.40 / 9.20 }
f 12.55		181.4	Ohio City .... MD	T181		f 8.30
f 1.35		189.8	Parlins .... TB	T190		f 7.45
		201.2	D. & R. G. R. R. Crossing			
		201.3	La Veta Hotel	T201½		
		201.6	D. & R. G. R. R. Crossing			
2.20pm		201.8	GUNNISON .... Gu DR	602		7.00am
	2.45pm		GUNNISON	602	6.00pm	
	f 3.27	209.9	Teachout	T210	f 5.25	
	f 3.45	213.4	Hinkles	T213	f 5.07	
	s 4.05	216.5	Castleton	T216	f 4.50	
	4.20pm	219.3	BALDWIN .... R	T219	4.30pm	
Arrive Daily Exc. Monday	Arrive Mon. Wed. & Fri.				Leave Daily	Leave Daily Exc. Sunday

Shown here is a sampling of memorabilia from the Colorado Railroad Museum collection: passes for transit over the South Park narrow gauge lines (and, by implication in one instance, the C&S' "merchant marine"), a tributary stage line, and "pie tickets" for meals at Como and at the Alpine Pass boarding house shown above.

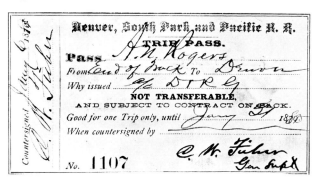

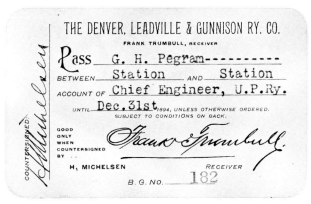

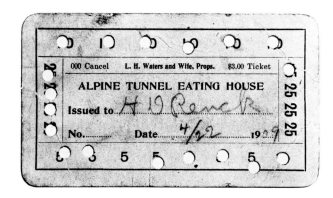

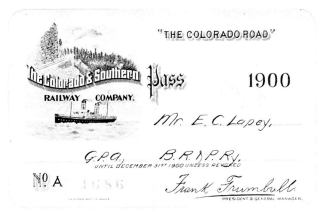

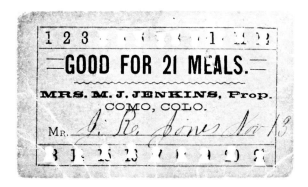

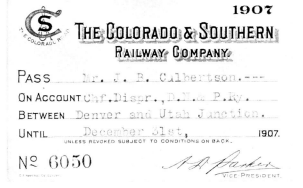

275

Acknowledgements

Many individuals assisted the authors in the preparation of the various chapters of this ANNUAL.

John Buvinger contributed the results of many long hours of research into early Denver newspapers, providing an important input of basic material for the first chapter.

The two principal libraries of historical material in Denver provided a great deal of assistance. Special thanks go to Agostino Mastrogiuseppe at the Western History Collection of the Denver Public Library, and to Opal Harber and the rest of the staff at the Library. Similarly helpful were Terry Mangan, Alice Sharp, Maxine Benson and others of the staff at the State Historical Society of Colorado.

Edwin Olmstead of Carlisle, Pa., and Ross Grenard of Camp Hill, Pa., assisted Mr. Chappell generously while he was working at Carlisle.

John Buvinger, Art Wallace, Bernard Corbin, Luke R. Sinclair and Stanley Yates of Iowa State University all contributed to the story about "South Park" engine number one.

For data on C&S operations, we are indebted to John W. Terrill, President of the Colorado & Southern; office manager Patrick Walsh; R. E. Hansen, retired Road Foreman; E. A. Graham, retired Chief Engineer; the late George E. Lundberg, Mechanical Engineer, and Mrs. Lundberg; Norman Heald, retired Roadmaster; and to many others who have contributed bits and pieces of information over the years.

We have attempted to correctly credit the source of each photograph used, and thank all of those who so contributed. In addition, special thanks are due to a number of people who were particularly helpful in this area — James R. Jackson, for his generosity in making all of his father's splendid photographs available to us; Lad G. Arend and Richard H. Kindig, for their substantial help; and John W. Maxwell and Gerald M. Best.

Bibliography

Athearn, Robert G., *Union Pacific Country*. Chicago: Rand McNally & Co., 1971.

Helmers, Dow, *Historic Alpine Tunnel*. Denver: Sage Books, 1963.

Kelsey, Harry, Jr., *Frontier Capitalist: The Life of John Evans*. Denver/Boulder: The State Historical Society of Colorado *and* Pruett Publishing Co., 1969.

History of the Union Pacific Coal Mines. Omaha: Colonial Press, n.d.

Kindig, Richard, E. J. Haley and M. C. Poor, *Pictorial Supplement to Denver, South Park & Pacific*. Denver: Rocky Mountain Railroad Club, 1959.

Overton, Richard C., *Gulf to Rockies*. Austin: 1953.

Poor, M. C., *The Denver, South Park and Pacific*. Denver: Rocky Mountain Railroad Club, 1949.

Poor's Manual of the Railroads of the United States. New York: (57 volumes) 1868-1924.

Reed, S. G., *A History of Texas Railroads*. Houston: St. Clair Publishing Co., 1941.

Reports of the United States Pacific Railway Commission and Testimony, Senate Ex. Doc. 51, 50th Congress First Session. Washington: 1887.

Archival Materials

Colorado & Southern Papers, Library, State Historical Society of Colorado (including John Evans-DSP&PRR letterbooks and Denver, Leadville & Gunnison papers).

Colorado & Southern Collection, Library, Colorado Railroad Museum

Denver, Leadville & Gunnison Collection, Library, Colorado Railroad Museum

Reports of Board of Equalization, State Archives of Colorado

Reports of the United States District Court, Archives Branch, Federal Records Center, General Services Administration

Union Pacific, Denver & Gulf Collection, Library, Colorado Railroad Museum

Newspapers

Colorado Springs *Gazette*
Denver *Post*
Denver Daily *Times*
Denver *Tribune*
Gunnison *News-Champion*
Gunnison *Republican*
Gunnison *Review*
Gunnison Daily *Review Press*
Gunnison *Tribune*
Holton *Signal*
Leadville Daily *Herald*
Leavenworth Daily *Times*
Pitkin *Mining News*
Railroad Gazette
Railway Age
Railway World
Rocky Mountain News

INDEX TO TEXT